PINCHBACK

PINCHBACK

AMERICA'S FIRST BLACK GOVERNOR

NICHOLAS PATLER

UNIVERSITY PRESS OF MISSISSIPPI / JACKSON

The University Press of Mississippi is the scholarly publishing agency of
the Mississippi Institutions of Higher Learning: Alcorn State University,
Delta State University, Jackson State University, Mississippi State University,
Mississippi University for Women, Mississippi Valley State University,
University of Mississippi, and University of Southern Mississippi.

www.upress.state.ms.us

The University Press of Mississippi is a member
of the Association of University Presses.

An earlier version of part of Chapter 9 originally appeared in
Before Obama: A Reappraisal of Black Reconstruction Era Politicians.

Any discriminatory or derogatory language or hate speech regarding race,
ethnicity, religion, sex, gender, class, national origin, age, or disability
that has been retained or appears in elided form is in no way an endorsement
of the use of such language outside a scholarly context.

Copyright © 2025 by University Press of Mississippi
All rights reserved
Manufactured in the United States of America

∞

Publisher: University Press of Mississippi, Jackson, USA
Authorised GPSR Safety Representative: Easy Access System Europe -
Mustamäe tee 50, 10621 Tallinn, Estonia, gpsr.requests@easproject.com

Library of Congress Control Number: 2025025159

Hardback ISBN: 9781496859907 | Trade paperback ISBN: 9781496859914
E-pub single ISBN: 9781496859921 | E-pub institutional ISBN: 9781496859938
PDF single ISBN: 9781496859945 | PDF institutional ISBN: 9781496859952

British Library Cataloging-in-Publication Data available

I DEDICATE THIS BOOK TO ALL TEACHERS AND HISTORIANS
WHO NEVER GIVE UP ON LIBERATING THE PAST
I ALSO DEDICATE THIS BOOK TO P. B. S. PINCHBACK,
WHOSE PAST I TRIED TO UNRAVEL

CONTENTS

Acknowledgments ix

Introduction 3

CHAPTER 1: Pinchback's Early Years:
From Caswell County, NC, to New Orleans, LA 11

CHAPTER 2: Pinchback Joins the Struggle for Liberation:
From Early Life on the River to Captain in the Army 26

CHAPTER 3: Pinchback, Nina, and the Rise
in the New Orleans Republican Party 40

CHAPTER 4: Pinchback and the Louisiana Constitutional Convention:
"All persons shall enjoy equal rights and privileges . . . without
distinction or discrimination on account of race or color" 51

CHAPTER 5: Pinchback in the Louisiana State Senate:
A Whirlwind Crusade to Bring Equality to the Deep South 64

CHAPTER 6: "Why, damn it, everybody is demoralized down here":
The Struggle for Louisiana Lieutenant Governor. 90

CHAPTER 7: Lieutenant Governor Pinchback and the Race to Save
the Republican Party. 103

CHAPTER 8: Thirty-Six Days that Changed History:
The First Black Governor 117

CHAPTER 9: "The Star of my Hope":
Pinchback's Fight for the US Senate 136

CHAPTER 10: After Reconstruction:
Pinchback's Post-Senate Career and Life 150

Notes 167

Bibliography 197

Index 209

ACKNOWLEDGMENTS

As much as we historians feel that our process is a solo endeavor, researching and writing history is a community affair. This book would not have been possible without so much voice and assistance—past, present, and even future. I wish to first thank P. B. S. Pinchback, whose remarkable and controversial life and work inspired me to delve into his story. I tried to listen deeply to him and his contemporaries.

I thank all of the staff at the indispensable repositories and archives that were the foundation for this book: Moorland-Spingarn Research Center, Howard University; Beinecke Rare Book and Manuscript Library, Yale University; Lexington, Mississippi, Public Library Archives; Wilson Library, University of North Carolina; Caswell County, NC, Historical Association; Holmes County, Mississippi, Chancery Office; Library of Congress, Manuscript Division; Louisiana State Archives, Baton Rouge; New Orleans Public Library, Louisiana Division; the University of Illinois Archives, Urbana; University of Virginia government records and documents; and many other secondary and newspaper sources that were crucial for helping to tell this story.

I am deeply indebted to so many historians, whose shoulders I stand on, including Carter G. Woodson, Agnes Smith Grosz, Lerone Bennett Jr., James Haskins, Charles Vincent, Philip Dray, Louis-Alejandro Dinella-Borrego, Ingrid Dineen-Wimberly, and many others.

I also want to express gratitude for the amazing editorial assistance I received from those who gave care and focus to this manuscript and research. It is a better book because of them: the University Press of Mississippi peer reviewers; editor and writer, Daphne Lavonia; my mother, Alice Patler, and aunt, Dr. Laten Bechtel; historian Sue Simmons; my friend Susanna Lord for making my research in the Delta possible; and my sounding board, Katie Savage. I cannot leave out those who believed in this story from the beginning and allowed me to write and share it: University Press of Mississippi acquisitions editor, Emily Snyder Bandy, and director, Craig W. Gill.

I want to express my deep appreciation for Matthew Lynch, Dean of Syphax School of Education, Psychology, and Interdisciplinary Studies at Virginia Union University. Dr. Lynch is the visionary behind the historical compilation, *Before Obama: A Reappraisal of Black Reconstruction Era Politicians*, and he gave me my first opportunity to research and write about P. B. S. Pinchback.

Finally, I want to thank the many people with whom I will share this story orally and whose questions and insights will continue making this book a community affair.

PINCHBACK

INTRODUCTION

Pinckney Benton Stewart Pinchback demonstrated to friend and foe alike that he could navigate the most volatile political terrain in the country to achieve power. Obsessively driven like few other political leaders of his day, this son of a formerly enslaved woman outmaneuvered his adversaries to make his way to the Louisiana governor's chair to become the first Black/biracial governor in history (1872–73). Even the white supremacist New Orleans *Daily Picayune* had to concede near the end of Pinchback's short term as governor that he was "a remarkably bold and decidedly smart man . . . a shrewd politician willing to assume any responsibility."[1]

Out of the ashes of the Civil War and through the smoldering fires of local racist violence, Pinchback worked feverishly to help create and nurture a democratized environment that made African Americans and Creoles the political and even social equals of white Louisianans. This was a sweeping change that only a few years earlier most people could have hardly dreamed possible. In every sense of the word, it was a revolution that reconfigured the political and social landscape and transformed life as everyone had once known it, particularly in New Orleans. Whether it was access to the military, transportation, public spaces, politics, or education, Pinchback believed that people of color must have absolute equality with their white peers. The moxie he demonstrated to confront and best his political enemies while blasting away at white supremacy deeply impacted his Black contemporaries and elevated him to celebrity status. One indication of his influence can be seen when a Black championship baseball team in New Orleans in the 1880s changed its name to the Pinchbacks, batting away in parks all over the South and Midwest while honoring their hometown hero.

With his reputation looming large on and off the field of politics, Pinchback was sometimes a lightning rod of intense controversy. His audacity not only to demand Black equality but to help make it a reality deeply offended the sensibilities of white supremacists who perhaps more than anything despised him for the most unforgivable offense of all, that of being unabashedly Black and bold. Pinchback was keenly aware of this when he told an audience during his tenacious fight for his US Senate seat, "I am bad because I have dared at times to advocate and insist on exact and equal justice to all mankind. I am bad because having colored blood in my veins I have dared to aspire to the United States Senate."[2]

Pinchback was also controversial because he operated in a corrupt and tainted political culture. Frederick Douglass, an intrigued observer of the New Orleans political scene, took it as a given that "the moral atmosphere in New Orleans has never been noted for its purity and freedom from vice." The dashing carpetbagger governor, Henry Warmoth, whom Pinchback would replace, brushed off charges of corruption directed at him by declaring, "Why, damn it, everybody is demoralized down here. Corruption is the fashion."[3] In this shady world of backroom deals and graft, where Pinchback was also known to have a penchant for gambling, allegations of corruption hovered over him ominously. Almost every time he achieved political success in Louisiana, his enemies were quick to cry bribery or fraud, claims which have been recycled in one form or another, ultimately becoming motifs used to delegitimize Pinchback and warning historians away from serious historical inquiry.

The specific charges against him during his political career are difficult to verify. The closest we have to a smoking gun is when Pinchback admitted that he took advantage of his office to successfully "speculate upon warrants, bonds, and stocks" and the controversial Norton bribery controversy, where Pinchback allegedly took a bribe to give up his US Senate ambitions.[4] Other than that, only rumors and allegations of fraud and bribery abound. It does appear that he accumulated a sizable fortune for an elected official. One reporter visiting his home in New Orleans sometime after he became lieutenant governor, looked around the room and remarked: "I see . . . that your circumstances have greatly improved since your entrance into political life." Pinchback strived for upward mobility, likely taking advantage of his offices for his and his family's economic benefit, not unlike other Louisiana politicians. At one point in his career, he acknowledged that he did "not possess all the honesty" in his state, but he stressed how most politicians of his day were worse, particularly those who were leveling charges against him.[5]

Pinchback was a complex person, perhaps even an anti-hero in the drama of reconstructed New Orleans. He was a heroic figure battling the daunting forces of white supremacy, never giving up on empowering the powerless and even supporting female suffrage. At the same time, he was perhaps the anti-hero greedy for profit and concerned with self-interest and who on occasion may have been indifferent to upholding the public trust. It was a seeming paradox that Pinchback's grandson, Jean Toomer, an icon of the Harlem Renaissance who authored the critically acclaimed novel *Cane*, grappled with as he struggled to define who his late grandfather had been. But reconstructed Louisiana, and New Orleans in particular, was not only the ideal place for such an anti-hero to emerge and survive; it may have been a time and place where only an anti-hero stood a chance of making a difference.

It took a certain kind of person to survive politically (and physically!) while navigating the morass of violence, corruption, competing factions, and fast-changing alliances that characterized Louisiana life and politics. It took an even more unusual personality to use and direct those forces for personal and public benefit. Pinchback was able to have as much success as he did in this challenging world because he was in some sense all the things that characterized that world—the good, the bad, and the ugly. He may have been just the anti-hero hero that his times—that the people of color of his times—needed.

In the 2000 study *Creole: The History and Legacy of Louisiana's Free People of Color*, Sybil Kein writes that Pinchback was "one of the most picturesque and splendid figures in the history of the state" and that "the history of Louisiana (during Reconstruction) is written around his name." This description has an obvious romantic ring. Still, it reflects the reality that Pinchback was a force of personality who helped shape the most inclusive democratic society the South had ever seen.[6]

But as influential and controversial as Pinchback was during his time in Louisiana, pushing democracy and even integration to a level not seen anywhere in the Reconstructed South, why hasn't there been more consideration of his life and work in the historical literature?

Beginning in the latter nineteenth and early twentieth centuries, white elite historians, known as Traditionalists, used their influence to convince Americans that Black suffrage "was a monstrous thing . . . , if not a sin" and declared Reconstruction as a "diabolical" failure "to be remembered, shuddered at and execrated." From their pens, visionary Black leaders were transformed into embarrassing anomalies, and those leaders' efforts and contributions were considered unworthy of serious and objective historical consideration. In what W. E. B. Du Bois described as "one of the most stupendous efforts the world ever saw to discredit human beings," these academic elites produced trusted scholarship that reinforced the narrative that Black inferiority and the debacle of Reconstruction were beyond dispute. And it was not just those in the school of racist historiography but everyday people who were pulled into the orbit by the powerful force of this dominant white narrative that would permeate the national historical landscape in narrative and monument.[7]

This has long since been completely discredited in historicism, but it is important to understand one significant reason why for so long there was little serious consideration of Pinchback in historicism. In their histories, Traditionalists either tried to enforce the invisibility of the man who was a force in Louisiana politics, erasing what was for them a troubling legacy of strong Black leadership, or they squeezed in a sentence or two only to discredit him as an unscrupulous and illegitimate leader.[8] And though the Traditionalist interpretation has no scholarly credibility today, the concept of Black inferiority that it engendered lingers in some of the white public imagination. The legacy of racism dies hard if at all, as we see all too well today in our political culture.[9]

Louisiana secondary school textbooks also played their part in erasing Pinchback from history. As late as the 1970s, Pinchback was not included in the roster of governors in secondary school history textbooks. All this enabled conscious amnesia among historians not to look too closely at Pinchback, saving them from confronting the heavy challenges he and his peers presented to the doctrine of white supremacy, particularly the disturbing reality that many of these Black leaders were equal if not superior to most of their white counterparts. "If there was anything that southern Whites feared more than bad Negro government," explained Lerone Bennett Jr., "it was good Negro government." Or, as James Lowen explains, the Reconstruction governments were ultimately "destroyed," not because they were inferior "but because they were succeeding." This troubling challenge to the doctrine of white supremacy contributed to the neglect and distortion of this successful Black leader, among others, through the first half of the twentieth century.[10]

Yet from the beginning of historical exile, Pinchback peered out from behind the heavy iron curtain of silence and distortion, usually in the narratives and memories of African Americans. As early as 1887, William J. Simmons, a Black educator and activist, credited the boldness of Louisiana African Americans to "assert their rights" to Pinchback's "bravery." Even before that, Pinchback's friend, Frederick Douglass, spoke and wrote favorably about Pinchback's work and tenacity. Following the leader's devastating political defeat as Reconstruction began to crumble, Douglass accurately prophesized in a speech he gave in Washington, DC, titled, "The Country Has not Heard the Last of P. B. S. Pinchback." Far from drifting into obscurity after Reconstruction, Pinchback and other African Americans would challenge discrimination in courts and support and participate in direct action for years to come. Because of the strength of Republican and Black power that Pinchback helped build and protect, African Americans would win elections to the Louisiana state legislature until 1896, even as white supremacy surrounded them. With the hardening of white supremacy in traditional white colleges in the South, Pinchback became one of the founders of Southern University in New Orleans, which has gone on to become one of the most flourishing math and science Historical Black College and Universities (HBCUs) in the country (and that today boasts the P. B. S. Pinchback Engineering building). Many Black writers and voices for the next fifty years offered revised accounts of Pinchback and other Black Reconstruction leaders that challenged white distortion and neglect, largely inspired by the brilliant Carter G. Woodson, the founder of the *Journal of Negro History* (today, the *Journal of African American History*) who laid the scholarly foundation in the 1920s for the slow demise of racist historiography.[11]

With few exceptions, however, Pinchback appeared only as a favorable side note or blurb (compared to other Black leaders of Reconstruction) in most historical compilations from the early to mid-twentieth century.[12] But that began to change near midcentury. In her well-researched 1943 thesis, "The Political Career of P. B. S. Pinchback," Agnes Smith Grosz considers Pinchback in more scholarly depth. Although she recycles some of the traditional white views of Pinchback, she concludes that "credit must be accorded his indomitable will and courage, his ability and personal magnetism." By 1967, Pinchback began to emerge more from the shadows when Lerone Bennett Jr. offered a deeply human account of Pinchback's work as a political leader. In *Black Power USA.: The Human Side of Reconstruction, 1866–1877*, he generally avoided the pitfalls of racist historiography that sometimes ensnared Grosz but took artistic liberty in an otherwise solid account. Bennett considered Pinchback one of the most "brilliant" leaders of the Reconstruction Era and "the best practical politician black America has produced." He goes on to demonstrate why in his riveting, lengthy chapter on Louisiana: "Pinchback . . . not only refused to stay in his place but denied by words and deeds that white or black people had any particular place." John Haskins has written the closest we have to a biography on Pinchback—categorized as a young adult biography—with his *P. B. S. Pinchback: The First Black Governor* (1970). Bordering on historical fiction at times, his work gave us even more insight into this important leader whom he credits with giving "much of his life to the cause of black people whom he loved and for whom he fought with all the energy he could summon." In *Louisiana Reconstructed, 1863–1877* (1974), Joe Gray Taylor contextualizes Pinchback and his contemporaries in what is still perhaps the most thorough scholarly narrative of Reconstruction in Louisiana. There has also been interest in examining Reconstruction through the work and visions of Black leaders, including Pinchback. These works include Charles Vincent's

Black Legislators in Louisiana During Reconstruction (1976), Philip Dray's *Capitol Men: The Epic Story of Reconstruction Through the Lives of the First Black Congressmen* (2008), and Louis-Alejandro Dinella-Borrego's *The Risen Phoenix: Black Politics in the Post-Civil War South* (2016). In 2019, Ingrid Dineen-Wimberly gave us a fresh interpretation of Pinchback and other mixed-race Americans in *The Allure of Blackness Among Mixed-Race Americans, 1862–1913* (2019). She writes that, in contrast to accounts that claim that Pinchback was ineffectual, her "research finds that he made significant civil rights strides for the benefit of Black people as a whole." Most recently in *America's Deadliest Election: The Cautionary Tale of the Most Violent Election in American History Election* (2024), Dana Bash and David Fisher focus their lens on the election of 1872 in New Orleans and Louisiana, which includes Pinchback's role in navigating what they describe as "the most contentious and deadliest election in American history." Interestingly and quite convincingly, Bash and Fisher find parallels to today's toxic political landscape.[13]

Aside from the historical literature, and perhaps most importantly, Pinchback and other Reconstruction leaders remained alive in the memories of formerly enslaved persons who lived through Reconstruction and who knew better than anyone that racist historiography was a lie. "'I know folks think the books tell the truth,' said an eighty-eight-year-old former enslaved woman, "but they shore don't."[14] Despite the white supremacist storm to ridicule Reconstruction and demean its Black leaders and participants, Black families kept the truth of Reconstruction alive. James Loewen writes that the "aging slaves whose stories were recorded by Works Progress Administration (WPA) writers in the 1930s remained proud of blacks' roles during Reconstruction. Some still remembered the names of African Americans elected to office sixty years earlier." Eighty-one-year-old Jeffries Moses recalled with pride during his WPA interview that "Many an ex-slave was elected sheriff, county clerk, probate clerk. Pinchback was elected governor of Louisiana. The first Negro Congress-man was from Mississippi and Methodist preacher, Hiram Revels."

Loewen stresses, however, that after this Delta generation passed away, the textbook view informed by racist historiography gradually took over even among Black students.[15]

History books may lie intentionally or by omission. But sooner or later those lies encounter scrutiny. Pinchback not only contributed to creating and maintaining one of the most interracial democratic environments in the Deep South during Reconstruction—or anywhere in America of his times; his and his contemporary's influence can be seen even after the end of Reconstruction and with the interracial democracy that would emerge in the second part of the twentieth century. In the 1940s, John Hope Franklin maintained that "the laws codified based on this constitution (Louisiana 1867–68), together with the laws adopted in three codes, remain even today the basic law of the state." Franklin explained that the new state constitution was written "soon after the overthrow of Reconstruction . . . (was) remarkably similar to the documents that had been so roundly condemned." There were many changes and revisions to be sure, the disenfranchisement of African Americans being the most blatant in the state's infamous 1898 constitution. However, many of the issues that African Americans like Pinchback had worked for doggedly as delegates at the 1867–68 constitutional convention, were maintained by their enemies, such as the public school system and the modernized machinery of local government. In short, white supremacists felt compelled to keep significant parts of the constitutions that were in part birthed and shaped by the Black minds that they now condemned.[16]

When another constitutional convention was held in Louisiana in 1974 to create a new document in alignment with civil rights, delegates largely adopted the same protections and similar language that Pinchback and his peers had worked out in the Louisiana Constitution of 1868, as well as the tone and guarantee of the civil rights that he had helped anchor in law. The 1974 constitution included most importantly a similar bill of rights, or declaration of rights, guaranteeing equality to all citizens before that law and banning discrimination in all forms. Thus, the visionary rights that Pinchback and others helped establish became normative rights throughout Louisiana and the South, often reflecting the tone if not the language of these reconstructionists in their new constitutions.[17]

Black Reconstruction leaders like Pinchback were by far the most consistent advocates for expanding democratic norms during the second half of the nineteenth century. Their legacies provide an important link to the greater fulfillment of democracy in America by creating a precedent and foundation for the inclusion of minorities in American political life. The powerful eloquence of these leaders, not to mention their ability to skillfully exercise power, anticipated the strong Black leadership that would arise in the twentieth century and galvanize millions to confront and sweep away de jure racism.

From the school of racist historiography to the important but incomplete attempts to tell his story, Pinchback has had difficulty emerging authentically and robustly in historicism. Without a deeper analysis of his life and his times, we have often ended up with the unfinished portrait of a one-dimensional leader whom we never get close to knowing and who is reduced to an anomaly of his times. Pinchback and his life are far more interesting and complex than most historians have portrayed, from the deep influence of a mother who had spent half of her life in bondage, to the ambiguity of racial identity and identification in Pinchback's life and world, to a political career that was as tumultuous and rich as any in American history.

This book will attempt to get closer to telling that story more fully, to explore the larger and more nuanced drama of how Pinchback—the hero or anti-hero of New Orleans—used strategy and skill, and force of personality, to navigate obstacles to obtain and maintain power and push an agenda of rights and equality during the Reconstruction Era. We cannot intimately grasp the history of Reconstruction in Louisiana nor, I would argue, the expansion and contraction of democratic values and praxis in the post-slavery period and beyond, without exploring his life and times. Sybil Kein may not be far off the mark when she declares that the history of this era and state is "written around his name."[18] Of course, that history involved many others, as well as the fact that that history had for so long been largely erased. But Pinchback was a tremendously effective egalitarian leader in Louisiana politics, perhaps not unlike his future successor, the charismatic and controversial Huey Long, and his obsession with uplifting the downtrodden and maintaining power while navigating with lively flair the tumultuous Louisiana political landscape of the 1920s and 1930s.

While the timeframe for this political biography is centered within the standard period of Reconstruction, roughly 1866–77 (which is in reality more fluid), when Pinchback's influence and agency were at their height, this book will also offer fresh consideration of Pinchback from his antebellum origins to his post-Reconstruction life. Indeed, to better understand how he navigated the challenges he faced in striving for the rights of the marginalized, it is necessary to know how the people and events in his life, particularly the impact racism had on him and those he loved, influenced his journey from obscurity to the echelon of power and beyond.

Significantly, the painful sting of racism and being plunged into poverty motivated him more than anything else to blaze a fiery trail in politics. According to his grandson, Jean Toomer, Pinchback seethed inwardly from how his mother and family were stripped of their dignity and possessions during his early teen years, which drove him toward his destiny. In a conversation he had with his grandfather in later years, Toomer recalled him explaining, "It was because we were classified as Negroes that we were powerless to prevent ourselves from being outraged, beaten down, and robbed and driven off . . . As a n----r, I was insulted. So then, as a Negro I will be respected. As a n----r I was helpless. *As a Negro I will be powerful.*"[19]

CHAPTER I

PINCHBACK'S EARLY YEARS

FROM CASWELL COUNTY, NC TO NEW ORLEANS, LA

Pinckney Benton Stewart Pinchback was born in passage on May 10, 1837, on one of the coldest nights on record for May that saw rare snowfall blowing across the east and parts of the South. He came into the world while his family was migrating from Caswell County, North Carolina, to their temporary home in New Orleans, Louisiana (to prepare to take over a plantation in Holmes County, Mississippi), shortly after the water broke around Macon, Georgia. The son of a white planter named William Pinchback and an enslaved woman he had freed from bondage, Eliza Stewart, his parents had transgressed the racist boundaries of the day to live openly as life partners on the Caswell County plantation. Making the transgression worse, William was still married to his first wife, a genteel, white, Virginia woman named Lavinia Rudd, with whom he had four older children when he began a relationship with Eliza in the late 1820s. Whether or not they were separated, his preference for Eliza and the family they had started together, caused some rumbling among his North Carolina kin, which grew intense some time before the family migrated to Louisiana and Mississippi.[1]

William's decision to relocate to Mississippi was partly influenced by a series of tobacco depressions, the worst of which occurred around the time of the family's migration. Tobacco planters like William Pinchback watched their profit margins dive as the state-owned tobacco industry in neighboring Danville, Virginia, shut its doors. A recovery would soon lead to the "Boom Era" for the local plantation-based tobacco economy, but in the middle of this latest depression there seemed to be anything but light at the end of the tunnel.²

If William foresaw an eventual revival for tobacco, its economic vulnerability, depletion of the soil, and constant need for fertilizer may have persuaded him to look for greener pastures. And Southern cotton looked like gold by comparison. The land was available, the soil was rich and required little cultivation, and cotton seemed less vulnerable to the economic declines experienced by tobacco. Indeed, the "Delta soil" was "so lush that without fertilizer it produced far more than other land did with fertilizer." For William and many other eastern tobacco planters, the declining price of tobacco and steady demand for cotton inspired an exodus of families, along with the forced migration of enslaved persons, to the thriving alluvial cotton lands of the Mississippi floodplain. With an already growing global demand, its potential seemed boundless. Cotton prices would not see a major drop in value until the severe economic woes of the 1870s, but that was still more than three decades away. Moreover, the devastating boll weevil would not wreak havoc on cotton and profit until the early twentieth century, and even then, some of the best Delta farms would still flourish. From the view of William's time and place, this tiny white fiber was a sure thing that presented unlimited wealth potential.³

Economic factors aside, another impetus for leaving his estate and the only world he knew came from the scorn of white relatives who disapproved of his interracial relationship with Eliza. It was not uncommon for a white master to maintain a dual relationship with his white wife and an enslaved woman without losing status among the community as long as he did not elevate the enslaved mistress to the status of a white person, such as in the famous case of Thomas Jefferson and Sally Hemings, in which Hemings remained in the traditional subordinated status. But for a married white Southern elite to leave his white wife for an enslaved woman, or to make her a priority over his white wife, was not only scorned, it was also sometimes cause to consider the white male as mentally ill. His status could be compromised.⁴

Further creating a sense of urgency to leave North Carolina was the law. As long as Eliza was a slave, William could keep her as his concubine without interference. But some time before heading to Mississippi, William had taken Eliza to Philadelphia where she was legally freed, which was a troublesome signal to his kin and community that he was bestowing onto her the benefits of white privilege. Making her a free woman revealed his emotional attachment to Eliza, along with a desire to create some sense of legitimacy and formality with his life partner, independent of marriage. But North Carolina law did not see it that way. The state mandated that freed slaves must leave

Tobacco Field, Caswell County, NC.

within ninety days of being manumitted or be sold back into bondage, which further pressed the couple to depart as soon as possible.[5]

It appears that it was on the Caswell County plantation where Eliza was born in slavery. Described by a contemporary as a "reputed beauty of mixed blood," she labored as a house servant due to her lighter complexion from her mixed ancestry, which included white, Black, and Native American heritages. The only physical account of Eliza is based on a description of a photograph of her later in life from her great-grandson, Jean Toomer, the celebrated Harlem Renaissance writer. Struggling to determine her heritage, Toomer wrote,

> The brow was broad and well-formed. The face was full (with) large pensive eyes spread rather far apart. The lips were held firmly, the chin set . . . there was not a sign of a wrinkle or a furrow. A well preserved woman, still capable, still in good health . . . . Her complexion was fair . . . I looked for some mark of Negro blood, of Indian blood. I could read into it whatever I pleased. . . .[6]

While the historical record suggests William was a benevolent slave owner who genuinely loved Eliza, profoundly unequal power dynamics characterized these relationships in antebellum times. Taking place within a system of oppression in which white males had complete power and control backed by law and custom, the Black female enslaved persons had no legal protection and often no power to resist. She bore their first child, Elizabeth, when she was only fifteen or sixteen and William was around fifty. Sexual abuse was the harsh reality for many enslaved Black women. Like other master/slave intimate relationships, William and Eliza's relationship emerges against the backdrop that she was his property to do with as he pleased. She was proscribed to a specific space that he controlled and dominated as a white master, no matter how benevolent he was. In this kind of relationship, she may not have been able to choose her marital destiny on the same level as a free woman or even a plantation woman independent of the severely restricted options presented to her as an enslaved woman whose master desired her.[7]

But we also do not know what Eliza thought and felt about her situation or how she defined her life. We can never be sure if she could have said no to William's sexual advances and if he would have abided by her wishes, or even the possibility that in Eliza's case, her options were not as restricted as we generally read into the lives of enslaved women (and men) and that William was who she wanted to be within a relationship where both had a genuine love for each other. In other, similar relationships, there appears to have been reciprocal love, such as the one between white planter Ralph Quarles and former bondswoman Lucy Langston, whose son would become one of the last Black congressmen of Reconstruction, John Mercer Langston. Enslaved women in Eliza's situation should not be viewed as never having any sense of agency and always consigned to a state of victimhood, even in a world with severely restricted options where they had virtually no legal power. The vulgarity of slavery does not define every aspect of an enslaved person's life. Doing so strips them of personhood, diminishing the vastness and complexity of their lives and identities and rendering the actual details of their lives insignificant. While the following is only conjecture, Eliza may have been the one who advocated for her freedom, as well as her children's, thus being an agent in their liberation and empowerment. She may have influenced William's noted view that slaves were "human beings, compared to his peer's natural contempt." She also could have been a partner in the decision to go further south and start a new life far away from the place of her former bondage and those that threatened her new freedom. It is important to keep in mind that Eliza would build with William a life, home, and family as a free woman, which is an indication that she likely lived a life not as one forced upon her but instead as one that she considered her own and had carved out of the challenges of the times.[8]

In April-May of 1837, pregnant with Pinckney and not far from giving birth, Eliza joined William in packing all their belongings. With their three children by this time, Elizabeth (1825/1829), Napoleon (1830), and Mary (1832), they began the laborious trek to Louisiana in the unusually chilly spring weather. About midway into their trip, around Macon, Georgia, Eliza started labor, and the family quickly found quarters. Pinckney was thus born in freedom in the antebellum South as his family made passage from their old world to a new one.⁹

Sometime during their journey, William's first wife Lavinia and her children joined the migrating party. According to Toomer, the families and enslaved persons journeyed together in a caravan to New Orleans before settling on the Holmes County, Mississippi, plantation. With the children from Lavinia adults by this time—the oldest son John was almost thirty—they took financial interest with their father in the cotton plantation and came to help him operate it. There are no accessible details about this cohabitation or how Eliza's family navigated the tensions that must have arisen from this arrangement. We also do not know how Lavinia dealt with losing her status to Eliza, who was a constant reminder of her demotion. Eliza's children from William would have felt the perpetual awkwardness if not resentment caused by this cohabitation, thus compromising the stable world she tried to build for them in freedom. Toomer writes that while William's two families "lived under an arrangement galling to both," they were "held apart by him during his life, and also somewhat harmonized all those years."¹⁰

After Pinckney's birth, the two families spent time in New Orleans prior to moving to Holmes County. During an interview in 1872, Pinchback says that he came to New Orleans with his family the "same year" of his birth "on the way" to his "father's plantation in Holmes County, Miss." It is unclear how long the families stayed in New Orleans, which was likely a layover as preparations were being made for their new home. Two to three years after the Pinchback family arrived in Holmes County, William purchased a 2,363-acre cotton plantation for under $30,000. His purchase may have included enslaved persons since those held in bondage on working plantations were often included in the sale price. The Holmes County census for 1840 lists seventy-seven enslaved persons owned by William, making this new cotton plantation owner one of the largest slave owners in the county at this time. The enormous sum paid for the plantation reveals that William was a man of means and that the family lived a privileged lifestyle in Holmes County. But William got this prime real estate at a bargain. If the Panic of 1837 was an impetus for William to flee the hard-hit tobacco region of North Carolina and Virginia, it may have also been a motivation to buy cotton land in Mississippi at reduced rates. Many new cotton planters had lost vast sums of money during the financial crisis because their plantations rested on credit from collapsing local banks. This sent land prices in the Delta region for a dive, though the price and demand for cotton were impacted very little. As a result, the price William paid in 1840 for the prime acreage making up the Holmes County plantation, one of the highest land values anywhere in the nation, appears to have been about a third of what it would have been before the crisis.[11]

Today Holmes County has been called the "poorest county in America's poorest state." During a recent trip there, this writer observed that it is a landscape still marred by intense poverty from the economic deprivation caused by the legacy of racism. But during antebellum times, it was one of the most prosperous regions in the country. When the Pinchbacks arrived in Holmes County in the late 1830s, Mississippi was "a frontier of vast and fertile lands tracts" where aspiring cotton planters had been flowing in for about a decade. Located in the central western part of Mississippi just Northeast of Yazoo City, Holmes County is hedged in by the Yazoo River on its western border and the Big Black River on its eastern border. Although it was frontier country with its "forbidding swamp forest full of immense trees and impenetrable canebrakes," cotton was already the commodity crop with plantations forming along the riverfronts of its silty Mississippi flood plain, worked laboriously by enslaved persons who formed the majority population.[12]

P. B. S., or Pinky as the family affectionately called him as a child, would spend close to his first decade of life on the Holmes County plantation. Without much information about this period of Pinchback's childhood, historian James Haskins creatively imagines what that childhood must have been like. He writes that Pinchback would have had much space to run and play and probably had many opportunities as a privileged child to cultivate an active and adventuresome imagination. Haskins surmises that while the child could possibly have passed for white, he may have nevertheless identified with his Black heritage early on: "One can picture him, curious about his black heritage, spending much time with the slaves in the quarters, listening to their songs and their stories—stories of their forefathers in Africa, stories of slavery, stories of joy and pain. Perhaps they helped him become proud of that part of him that was them."[13] This is speculative and an overly romantic description to be sure. One longs to hear Pinchback's recollection from his childhood on the Holmes County plantation, which, unfortunately, is not part of the accessible historical record. His Black heritage and the grinding reality of slavery likely prevented him from living in an insular world, not to mention the backdrop of his mother's time in bondage while now living in cohabitation with his father's white family that once benefited from her enslavement. Toomer writes that Pinchback "did not fit in any too well" on the plantation because his family was likely "subjected . . . to open prejudice and frequent insult on the part of those who felt themselves legitimate, white, and superior." According to Toomer, at some point in his grandfather's

Pinchback Lake on Pinchback Plantation, Holmes County, Mississippi. Courtesy of the author.

childhood, the harmony that William had maintained gave way to frequent clashes between the white and Black families until it all became so unbearable that Pinchback ran away from home for several months. He believed that this fostered a rebellious spirit in the young man that he would carry throughout his tumultuous political career. "Yet there may be a gleam of truth in Haskins' romantic description. Rather than disappearing into a white world as an adult, or even into a respected Creole planter world, as one contemporary noted he could have done,[14] Pinchback embraced his Black "heritage more fully." Toomer writes that his grandfather "claimed he had Negro blood, linked himself with the cause of the Negro and rose to power."[15] All of this is speculative, but it is possible that his racial consciousness was first formed on the plantation in Holmes County and perhaps in no small part by the enslaved persons with whom he interacted.

Pinchback's consciousness was undoubtedly shaped by his mother who had spent half of her life in bondage. A strong influence in his life, Eliza encouraged him to expand his educational horizons. She planted the seeds for his abhorrence of racism as well the structures and behavior that degraded Black people, not only by word but also by her own enslavement.

Once Pinchback established a home in New Orleans and entered politics, Eliza would reside with the family until her death. She was a source of encouragement for Pinchback; it always pleased him to make her proud, and he would always consider himself her protector. He told his grandson later in life that he was "more attached" to her than his father and identified with her throughout his life. Thus, it was a mother who had been born in bondage that had shaped her son's character and confidence in freedom.[16]

Remarkably, the Holmes County plantation today still maintains the deep imprint left by the Pinchback family more than one hundred and fifty years ago. Although they were there for a little less than ten years until William's death, the plantation is still referred to as Pinchback Plantation with a designated Pinchback Lake full of moss-draped cypress trees, stretching from the water as they did back in the antebellum days. Presently, Pinchback Road winds past the lake, through the middle of sprawling cotton fields speckled with seasonal white blossoms stretching as far as the eye can see. Other than wider dirt roads, telephone poles, and a few homes, the dominant cotton field landscape of Pinchback Plantation harkens back to the past when Pinchback lived there as a child.[17]

At the age of nine, Pinchback's life on the plantation in the rural slaveholding South would be replaced by one in the urban free North. In 1846, William and Eliza sent Pinckney and his brother Napoleon, who was around sixteen, to Gilmore School in Cincinnati. Founded by abolitionist and philanthropist Hiram Gilmore, the curriculum was structured around a liberal arts education modeled after prestigious white private schools. With a national reputation for having the best teachers at any African American school, and funded by donors nationwide, Gilmore taught students "Latin, Greek, music and drawing" as well as algebra and advanced courses in English. Gilmore was importantly an early college preparatory school where a "significant proportion" of pupils, many of whom were fathered by Southern white planters, would go on to the few colleges like Oberlin "which drew no color line on matriculation."[18] Many of the future Black elites would pass through Gilmore High School, such as John Mercer Langston, who would go on to become minister to Haiti under President Hayes in 1877 as well as a Virginia congressman in 1888.[19]

William and Eliza clearly desired for their sons to have the best education possible. Before that, under Eliza's oversight, the boys were educated at home by tutors, which was common for aristocratic or privileged households of that time. Gilmore was not only an elite school that offered advanced academic training; it was a stepping-stone for a better life and even college. While there is no information about how Napoleon did at Gilmore, Pinckney

Cincinnati around the time that Napoleon and Pinckney attended Gilmore School.

was far from the ideal student and did not seem to fit into the structure and discipline of the school. The familiar story goes that he paid little attention in class and skipped whenever he could get away with it to play dice with other truants down by the docks of the bustling port city.[20] Only nine years old, Pinckney was more attracted to the glitz and freedom of urban Cincinnati Pinckney than the stuffy classroom or the predictable drabness of the rural Mississippi plantation.

But Cincinnati also presented lurking danger. The city was not much more than a stone's throw across the Ohio River from the slaveholding state of Kentucky. Slave catchers crossed over regularly and roamed the city in search of runaways, often aggressively accosting free African Americans suspected of harboring runways and sometimes kidnapping them if they could get away with it. Cincinnati was also a city with a rising tide of anti-Black sentiment, which at times erupted into white mob violence against African Americans and Black communities. As much as it was an adventuresome place for Pinckney, it was a hazardous world where he had to be on guard and navigate ubiquitous anti-Black dangers.

In 1848, Pinckney and Napoleon's time at Gilmore would be cut short when they were summoned home. Their father was dying, and shortly after the boys arrived home, he passed away. Eleven-year-old Pinckney escorted his father's body, along with family and friends, to the "highest peak" in Holmes County, one of the familiar craggy bluffs in that part of the Delta overlooking the flatlands below where he was buried in a cemetery that today still bears his name. Surrounded only by a handful of neighbors interred nearby, William would be left in this lonely place "far into the woods" with no kinfolk to visit, as his family would forever leave Holmes County.[21]

Only days after his burial, William's sister, Lydia (Pinchback) Holman, inherited the land and appears to have refused to disperse anything substantial to his interracial family and wasted no time in selling the plantation. The white family, according to Toomer, "rose to arms against what they regarded the bastard n----r family." He continues: "Their pent up sense of wrong, humiliation, injustice, outrage broke bonds and now struck at the defenseless family of Eliza Stewart." White relatives not only left Eliza and her family destitute; they also made moves to force the family into bondage. Toomer writes that "suddenly . . . she found herself in a vortex of grief, rivalry, urgent needs, apprehension, threats, the odds stacked against her . . . ." But William had had enough foresight to plan for their protection by creating a way to usher them to a free state "beyond the reach of their possible captors." He accomplished this by creating a legal document, confusing at first glance, where he appears to have sold his free family as slaves to two local men named David Holeman and William Jacobs.[22]

This document was created in 1845, three years before his death. In it, William arranged to receive "the sum of one Hundred dollars" from Holeman and Jacobs in exchange for "the following Negro slaves to wit: Eliza, a woman now about thirty-five years of age and her children Napoleon now about fifteen years of age; Mary Louisa about thirteen years of age; Pinckney Benton ten years old and Adeline four years old."[23] Two other twin brothers, William Henry and Nathaniel, were born after this document was created sometime around 1847, perhaps shortly after William passed away. The oldest child, Elizabeth, who may have been around twenty years old, according to the earliest birth date we have for her, is not included in this document either, possibly because she was not living with the family at this time.[24]

In this deed, William gives these two men "good and lawful right and title to said Slaves," including the explicit right to "sell and dispose of them." William then does something unusual which contradicts the right of Holeman and Jacobs to "sell and dispose" by stating that they are to agree that "should in some convenient time at the request of each and all of said slaves remove them to one of the non-slaveholding states . . . and truly set free and Emancipate each all of said Slaves with their future increase (meaning children) . . . as to discharge and acquit them from all bonds of Slavery and to make them and each of them free." William concludes this document by essentially repeating the part about setting his family free in a free state on their own terms. In short, William legally makes his family slaves but then gives them the power to eradicate their bondage.[25]

Holeman and Jacobs were trusted friends who assisted William in creating this shrewd document. Holeman was also the husband of Pinchback's sister Lydia, who appears to have been the one who would make sure that Eliza and her family would get nothing, an interesting twist of different loyalties in the same marriage. Eliza was free by this time for almost ten years, and the children were also likely free. Mary Louisa and Napoleon may have been manumitted with their mother, and Pinckney was born free. But without William's protection, that status could become precarious if his white relatives tried to claim them as property, particularly in a state that frowned upon Blacks living there as anything but slaves. Indeed, by the time of this deed, there were virtually no documented free Blacks in Mississippi. William understood that to protect his mixed-heritage family in the event of his death—he was seventy years old when he created this document—he would have to create a legal shield to protect them from being enslaved. He made sure that his family would be considered the legal property of Holeman and Jacobs, hoping to create a safeguard that would protect them from being left vulnerable as property in his estate, which could be confiscated by his white relatives and/or the state. In reality, the three men created a guardianship under the guise of a slave sale to protect the family that would be eventually transported to a free state.[26]

Shortly after William's death, the family hastily left Holmes County for Cincinnati, desperate and humiliated by their mistreatment and forced exodus, a scar that Pinchback would carry for the rest of his life. While his father had created the will to protect his family, Pinchback would go on to feel that it prevented any chance for an inheritance because they were misclassified as slaves. Pinckney and Napoleon never imagined that they would be returning to Cincinnati with their family in tow, particularly under such dire conditions. According to one source, Eliza was close to forty by this time, and the migrating family included sisters Mary and Adeline and possibly the two brothers (either still infants or very young children).[27] It was one thing for two young schoolboys on their own to navigate the dangers as well as the opportunities in Cincinnati. But a migrating Black family with more mouths to feed faced greater challenges in a city that was no utopia for Black residents. By the time the Pinchbacks arrived in 1848, the city had endured three racial riots and was far from the most welcoming place to a family of Black Southern transplants. Toomer believes they arrived in the city as a white family, but this has been difficult to confirm. Whatever the case, without the adequate resources they had been denied, they were thrust into a life of poverty in a world of profound uncertainty in a crowded urban setting.[28]

Things would get even tougher for Pinckney. When nineteen-year-old Napoleon, overwhelmed with the burden that now fell on his shoulders, sunk into despair, twelve-year-old Pinckney was forced to take responsibility for keeping the family afloat. What an enormously heavy responsibility to help his mother and five siblings, particularly at such a young age. In addition to Napoleon, Mary, and Adeline, the family included two infant twins, born shortly before or after the family migrated to Cincinnati. But his time on the city's streets may have equipped him well for hustling money. Street-savvy from navigating areas of Cincinnati while skipping school, Pinckney quickly began earning money by running errands for street vendors and local merchants and carrying bags for travelers disembarking riverboats and steamboats.[29]

Less than a year later, in 1849, Pinckney would find a better paying job with more stability working on the boats plowing the Ohio canals. Here he earned eight dollars a month shining shoes in a barbershop, most of which he used to help his family in Cincinnati. In 1854, after more than five years working the canal boats, the now seventeen-year-old Pinckney was old enough to get a job working as a steward on a steamboat plying the Mississippi, Missouri, and Red Rivers. He had reached the highest position for an African American in the steamboat world, supervising enslaved workers and free African Americans, which was common for Black stewards.[30]

Highly prized by African Americans in the mid-nineteenth century, steamboat jobs provided an escape from the harsher aspects of social and cultural racism on land and stirred their imaginations for freedom and self-determination. Pinchback was one among thousands of free and enslaved African Americans who worked on these cosmopolitan centers roving the superhighways of the day, carrying travelers from all over the country and even Europe. Steamboats gave African Americans a rich point of observation and encounter that they may not have had otherwise. Thomas Buchanan writes that it was a "proud thing to be part of the crew" and that "African American river workers were heroic figures in the slave community."[31]

Some of the most prominent future Black politicians during Reconstruction had spent their obscure teens and early adult years working on steamboats, forming lifelong friendships and alliances. During his own time sailing the Mississippi and other rivers, Pinchback became friends with future Black leaders such as Norris Wright Cuney, who would go on to become the most influential Black leader in Texas during Reconstruction; future South Carolina Lieutenant Governor Richard Gleaves; Josiah T. Settle, who would become a district attorney in Mississippi and member of the state house of representatives and then assistant attorney general in Shelby County,

Tennessee; and James Lewis, a future fellow Louisiana state senator who would struggle for civil rights and one day provide the crucial vote that would make Pinchback lieutenant governor of the state.[32]

Working on a steamboat offered Pinchback a more unconventional opportunity—one that gives rise to the most colorful story of his early years. One day while he was busy with his duties, Pinchback met the legendary riverboat gambler, George Devol, who took a strong interest in the young steward. Self-proclaimed as the "most daring gambler in the world," the audacious braggart Devol had been playing cards for money since he was eleven, skillfully cheating his childhood companions to get the best of them.[33] He had shared with Pinchback a strong dislike of school as a child, preferring to play "hooky," and was wildly precocious. He refused to conform and got into trouble daily for fighting and mischief, and the more austere members of his church-going Ohio community predicted that the troublesome youth would "be hung if he lives to be twenty years old." Evading their prophecy of early death by lynching, Devol became a larger-than-life personality after he made his way to the riverboats where gambling was the sport of the day. According to his narrative, he hired Pinchback as his personal steward and became a surrogate father to "Pinch." Devol and some of his cohorts "instructed him in the mysteries of card-playing," and practiced together daily while smoking cigars, sipping whiskey, and telling colorful stories.[34]

Pinchback's gambling in this seedy world began to stir up trouble for him. With a knack for cards, he quickly became an expert at poker or any other card game he learned, and he knew how to get the best of his opponents. It was common for other African Americans in the steamboat world to take up gambling as well, often entertaining white passengers with marathon gambling sessions. Sometimes fights would break out around the gambling table, and the table Pinchback played at was no exception; he would sometimes provoke the ire of opponents after beating them and taking all they had. Whenever the riverboat docked, Pinchback would put on his dapper best and stroll into the saloons at places like Memphis and New Orleans with his winnings to live it up and where, according to Toomer, he would go "whoring." On one occasion, according to a story, the deckhands decided they wanted to keep their money as the riverboat was about to reach the port and tried to take back what they had lost to Pinchback. The gambler managed to get away with his winnings, so the story goes, but not without an alleged shootout that left one man dead, though it is not clear who did the killing. Whatever truth there is to this story, this was the sometimes-perilous world of riverboat gambling, where desperation and anger could sweep in in an instant and where only a certain type of man had the nerve and skill to navigate the turbulence. It

Pinchback in his twenties. Courtesy of University of Tennessee, Knoxville. Special Collections.

was also a world where strange bonds of genuine friendship could be forged around the gambling table, ones that transcended racial barriers at times, and where predatory gamblers like Devol and Pinchback would take care of each other and even act as a surrogate family.[35]

By the latter 1850s, around the age of twenty, Pinchback left the world of steamboat gambling on the Mississippi and took a job as a waiter at the Stewart House Hotel in Terre Haute, Indiana, located in the southwestern part of the state, not far from the Illinois border. Pinchback's movements and motivations here are a mystery. It is not clear why he came to the far western Indiana city.[36] Sometime before or after his arrival, he began going by Pinckney Stewart, dropping his father's name, and using only his mother's maiden name. This change might indicate that at this stage of his life, he was grappling with less-positive feelings about his slave-owning father and wanting to identify wholly with his mother, a "devotion" to whom he maintained for his entire life and whose past enslavement and mistreatment by his father's white family he deplored. Taking on the name Stewart could also imply that he was trying to conceal his identity. If there is truth to the story of his shootout that left one man dead, this or possibly a similar episode in the heated aftermath of a gambling night turned bad may offer one explanation why Pinchback suddenly fled the lucrative world of riverboat gambling to be a porter at a hotel under a different name in an area that was still considered the fringes of civilization.[37]

There is a printed pencil drawing of Pinchback in his papers at Howard University from around this time where he appears to be in his early twenties. It shows a youthful young man with wavy black hair, a bushy mustache, intense eyes, and bronze skin. It is not clear where the young man in this drawing went next. According to a few solid accounts, he moved from Terre Haute to Memphis in 1860. Even though Memphis was a Southern slave city teeming with anti-Black sentiment, it was also a "Black Mecca." With its politically astute free African American population, Black Memphis flourished with hundreds of fraternal and mutual aid societies, along with a community that was known to harbor runaway enslaved persons. It was while living in Memphis, according to one account, where the young Pinchback met his future wife, the sixteen-year-old Nina Emily Hawthorn.[38] (Other accounts maintain the two had met and married in New Orleans in 1860, which will be considered later.[39]) Pinchback resided briefly in Memphis before he found work again on a steamboat at the beginning of the Civil War. And it would be from the turbulent waters of war that stirred during his time on a steamboat that he would embark on a stormy military career that would fuel his passion, if not rage, and launch him into politics.

CHAPTER 2

PINCHBACK JOINS THE STRUGGLE FOR LIBERATION

FROM EARLY LIFE ON THE RIVER TO CAPTAIN IN THE ARMY

Pinckney Pinchback understood clearly what the fall of New Orleans meant. When General Benjamin Butler marched into the city on May 1, 1862, he brought with him more than an occupying army; he created a space for a revolution that would transform this Southern world from a restricted land of slavery to a new one of freedom and inclusion. During this time, Pinchback, who now resided in Memphis, was working as a steward on the *Alonzo Child*, a large side-wheel steamer, later made famous by Mark Twain, who would pilot the boat for a time. When the steamer ran into a Confederate blockade at Yazoo City, not far from the Holmes County plantation where Pinchback had spent his childhood, he jumped ship and made his way through the blockade to reach New Orleans on May 12.[1]

In New Orleans lived the wealthiest and most educated free Black community in the Deep South. Pinchback knew they were restless to join the Northern cause and that the occupying Union army would have to accommodate their aspirations. Less than two weeks after Butler had arrived with Union forces, Pinchback was in the Crescent City to fight for the North, apparently enlisting in the military shortly after his arrival. His rise in this world would be meteoric, perhaps assisted by the connections and friendships he had made on the riverboats and possibly from his father's influential circle of friends and associates in the city. Most importantly, his rise was due to his moxie and determination. However, trouble stirred for him from the start. Four days after his arrival, on May 16, Pinchback was accosted by a "free man of color" named John Keppard, who was brandishing a knife and who by some accounts was Pinchback's brother-in-law. While defending himself, Pinchback stabbed Keppard and was immediately arrested. Released on bond, he was arrested by military authorities and sentenced to two years of hard labor for "assault with intent to kill." When the sentence was handed down, he "nearly fainted in court, having pleaded guilty on the advice of his lawyer that the judge would show leniency." Serving only two months of his sentence, he was released from jail. What transpired during those two months to get Pinchback out of jail after such harsh sentencing is a mystery. He claims that he "effected" his "release," though how he did it is unclear.[2]

On July 28, two days after his release, Pinchback became a private in the newly organized First Regiment Infantry. This was a white unit, as were all Union military units that were being raised in Louisiana at that time. Because of the ardent racism of white soldiers and officers, it is unlikely that a white regiment would have tolerated a Black soldier in its ranks. General Butler also still opposed arming African Americans, and it would be another month before he finally changed his mind and issued Order 63.[3]

"AS A NEGRO I WILL BE POWERFUL": PINCHBACK'S FINAL PASSAGE INTO A BLACK IDENTITY

With all considered, was the man who would become one of the most definitively Black leaders of Reconstruction passing for white during this time? Pinchback's prison record does not refer to him as "colored" or "negro," as we would expect to see, only a generalized description: "age 24; height, 5 ft. 9 ¼ in.; the color of hair, black; the color of eyes, black." He may have very well been arrested as a white man, which makes sense since he would go from jail to a white regiment. Pinchback's fellow white soldiers and officers apparently believed he was white until "it was discovered that he had Negro blood" about a month into his service. This discovery coincided with Butler's change of mind about recruiting African Americans. Shortly after, the newly identified Black Pinchback was tapped to "recruit a company of (Black) Louisiana volunteers for the United States Army," which began a short military career that would transform his life and launch him into politics.[4]

All this begs the question: did Pinchback look white? In a pencil sketch where he appears to be in his mid-twenties, his skin tone appears bronze-colored, and his features reveal more of his African heritage.[5] This sketch is consistent with a few later photographs of an older Pinchback. However, the most reproduced image is a photograph taken in his mid- to late thirties at the height of his political career. In this photograph, Pinchback has an angular nose and a neatly trimmed beard, appearing as a Gilded Age white aristocrat with no hint of his African heritage. This photograph was taken by Matthew Brady, who photographed many famous people of his time, Black and white, and who is most known for capturing gruesome scenes of Civil War battlefields.[6] By the time of the Pinchback photograph in the 1870s, Brady was experimenting with innovative lighting techniques that tended to wash out natural color tone, giving skin tone a lighter appearance. This is likely why Pinchback appears white, or lighter, in this familiar photograph.

Many firsthand impressions reflect ambiguity over Pinchback's ethnic/racial appearance and surmise his passing potential. One newspaper reporter described him "not darker than an Arab" whose features are "just perceptibly African" and who could "pass for a wealthy Creole planter." Shortly after spending time at Pinchback's residence in New Orleans, Frederick Douglass wrote in an article for the *New National Era*, "Mr. Pinchback is a colored man, but only colored enough to be thus classified by the most skillful discerners of proscribed blood." He continued: "Anywhere outside of the United States he might pass for a Spaniard, Frenchman, an Italian, or an East Indian, but here, where color is more important than character, he is easily and quickly coupled with the hated race."[7]

Revealing racial indeterminacy to even the most casual observer, Pinchback recounted a story of a policeman stopping him on a New Orleans street, asking, "Are you a white man, or what are you?" Pinchback's grandson, the Harlem Renaissance writer Jean Toomer, remembered how as a child he witnessed his grandfather happily mistaken for the white industrialist, Andrew Carnegie, while riding streetcars in Washington, DC. Indeed, pictures of the two men during their later years look almost identical. Many of these accounts reflecting ambiguity over Pinchback's racial identity likely convinced even the astute W. E. B. Du Bois to write in his study, *Black Reconstruction*, that Pinchback for "all intents and purposes . . . was an educated, well-to-do congenial white man, with but a few drops of Negro blood, which he never stooped to deny . . . ."[8]

Pinchback's response to a white reporter's question about his racial identity is revealing. During an interview in 1872, the reporter asked, "In what proportion is your blood colored?" Pinchback responded, "I regard myself as a quadroon, or about one-fourth colored." The reporter then tried to push him to identify with one or the other: "Of which you are the proudest, the African or the Anglo-Saxon blood in your veins?" Not taking the bait,

Matthew Brady's photograph of Pinchback. Library of Congress, Prints & Photographs Division, LC-DIG-cwpbh-03857.

Pinchback answered, "I don't think the question is a legitimate one, as I have no control over the matter."⁹

For Pinchback's sister, Adeline, her brother not only looked white; she tried to convince him that he was white. In a letter dated April 30, 1863, Adeline pleads with her brother to take his "position in the world as a white man as you are." Written in response to the racism Pinchback and other Black officers were encountering from white Union officers in Louisiana, Adeline stressed to her brother that "you will <u>never</u> get your rights." She explained that "<u>mobs</u> are constantly breaking out in different parts of the North and even in Canada against the oppressed colored race." Even in Cincinnati, her hometown and supposed free territory, African Americans "can hardly walk the streets but they are attacked." Adeline goes on to explain that her husband Reuben had decided to pass for white in Cincinnati to the bitter consternation of the Black community. She tries to convince her brother that African Americans "will never be righted in the world" and urges him to "have as little to do with the Negroes as you can" and urges him again to pass into the white world. "You will fare better in the end," she writes. Adeline explains that she has not only passed into the white world, never to return, but that she also considers herself white: "I have nothing to do with the negroes, am not one of them." She closed with a plea to Pinchback: "Take my advice dear brother and do the same."[10]

Adeline's abandonment of that part of her heritage, while tragic in one sense, was also an act of survival in a deeply racist world, as her letter to Pinchback implies. Many who could pass felt that there was no choice, no in-between, only Black and white. If you were the former, which meant a drop of Black blood according to the white American racist lexicon, life could be exceedingly difficult and dangerous, as she stressed in her letter. Passing was a controversial strategy to escape the harsh reality of living Black in a deeply racist society to enjoy the rights and privileges of living white. This is the reason that African Americans even without the option to pass rarely betrayed those who did, understanding why they did it, even if provoking their ire, as was the case with Rueben who "was called every insulting name" for passing.[11] Adeline was only one of many whose faint appearance of African heritage, if even that, gave them the option to permanently pass into the white world for a chance at an easier life with more opportunities, and one that was much safer. According to Toomer, two of Pinchback's brothers also "left home . . . and were thereafter known as white." These may have been Pinchback's two youngest twin brothers, William Henry and Nathaniel, who disappeared without a trace. Toomer recalled his grandfather explaining without judgment that "they saw it to their advantage to do what they did."[12]

The oncoming Reconstruction period would present for some the possibility of Black identity as an asset. But in such a racialized climate before this (and after), where much of white society was determined to degrade Black humanity, there was a great incentive for many to distance themselves from their Black communities and even families by passing. The tragedy, then, was not only turning from their Black heritage but also living in a corrupt society that so normalized the degradation and dehumanization of African Americans that, given the choice, some would abandon all they knew for a better life.

Pinchback may have passed into the white world by joining the First Infantry, which, according to Toomer, he had done several times "between the ages of 12 and 21." However, by the time of Adeline's letter, as she passed forever into the white world, he had definitively crossed back over to the Black world, which deeply angered his sister. Toomer believed that Pinchback's decision may have been interwoven with how his family was mistreated after the death of his father, particularly the distress that it caused his mother Eliza, whom he described as "beaten down" by the loss and displacement. "It was an ugly situation for the Stewart family," he wrote, "and a dangerous one, since the law, public opinion, and money were all on the side" of the white family. Because of Pinchback's deep attachment to his mother, he was powerfully motivated to identify with the Black rather than the white aspects of his heritage. He seems to have seethed inwardly with anger against the indignities that his family suffered, and it may have driven him to achieve against such odds the liberation of Black people. "His fighting blood was aroused," wrote Toomer. "It remained aroused for forty years or more." Pinchback would write in an editorial that appeared in the New York *Herald* in 1876 that he had been "[r]obbed of a competency in my youth by my father's kindred," meaning deprived of education and opportunities by his white relatives, who forced his family into dire poverty. According to Toomer, his grandfather explained, "It was because we were classified as Negroes that we were powerless to prevent ourselves from being outraged, beaten down, and robbed and driven off [from the Mississippi plantation]. As a n----r, I was insulted. So then, as a Negro I will be respected. As a n----r I was helpless. *As a Negro I will be powerful.*"[13]

Less than a week after General Butler had opened the door by issuing General Order No. 63, officially authorizing the enlistment of Black troops in the Louisiana Native Guards, Pinchback, on August 27, 1862, was "authorized" to raise a company of Black soldiers for the Second Louisiana Native Guards. In the weeks that followed, while thousands of African Americans joined to fight for the North in the First Louisiana Native Guards, Pinchback was actively recruiting African Americans to fill the ranks of the Second Louisiana Native Guards.[14]

Butler was initially reluctant to enlist Black soldiers in Louisiana. The stolid, droopy-eyed general from Massachusetts hated slavery, but he was only willing to go so far. President Lincoln still objected to arming runaways for fear that it would push teetering border states to side with the South, and Butler oddly believed African Americans lacked a propensity for military service. While commander of Fort Monroe at the southern tip of the Virginia Peninsula in 1861, he had declared runaways flowing into his camp as contraband of war, which gave him justification for refusing to return them as mandated by federal law. Acting on his own accord to free enslaved persons impressed abolitionists, including the Northern free Black community, and set a precedent for freeing all runaways coming into Union camps and controlled territory. Significantly, Butler's action was the first step leading toward Lincoln's Emancipation Proclamation. But he resisted demands from Northern abolitionists to enlist runaways as soldiers, employing them only as laborers to cut down trees and strengthen fortifications. And once in New Orleans, he maintained this policy of Black labor.[15]

General Benjamin Butler, Union leader in occupied New Orleans, who paved the way for Black soldiers and officers to serve in the Civil War. Library of Congress, Prints & Photographs Division, Civil War Photographs, LC-DIG-cwpb-04895.

A potential threat soon prompted Butler to have second thoughts. The general feared that a Confederate army thwarted by Union forces in Baton Rouge might eventually make its way to New Orleans. His appeals for Union reinforcements were answered with a directive to recruit loyal Irish and German immigrants in New Orleans. Butler quickly learned that this potential pool was dry, and he immediately turned to the city's free African American community, most of whom were light-skinned descendants of French settlers and Black women, or Creoles, along with others of mixed Black and white heritage. Before the fall of New Orleans, this community, some of whom were slaveowners, had pressured local Confederate forces to enlist them to protect the city "against any enemy who may come and disturb its tranquility."[16]

In the early days of Louisiana secession, fifteen hundred free African Americans in New Orleans took it upon themselves to form a Confederate military unit before recognition and called themselves the Native Guards. Louisiana governor Thomas D. Moore responded to their appeals to serve on May 2, 1861, by recognizing the Native Guards as part of the Louisiana militia.

Thus, one of the most unprecedented social movements in American history up to that time, which quickly elevated African Americans to be officers as well as enlisted men, began not in the North, but with a Confederate governor's recognition of African American soldiers in the Louisiana militia.[17]

Shortly after the Union occupation of New Orleans, the Native Guards disbanded and returned to their homes. When Butler put out feelers to enlist Black soldiers for the Union cause, he found the precedent created by the city's free Black population and authorized by the Confederacy. While Butler claims that he approached the city's free Black leadership after learning "they had raised a colored regiment," it appears that a committee composed of Black officers surrendered their weapons to Butler; during the weapons surrender, they explored the possibility of reorganizing the Native Guards for the Union army. Butler recounts asking them, "How come you, free colored men, fighting here for the Confederacy—fighting for slavery?" They answered that they did so out of self-preservation and self-interest, fearful that if this free class of property owners living in precarious freedom declined to show allegiance, their lives and wealth would have been vulnerable to white hostility.[18]

There is certainly truth to this fear. While many Creoles identified with whites of similar economic and social status, most of the wealthiest members of the New Orleans free Black community did not have the same vested interest in protecting their slave-based wealth as white planters. Free Blacks in New Orleans owned about two thousand slaves. But most had only a few slaves who were "usually members of their own families whom they often manumitted" whenever they could traverse the law against manumission. Wealth in slaves was not concentrated within the New Orleans free Black community, as was the case with white planters. Many Black slaveholders were committed to emancipation, submitting "501 of the 1,353 manumission petitions in the emancipation courts between 1827 and 1851." The fact that the Creole elite went so easily over to the Union side when their white counterparts remained loyal to the Confederacy reveals that they still suffered limitations by white society because of their mixed heritage.[19]

With all considered, it is no surprise that many of this free Black community were ready to enthusiastically commit to the Union, whose principles aligned much more closely with their own. As free African Americans flowed into the Union ranks early on, at least as many runaway slaves joined as well, soon making up more than half of the First Louisiana Native Guards.[20] Runaways thus pushed to another level the social movement that had begun with free African Americans in the Confederate militia, emancipating themselves and compelling Butler to accommodate them as soldiers in the Union Army, even with no authorization from Washington.

2nd Louisiana Native Guards, the Union regiment that PBS Pinchback inspired and built.

With this strong trust from free and formerly enslaved African Americans, Butler accepted arming runaway slaves, still without authorization from Washington, which refused to answer his requests on the matter. It would not be until a month after the Native Guards were mustered that he would finally get a green light from the Lincoln Administration that it was leaving the matter of recruiting Black soldiers to Butler's "judgment and discretion."[21]

After Pinchback got authorization to raise Company A for the Second Louisiana Native Guards, he opened a recruiting headquarters on the corner of Bienville and Villeré streets in New Orleans. The funding likely came from the Union army, though some accounts maintain that Pinchback used his resources. He was incredibly good at persuading men to join the fight. In a little over a week, Pinchback had recruited a company "made up almost entirely of men who had been slaves only months before." On October 12, the Second Louisiana Native Guards, which included Company A, was mustered into the army. On that same day, Pinchback was commissioned captain and commander of the company and would be one of at least seventy-six Black officers, including at least twenty-five Black captains serving in the Native Guards during the Civil War. Three weeks later, the third and final regiment of the Louisiana Native Guards was mustered into the army, altogether contributing thousands of African Americans to the Union Army.[22]

As Pinchback organized Company A of the Second Louisiana Native Guards, he and other officers trained and drilled recruits. While most of these soldiers were native to Louisiana, two of them had been recently taken from the Congo region of Africa aboard an illegal slave ship and sold to a planter on the Mississippi River. Known as Wimba and August Congo, they escaped bondage soon after their arrival and followed Butler's trail to New Orleans where they tried to enlist in Company A. Pinchback was initially reluctant because their English was difficult to understand. But the Congos persisted, and the captain finally gave in and allowed them to join the crowd of recruits after Lieutenant William F. Keeling "insisted on taking them." Natural storytellers, these "patriotic sons of Africa," as one Black officer called them, captivated their fellow soldiers with tales of "ancestors in Africa, their customs, their tribes, and their kings." This infusion of Black history, reconnecting formerly enslaved persons with their African roots, which had been denigrated and erased by whites, kept morale high in Pinchback's company.[23] (This writer yearns to hear more about Wimba and August Congo, these enslaved immigrants who freed themselves and then joined the crusade for freedom, but, unfortunately, they seem lost to history).

Like Pinchback, most of the officers had been free men and were of mixed ancestry, with lighter skin than the mass of enlisted troops, who had been enslaved persons and who had darker skin. Heavily representing the Native Guard officer corps were African American/French or Creoles and African Americans mixed with other white lineages. This elite reflected the connection between skin color and free status that existed in antebellum New Orleans, which sharply distinguished more privileged free people of color from slaves. During the occupation and immediately postwar periods, this elite was reluctant to make "common cause with the masses of freed slaves," and it has been suggested that this divide between the two was never bridged. Yet as they became one military unit, their shared sense of purpose, along with racism from white Union officers and enlisted men and the intense hostility from white citizens of New Orleans, forged solidarity among the Native Guards of all complexions and status. This solidarity would not only grow stronger in the post-Civil War period, with the free Black elite declaring that its "future is indissolubly bound up with ... field-hands on sugar plantations,"[24] but formerly enslaved persons and darker-skinned African Americans would assume leadership roles in New Orleans and Louisiana. One of the most famous of these darker-skinned leaders would be the first African American lieutenant governor, Oscar Dunn, whom Pinchback described as "black as the ace of spades."[25]

Despite their lighter skin, education, and wealth, mixed-heritage officers quickly discovered that they were not immune to racism from their white peers of equal military status. Believing they were the same as all officers of equal rank, they were disheartened when white Union officers treated them with contempt and considered it "an insult" to be addressed by any Black officer. In one case, a Black officer was appointed duty officer of the day, giving him command of white soldiers from the Thirteenth Maine. The Northern white soldiers refused to acknowledge his authority. But the Black officer persisted, and the white soldiers responded by grounding their rifles and threatening to kill him if he continued. Racism became such a high-pitched issue that Black officers in the Native Guards began to resign in protest. One officer declared in his resignation statement that "prejudices are so strong against colored officers that no matter what be their patriotism and their ability to fight . . . they cannot serve with honor to themselves." The entire Black officer corps of the Third Louisiana Native Guards eventually resigned because they were "met with scorn and contempt, from both military and civilians," and these officers blasted their "regimental commander" for abusing them "under the cover of his authority."[26]

Pinchback tried to dig in his heels for as long as he could. Despite racism from his white counterparts, he was proud to serve the Union cause and was grateful that he was making enough money to send back to his family in Cincinnati to purchase a "little 'Home.'" Yet he refused to remain silent. In a series of resolutions to the department commander, Pinchback complained that Black officers were being held to higher standards than white officers and that he believed that behind it all was an effort to eliminate the Black officer corps. Indeed, white officers got support from the top. General Nathaniel Banks, who had replaced General Butler as commander of the Department of the Gulf in December 1862, initiated a purge of Black officers in the Native Guards and replaced them with whites. Rather than defending his Black officers who were by most accounts serving honorably, he claimed they were "a distressing failure." In a striking revelation of his racism, Banks blamed the growing tide of racism in his ranks on their own "arrogant and intolerant self-assertion" and declared that they were "unsuited for this duty."[27] Consequently, by the summer of 1863, only seven Black officers, including Pinchback, remained in the Second Louisiana, and it would not be long until he found himself the "only black officer left" at a dreary outpost surrounded by arrogant white officers who wore their racism on their sleeves. Finally, Pinchback had his fill. On September 10, 1863, he too resigned:

> General: In the organization of the regiment, I am attached to I find nearly all the officers inimical to me, and I can foresee nothing but dissatisfaction and discontent, which will make my position very disagreeable indeed. I would, therefore, respectfully tender my resignation, as I am confident by so doing, I best serve the interest of the regiment.
> I have the honor to be, sir, very respectfully, your obedient.[28]

This may seem like a tame and overly deferential resignation submitted to a man who had used his power to abandon and humiliate Black officers. But Pinchback was strategizing his next move to organize another Black military unit, which he hoped would involve assistance from General Banks. And he may have had good reason to believe that Banks would be receptive to the idea. On May 27, 1863, the Third Louisiana Native Guards helped defeat Confederate forces at Port Hudson, Louisiana, fighting tenaciously and suffering great losses. Impressed by their fighting, Banks described these Black soldiers as nothing short of "heroic," and news of Black courage spread across the nation like wildfire, shattering the racist myth that African Americans were only suited for noncombatant roles. Banks almost immediately implemented a recruitment campaign targeting African Americans while changing the name of the Louisiana Native Guards to the Corps d'Afrique. With this positive shift in the perception of Black soldiers, Pinchback bombarded Banks with requests to raise a regiment of Black cavalry, finally getting authorization but with no commitment of material support. After creating the "First Calvary Regiment Corps d'Afrique" at his own expense, Pinchback officially applied for his commission as captain. Despite the hard work he had put into recruiting, organizing, and training men for this Union cavalry, Banks rejected approving the commission, claiming it was out of his hands, rather than a policy that he had created and implemented and that he could alter if he chose to do so: "No authority exists for the employment of colored people in any capacity except as noncommissioned officers and privates." Banks's assistant adjunct-general put the rejection this way in an official response from his boss: "The application is *disapproved*, the commissioning of negroes as commissioned officers being contrary to law."[29]

Pinchback fumed, complaining that Louisiana Black officers "had given up a lucrative situation, quit a remunerative business, spent all or nearly all they possessed" to serve their country. Now Banks's most recent rejection meant white officers would lead the First Cavalry Regiment. Pinchback thus washed his hands of having anything to do with a regiment that would most likely be led by whites who would hold their Black subordinates in disdain. Racism from white Union officers reinforced by Banks's belief "that only white men are fit to command" drove Pinchback out of the military and down the path of political activism. Toomer believes that, apart from the family's forced displacement from Holmes County, Mississippi, to Cincinnati, no experience "so snubbed, insulted, and humiliated him" as did the racism he encountered in the military. He understood more clearly than ever that Northern whites could not always be depended upon, even the best of them, and he would say so at rallies. After all, Banks was an abolitionist who nevertheless added fuel to a racially charged atmosphere and intentionally reversed the progress that people of color had made in the officer corps. African Americans now had to organize, Pinchback believed, and demand their rights and protections without haste.[30]

On November 5, 1863, Pinchback helped organize a mass meeting in New Orleans. If he could not use the leverage of Black soldiers in battle to advance African Americans in the military, he would use it as leverage to advance Black political rights. He declared that because African Americans had fought and died for the Union, they earned "the right of suffrage." In front of a packed audience in the city's Economy Hall, he bellowed, "They did not ask for social equality and did not expect it, but they demand political rights—they wanted to become men." After this mass meeting, African Americans resolved to petition the military governor for "permission to register as voters, a right which they considered themselves entitled," particularly considering their service in the Civil War. When their request for suffrage was denied, they continued their drive for political rights undeterred until they grabbed the attention of the Lincoln Administration, which sent a commissioner to New Orleans to consider their demands. This resulted in the unprecedented recommendation that partial suffrage be granted, a victory that was accomplished because of the efforts of Louisiana African Americans.[31]

Pinchback also participated in one of the earliest direct-action protests of segregation in the Deep South. Since they began operating in the 1820s, streetcar companies enforced a strict segregation policy. Some even excluded African Americans altogether. The free Black community in New Orleans bitterly resented this humiliating policy. During the war years, streetcars displayed a star on the cars designated for Black riders. In 1862, African Americans began to resist streetcar segregation. Pinchback was one of the Black military officers during this time who refused to get on streetcars in New Orleans designated for Blacks and instead rode the ones for whites only. His protest was one of the earliest sit-ins against racism in the Deep South. The streetcar operators generally did not make a ruckus, letting Black officers ride. But when they were aboard, they either refused to pick up white passengers or created makeshift barriers between their seats and the seats occupied by whites to create the appearance of segregation. Pinchback, with other New Orleans African Americans, not only demanded equal access and treatment by using his body to violate streetcar discrimination; he also joined with others in petitioning General Butler to use his authority to desegregate the streetcars. While the general eventually responded with an official desegregation order, streetcar companies resisted and enlisted a local judge to table the order, thus for the time being keeping the racist policy in effect. Yet local African Americans, Pinchback among them, continued to violate the policy, setting in motion a pattern of resistance that would continue for another four years. In April of 1867, that resistance paid off. On a rainy afternoon, a conductor forcibly removed William Nichols from a streetcar and had him arrested, after which Nichols sued the conductor for "assault and battery," stirring up loud verbal and direct-action protests from allies across the city. The streetcar company finally responded by dropping its racist policy, though racist incidents such as sneers, rebuffs, and clashes would still occur on streetcars.[32]

Weary from the racism he encountered on all levels in New Orleans, which had stripped him of his right to be an effective officer in the Union Army, by late 1863, not long after he resigned from the military, he shook from his shoes the dust of the city of disappointment and went with Nina to Cincinnati to be with his mother. From there, he stayed abreast of the fast-moving events including Robert E. Lee's surrender at Appomattox, President Lincoln's assassination, and the recalcitrant Andrew Johnson's swearing-in. He was deeply troubled by Johnson's appeasement of the South, allowing former rebels to return to power, armed with a mandate to restrict and control the freedmen with Black codes that in his view, as well as that of many others, was "worse than actual slavery."[33] Such horrific bloodshed and sacrifice could not have been simply for a new version of the old order. As Radical Republicans began to push back against Johnson, calling for harsher measures against the South and for protections and rights for African Americans, Pinchback was more driven than ever to advocate for Black political and civil rights. Sponsored by the Republican Party, he took his speaking tour in New Orleans to cities throughout the Cotton Belt of Alabama, as we will see. Here he delivered fiery speeches to audiences packed with freedmen, calling on them to recognize, embrace, and push for their own equality. And it would be during his equal rights tour that he would find his voice and talent for inspiring action and change.

CHAPTER 3

PINCHBACK, NINA, AND THE RISE IN THE NEW ORLEANS REPUBLICAN PARTY

Nina Hawthorn's origins are a mystery. Some accounts maintain that she was from Memphis; others claim that her birthplace was New Orleans. Pinchback's grandson, Jean Toomer, writes that his beloved grandmother was from New Orleans and that Pinckney and Nina had married there in 1860, which other sources maintain as well. The couple did indeed marry in New Orleans, but according to their marriage license not until almost a decade later in 1869 after all their children had been born—another mystery that we will get to in a moment.[1]

The most enduring mystery that hovers over Nina Hawthorn's origins is the ambiguity over her racial identity. Toomer writes that Nina was "white Creole . . . reputed to be English or French" and that he "never heard any implication that she had Negro blood," though he qualified this by saying, "I do not say she was completely white." Historian Anna Bontemps also stresses the dominance of Nina's white heritage: "When he was about twenty-three, [Pinchback] married beautiful Nina Emily Hawthorne [sic] who, like himself, was practically white in appearance." Further descriptions of Nina, and two photographs taken possibly in her twenties, only add to that ambiguity. Consistent with Toomer's claim that his grandmother was a white Creole—meaning no or very limited African in her combination of French, Spanish, and other white heritages—Toomer biographers Cynthia Kerman and Richard Eldridge describe Nina's "racial heritage" in these photographs

Portrait of Pinchback's grandson, Jean Toomer, a Harlem Renaissance writer.

as "indistinguishable." They observe that she has a "fair complexion and lightly rounded nose, smooth straight hair" and "a sharp chin."[2]

Indeed, in these photographs, there seems to be no hint of Nina's African heritage. Toomer wrote that Nina identified as white for most of her early life and spoke French fluently, including at her family gatherings. John Chandler Griffin goes as far as to argue that this white woman "assumed the man she married was a white man," but it is difficult to imagine that she would have married Pinchback without a clue to his heritage and background. Toomer also claimed that Nina resisted Pinchback declaring "himself as a Negro," which meant that he was making the "decision for her too" to be Black, thus implying that she would have preferred to have been considered white. None of this is for certain since Nina's background is difficult to unravel. In census records between "1850 and 1920," Nina and her husband "are identified as black or as mulattos," with Nina identifying as mulatto years before her marriage to Pinchback.[3] The most likely possibility is that Nina was a Creole with French, Spanish, and African heritage, and her appearance was like many other Creoles with the same heritage whose appearances were depicted as white. Undoubtedly, Nina could have passed if she had chosen to do so like her sister-in-law Adeline and husband Rueben. Instead, she devoted her life to a man who would become one of the most definitive Black leaders in Louisiana politics, making it clear that if not unambiguously Black by heritage, she was *de facto* Black by her choice to be so in that world.[4]

The date of Nina's marriage to Pinchback is also a mystery. Despite the consensus that they married in 1860, the official year according to their marriage license is 1869. What accounts for this discrepancy, particularly with the earlier date coming from Toomer who was raised by his grandparents and likely got the 1860 date firsthand? Toomer mentions the 1869 marriage license but says that they "found it expedient to do so," which contradicts his claim that they were ceremonially married in 1860. However, Toomer finds it curious that for years after 1860, Pinchback appears to have not mentioned his marriage to Nina or anything about their relationship to his family, "keeping it a secret," another possible indication that the couple may not have been officially married but were perhaps cohabitating together. By the time of their marriage in 1869, Nina had given birth to all four of their children: Pinckney Jr. (1862), Bismarck (1864), Nina (1866), and Walter (1868). If Pinckney and Nina were not married, their children would have been born out of wedlock. At that time, this would have been more of a social taboo and could have stirred unwanted controversy since Pinchback was then a rising star in the New Orleans political world. They may have passed down the earlier date to protect their public reputations and to preempt a potential danger to Pinchback's political ambitions. There is also the possibility that they may have had to wait until the passage of Act 210 in early 1869, which Pinchback sponsored as a state senator, and that legalized Black and interracial common law marriages (we will consider this more in Chapter 5).[5]

Toomer describes Nina in striking contrast to her husband. Comparing youthful photographs of the couple later in his life, he superimposes the memory of their personalities onto their images, describing Pinchback with a "strong headstrong self-confident face . . . suggesting physical courage and a sort of picturesque recklessness." In contrast, he described Nina with a "soft gentle face, sensitive and delicate, touched with a strain of timidity or meekness." But that was not the only Nina, according to Toomer. He goes on to say that she also had "surprising courage and fortitude," and had expressed abiding faith in him as an emerging writer during his drifting young adult years when no one else did and that she "stood without flinching at Pinchback's side all through his stormy and dangerous political career."[6]

Pinchback did indeed lean on Nina throughout his life. Toomer writes that shortly after the birth of the couple's son in 1862, Pinckney Napoleon, Nina joined Pinchback at a "war camp" during the Civil War, enduring mosquitos and stifling heat to be by her husband's side. She would also stand by his side as he turned disappointedly from any hopes of a Civil War military career to his fiery entrance into the world of political activism before the war ended, traveling with him as he became an early spokesman for the Republican Party.[7]

Following Pinchback's resignation from the Second Louisiana Native Guards in late 1863, he would spend the next year addressing mass meetings in New Orleans advocating for immediate suffrage and Black political rights while signing numerous petitions and resolutions calling for the "equalization of human rights." Here he would sharpen his oratorical abilities through practice and voracious reading, impressing audiences with quotes from his ever-growing repertoire that included John Milton, William Shakespeare, Frederick Douglass, Abraham Lincoln, and others. The largest free Black community in the Deep South, numbering over ten thousand, New Orleans was more than ripe for activism. This community was bound together by ties of kinship and personal acquaintance, including in many cases with the enslaved population despite the class gap between the free Black and Creole elite and the enslaved community. Black politics had advanced more here than in any other city during the Civil War. New Orleans African Americans had been demanding suffrage and equal rights as citizens since Butler's arrival in the Spring of 1862. Adding their voices to these demands were the self-emancipated who had been flowing into the city since the Union occupation. The short-lived newspaper, *L'Union*, was formed in September of 1862 by the city's French-speaking free Black population to "mold the energies of the black race into a political force." Mostly focused on the free Black community, this first attempt was followed by its more prosperous and inclusive successor in 1864, *The New Orleans Tribune*, whose white Belgian-born editor, Jean-Charles Houzeau, would be mistaken for African American because of his ardent defense of Black liberty. Incidentally, Houzeau did nothing to correct this mistaken identity, perhaps even encouraged it, in what was an interesting case of a white man with no African heritage passing for Black. By the mid-1860s, the *Tribune* had become a "vanguard" of equal political rights throughout the South. Moreover, African Americans in New Orleans, tired of being treated as inferior, were challenging segregation in retail establishments and public schools. In this progressive climate where African Americans were forcing open space to accommodate their vision and demands, and where community ties going back generations were fostering mobilization around demands, Pinchback urged his Black audience members to continue organizing and struggling for suffrage which, he stressed, was crucial for protecting their liberty.[8]

Pinchback's oratorical skills and vision impressed local Republican Party officials who enlisted him to speak at Black rallies and conventions in Alabama cities, eager to build the Republican Party in the South. The votes of former enslaved persons, particularly in the Black Belt region, were crucial to restoring loyal Union government throughout the South. Shortly after the passage of the 13th Amendment abolished in 1865, Pinchback left New Orleans and made his way to cities that would become famous in the 1960s as the "Cradle of Civil Rights." According to his grandson Jean Toomer, as mentioned above, he was accompanied by Nina and their two-year-old, Pinckney Napoleon, and infant son Bismarck. If this is true, it was remarkable that his family, particularly with a small child and infant, would endure what was likely an exhausting speaking tour to keep the family together.[9]

Pinchback spoke on the importance of equal rights and voting to audiences in Montgomery, Mobile, Selma, and other Black Belt towns and cities. The family arrived in these cities just as a handful of Freedmen's Bureau agents and missionary groups were helping the newly emancipated build schools. It was also a time when African Americans in these towns and cities were quickly establishing their independence from whites by forming their own churches and fraternal societies that were crucial in providing self-governing spaces for religious and community activities, and a springboard for organizing politically. Church communities and fraternal societies also provided them with a platform to the forthcoming Union Leagues (or their equivalent) and Republican clubs that would be important for mobilizing Black and white Republican voters and officeholders. Using their autonomous spaces, African Americans were quickly "organizing a seemingly unending series of mass meetings." In Alabama, as in other parts of the Deep South, they were organizing statewide conventions in 1865 that brought African Americans together who "ranged all colors and apparently all conditions" regarding how to advance their rights while navigating white resistance and the Black Codes that sought to restrict those rights. Some advocated a cautious approach for moving forward so as not to provoke the ire if not the rage of whites now empowered with this post-slavery tool of control. "Ironically, the end of slavery actually had placed freedman in greater mortal danger," explains historian Douglas Egerton, "since they were no longer the expensive chattel of politically influential planters." Pinchback stepped into this expanding space and pushed attendees beyond their hesitancy if not fears, becoming a featured speaker where he inspired and electrified crowds by denouncing racism, and where he thrilled them with his vision of a new day in freedom if they would organize and struggle for rights. "You are men! You are equal!" he bellowed to the crowds. "Protest against this treatment, against these outrages, and make

Pinchback's wife, Nina Hethorn (Hawthorn). Courtesy of the Cynthia Earl Kerman Papers Relating to the Lives of Jean Toomer. Yale Collection of American Literature, Beinecke Rare Book and Manuscript Library.

your voices heard!" These words were transformative to people treated as anything but men. One former enslaved person in the audience at an Alabama mass meeting recalled how Pinchback delivered the first "Republican speech" he had ever heard about Black equality, and how it stirred him to the "highest pitch of enthusiasm."[10]

While Pinchback stirred audiences and helped create Black solidarity and political awareness, he was for now fighting an uphill battle. He had earlier been part of the momentum in Louisiana that had forced Black suffrage to the forefront of state and national politics. In 1864, New Orleans African Americans, including former Black officers, had petitioned President Lincoln to support Black suffrage in Louisiana. Persuaded by their appeals, as well as their service in the Louisiana Guards, Lincoln changed his position from only supporting white suffrage to now accommodating limited suffrage for educated African Americans and Black soldiers in Louisiana, which by war's end he would extend to all Southern states. General Nathaniel Banks, the Union district commander in New Orleans, made a series of efforts at the Louisiana constitutional convention in 1864 to adopt limited Black suffrage, mostly aimed at Creoles who he tried to have classified as white. His efforts, however, were soundly defeated by white Southerners who dominated this early convention, and the new constitution was approved without recognizing Black political rights in any form. Following President Lincoln's assassination in April of 1865, his successor, President Andrew Johnson, had no intention of using executive power to advance or protect Black political rights. Though he had earlier believed that the white South should be punished and had for a moment supported limited Black suffrage, his plan for Reconstruction as president changed to now confer amnesty on former Confederates if they pledged allegiance to the Union, including voting rights, and to restrict the rights and movement of formerly enslaved persons. This meant that executive power would be propping up white power, leaving the "Southern states in the undisputed management of their own affairs," while relegating Blacks to an inferior status with no protection.[11]

As Pinchback, along with possibly Nina and the children traveled throughout Alabama in 1865 and 1866, things were beginning to look bleak as white supremacy struggled violently to assert itself throughout the South. Black efforts to peacefully organize and exercise their freedom provoked white violence, as African Americans endured assaults and terror. Two of the bloodiest episodes of mass violence at the hands of white aggressors occurred in Memphis and New Orleans in 1866, leaving African Americans dead and wounded and Black homes and businesses destroyed and looted. In New Orleans, as Pinchback was on his Alabama tour, more than a hundred African Americans were murdered and wounded, including by police, while peacefully supporting a convention held at the city's Mechanics Institute to consider their empowerment. One African American who was present in the convention hall when it was attacked described the floor as "slippery with blood." Because of ubiquitous violence and the solidification of white power, Black mass meetings and conventions began to fade as the newly reorganized state governments ignored their pleas and instead used arbitrary power to severely proscribe the freedom of emancipated with Black codes and violence. In short, Johnson's plan of Presidential Reconstruction unleashed white domination and brutality upon the newly freedmen and free people of color.[12]

Yet a glimmer of hope emerged from these ashes of brutality. The violence in Memphis and New Orleans was like a clap of thunder, sounding the failure of President Johnson's plan to reconstruct the Southern states. African American leaders such as Pinchback and the white Republicans in Congress had been advocating Black suffrage and more stringent measures against white Southerners. Their voices were growing louder as things continued to worsen in the South. With white aggression so visible and the blood of

Port of New Orleans around the time of the Civil War.

innocent African Americans in the streets, their arguments acquired a sense of urgency with white Northerners. Something needed to be done to protect the rights and lives of emancipated African Americans. Public opinion began to shift in the wake of racial violence and President Johnson's stubborn resistance to changing his course. Repulsed by the violence, Northerners elected a majority of Radical Republicans to both houses of Congress in November 1866. This new Congress wasted no time usurping executive power, going to work almost immediately to create and implement its plan to reconstruct the Southern states known as "Congressional Reconstruction." Their plan created five military districts in the South under the control of appointed federal commanders and sustained by armed Union soldiers. It ordered new constitutional conventions, disenfranchised former Confederates (but never as many as southern critics of Reconstruction have charged), and mandated Black voter registration. African Americans would be invited to play a part in creating new state constitutions, thus helping to shape an equalitarian environment in their states and communities. In "a stunning and unprecedented experiment in interracial democracy," Congress had essentially turned Presidential Reconstruction on its head, stripping the oppressors of power and giving the oppressed protection and the unhindered opportunity to participate in creating a democratic future of the South.[13]

With the human and structural obstacles to Black empowerment being removed, the Pinchback family made their way back to New Orleans sometime in late 1866 or early 1867. Now thirty years old, Pinchback felt more than ever a sense of destiny in the wake of this unprecedented transformation. The city of past disappointment now beckoned him back with the possibility of helping to shape this new world of equality.[14]

Shortly after their return, in April 1867, Pinchback organized the Fourth Ward Republican Club in New Orleans where during the early years of the Civil War he had successfully recruited Black soldiers for the Union Army. Winding narrowly from the Mississippi River in the North to Lake Pontchartrain in the south, the Fourth Ward was created as part of an enforced divide to separate Black Creoles from whites to "prevent racial ill-feeling." By the time Pinchback was there, the ill-feeling between the two had subsided, however, the ward was still composed predominantly of Creoles along with a recent influx of emancipated African Americans, making it a fertile ground to recruit for the Republican Party. Also making it fertile ground was that New Orleans Creoles and African Americans had been organizing and mobilizing for several years and had a stronger Republican Party structure than any other area of the South.[15]

With his hopes high and taking advantage of the structure and networks in place, Pinchback worked incessantly to organize Fourth Ward African Americans and sympathetic whites for the burgeoning local Republican Party, which continued to impress local and regional party elites. With his talent on display and popularity growing, Pinchback was offered an appointment for Inspector of Customs of New Orleans in late May. But he declined this impressive local appointment because he had his sights on strategizing his way to the Louisiana constitutional convention in November where he could have a hand in directly shaping the state's equalitarian future.[16]

About a week after he declined the appointment, Pinchback was elected as a delegate to the Republican state convention in mid-June, a preliminary to the constitutional convention in November. This convention brought together loyal Republicans who supported Congressional Reconstruction to strategize the future of the Republican Party and a new state constitution. Speaking to those gathered, Pinchback stressed the revolutionary role of Black suffrage and admonished some African Americans for their false "sense of security" that because the Civil War had been won "that all is done." He understood that Louisiana native whites would do everything in their power to prevent Blacks from participating as citizens. Stressing the immense work necessary for protecting equality in this unstable climate, he warned, "Gentlemen, this is a fallacy. The Great Contest had just begun!" The preliminary convention proposed a sweeping "platform that advocated equality for all men, the opening of all public schools to all children, and an end to class distinction." Pinchback worked with others to secure the controversial agreement that the number of delegates to the November constitutional convention is equally divided between Black and white. He was also elected as "one of the ten vice-presidents of the assemblage" and by the end of the convention, he had been selected to serve on the Central Executive Committee of the state's Republican Party, which placed him directly within the inner circle of local and state party elites. Pinchback was now well-positioned, both as a visible leader in the Fourth Ward and a newly tapped powerbroker of the local Republican Party, to make his way to the November constitutional convention as an influential delegate who could help shape the interracial democracy of his state.[17]

Shortly before the convention, the recently appointed military governor of the Fifth District that included Louisiana and Texas, Philip Sheridan, had set in motion the registration of voters which opened voting to African Americans. Consequently, thousands of African Americans registered and were "intense" in their commitment to voting for Black delegates to the November convention. One Democratic newspaper that was less than enthusiastic about the Black voter turnout in Rapides Parish, observed that African Americans from all walks of life registered to vote, albeit in a disdainful tone: "They came from every portion of the parish, and none were left home. The lame, the cripple, the blind, the halt; old, young, one-eyed, one-legged, no legs, no arms, deformed, diseased, sick, well, dressed, ragged, barefooted all, all were on hand eager and panting from freedom's boon!"[18]

These African Americans were far from the pathetic humanity that the Democratic newspaper wanted its readers to believe. They included free men, educated and skilled, politically astute, many bilingual, and former enslaved persons, some of the poorest of the poor, but many of whom had been attending Freedman's Bureau and missionary schools for years by this time, and who understood clearly what the power of the vote meant in their time and space. Like African Americans all over the South, most had been preparing and organizing for several years under local Black leadership in churches and Republican and community organizations. They were more than ready to mobilize en masse to vote and take their place in political leadership roles. In many cases, they were more prepared and politically cultivated than their white counterparts, despite being portrayed in the media as well as later historicism as naïve and incompetent. With half of the ninety-eight delegates elected African American, the Black majority of the Fourth Ward elected Pinchback as their delegate to the convention—the prize he desired above all else at this stage of his early political career. Black and white delegates were now poised to create the most revolutionary interracial document the Deep South had ever seen at the November constitutional convention. Pinchback's "strong headstrong self-confident face," as his grandson Jean Toomer described him, would be one of the most conspicuous during these intense proceedings hashing out constitutional human rights, launching one of the most remarkable political careers in American history.[19]

CHAPTER 4

PINCHBACK AND THE LOUISIANA CONSTITUTIONAL CONVENTION

"ALL PERSONS SHALL ENJOY EQUAL RIGHTS AND PRIVILEGES . . . WITHOUT DISTINCTION OR DISCRIMINATION ON ACCOUNT OF RACE OR COLOR"

The Louisiana Constitutional Convention of 1867–68 was one of the most progressive of any Southern state constitutional conventions during the Reconstruction Era. It is also considered the first if not the most advanced interracial document until after the second half of the twentieth century because of its bill of rights that included civil rights provisions, broad application of citizenship status, and support of integrated public schools. Delegates created a constitution that was, in the opinion of one astute observer, "magnificent for its liberal principles." Shortly after the convention opened, delegates adopted a resolution that declared their vision for what they were determined to accomplish at the convention: "*Resolved*, that all we claim is equality before the law for all men without distinction of race or color or previous condition, and shall endeavor to secure this great consideration of all just men, and to inaugurate a system of government that will secure the great political, social and industrial welfare."[1]

While the work of the convention depended, remarkably, on interracial cooperation, the tone and agenda had been largely set by Louisiana African Americans, particularly by those living in New Orleans. They were not only active on working committees but articulated and pushed for the most inclusive and embracing reforms possible. For several years prior, local African Americans had been holding conventions and mass meetings, writing articles and op-eds, where they called for political equality, integrated public schools, and equal access to public accommodations. These activists included the largest free urban community in the Deep South, led by the French-speaking Creole elite, augmented by an ever-increasing population of formerly enslaved persons. They were bound together by kinship and community ties, and in some cases, by master/employer and servant relationships that were often more paternalistic and benign compared to the harsher and exploitive ones that typified white masters. General Butler's occupying Union troops in New Orleans so early in the Civil War in 1862 had created a protected free space for this remarkable vision and energy, which was already stirring, to unfold. With the old world now swept away, African Americans believed that the time had "come when any citizen should enjoy his full rights as well as every other citizen." The number of Black delegates elected to the 1867 Louisiana constitutional convention was higher than for any Southern state constitutional convention, accounting for half of the ninety-eight delegates in attendance. Eager to shape this new world, these delegates would dominate the debate and often outmaneuver whites to push to the forefront of the agenda not only universal male suffrage but also access to education, integrated schools, and the elimination of racial discrimination in the public sphere. In short, what these delegates demanded and achieved was inclusive democracy.[2]

Pinchback was eager to help remake this world in Louisiana, quickly becoming a leading force behind some of the convention's most progressive reforms. The opportunity to officially play a role in transforming Louisiana from a slave-based aristocracy to a free democracy was the prize he desired from the time he arrived back in New Orleans after campaigning for the Republican Party in Alabama. Since that time, he had quickly risen from a local party recruiter to delegate at the June Republican convention, to being selected for the Central Executive Committee of the Louisiana Republican Party, to now delegate to the official convention that would create a new state constitution, which meant reconstructing a new world. Representing the Fourth Ward in New Orleans, the rising Republican powerbroker went to work, determined to empower African Americans with rights equal to whites.

One of the first issues Pinchback expressed his voice on was a proposal that all subordinate officers be drawn equally from both races. Pinchback opposed the proposal, insisting that all officers should be chosen by merit and general ability above color. This likely reflected both elitism and strategy on his part. Years later he would claim that "Democrats instigated and thrust

Delegates of the Louisiana constitutional convention, 1867–68. Library of Congress, Prints & Photographs Division, LC-USZC4–5947.

forward the most ignorant Colored men that could be found for election to the Constitutional Convention with the view of making that constitution a farce" and that some Black delegates, in his view, were unqualified because they did "not know one letter of the alphabet." However, Pinchback's claims here are dubious. It was not unusual for Democrats to push forward oppositional Black delegates in hopes of dividing the Black vote. But most importantly, it appears that over three-fourths of Louisiana's Black delegates were literate with only one known to have been definitively illiterate. Moreover, only seven out of the thirty-six delegates had been enslaved, which meant that the vast majority who were free before the Civil War likely had at least some education. Pinchback may have formed his judgment based on how the press comically mocked (with racially charged overtones) the appearance of some of the rural Black delegates attending the convention. Many of these less prosperous Black delegates came from districts where their lives and the lives of their constituents were bound to the land, and where they desired to benefit from their labors free of white control, coercion, and violence. These delegates understood perhaps as much as he did the importance of economic and political reforms that would protect their right to free labor and suffrage, and they participated in promoting and supporting these rights. They certainly had an instinctive thirst for political and civil rights that was not dependent on status or formal education.[3]

Most delegates agreed with Pinchback's surface argument of merit and followed him in voting the proposal down. With the equal proportion issue defeated, Pinchback steered those African Americans he deemed to be of higher caliber into leadership roles. He also hoped that the press would take their attention off those "ignorant" delegates and focus instead on the more visible Black delegates overseeing the important work of the convention. If efforts to marginalize these Black delegates reveal elitism, they also reveal Pinchback's skill and leadership at this early time to mitigate what he saw as a potential obstacle—rightly or wrongly—to push an agenda he believed necessary to create interracial democracy in Louisiana. A few years later, however, he seemed to take the opposite position regarding Black officeholders. In response to a white interviewer who questioned the ability and qualifications of some local Black leaders, Pinchback would defend the right of even "ignorant men" as "justly entitled to recognition in office."[4]

The first important issue that delegates tackled was suffrage. In the Reconstruction Act of 1867, Congress had defined the expectations by which Southern states were to follow when forming their new constitutions. This importantly included male suffrage without racial distinction and ratification of the Fourteenth Amendment, which guaranteed citizenship rights and equal protection of the laws. States were expected to follow suit by guaranteeing the ballot for African American male citizens while protecting African American citizenship rights.

Without serious controversy, delegates incorporated these rights and protections into the new Louisiana constitution. However, there was one issue revolving around suffrage that did stir up controversy. Known as Article 99, it mandated that former Confederates and those who gave comfort to Union enemies were ineligible to hold public office or to vote. Stripping former Confederates of the right to vote was seen by many as crucial for assuring the electoral success of the emerging Republican Party. Delegates in all Southern constitutional conventions grappled with the issue and eventually voted to enforce disfranchisement with slight differences. Yet four Black Louisiana delegates, led by Pinchback, vehemently opposed this restriction and together submitted a protest: "We are now, and ever have been advocates of universal suffrage, it being one of the fundamental principles of the Radical Republican Party."[5]

With most Black delegates and many whites supporting disenfranchisement, why did Pinchback oppose a restriction that without it could work to the detriment of his goals? First and foremost, Pinchback had faith in the democratic process and constitutional mechanisms. He believed it was simply undemocratic to deprive suffrage to a class of people, the way it had been denied to African Americans. How could they argue so passionately and eloquently for Black suffrage with the integrity of universal suffrage as the basis of their argument, and then turn around and deprive others of that right without being hypocrites? In a similar tone, *The New Orleans Tribune*, the vanguard of Black equality in Louisiana, argued, "If we refuse the franchise to any class, it can be as well withheld from us." Pinchback also believed that once Black rights were firmly embedded in the Constitution, and then reinforced by legislation that included the participation of Black political leaders, it would be enough to protect and advance Black interests without any threat of infringement from opponents. He likely shared Frederick Douglass's opinion that with capable Black leaders in the South, "it would not be easy to reverse the wheels of liberty in that region." Moreover, supporting the integration of former Confederates back into the body politic would demonstrate goodwill to whites, rather than antagonizing them, which could suppress the secessionist impulse. But this seeming paradox was not unique to Pinchback. Many Black congressional leaders during Reconstruction would support leniency for former Confederates, as well as opportunities and rights for Southern whites in hopes of not alienating white support and engendering opposition. Mitigating opposition may have been one reason why Black delegates sidestepped land and labor reform in their pursuit to embed political and civil rights in the constitutional fabric. With that olive branch established at the convention, Pinchback hoped native whites would be more inclined to work with African Americans as part of an interracial effort in shaping the future of Louisiana, which, he believed, was inevitable. Pinchback was confident that the alignment of African Americans and whites into the burgeoning Republican Party would be strong enough to prevent the domination of white Democrats. He had a devoted, almost blind faith in democracy during this time, imagining a better future where discrimination and injustice could not withstand the force of inclusive democracy.[6]

Pinchback was certainly principled in his ideas during this time, but he was also naïve. It had only been less than a year and a half since whites demonstrated how willing they were to use violence against African Americans during the New Orleans Riot, demonstrating disdain not only for Black equality but also for Black humanity by the blood that flowed in the streets. White Southerners were aghast at the transformation of their world, resisting it in editorials, through intimidation, and by overt violence throughout Louisiana. They made it clear that they were waiting for the day when Union troops were gone, and white supremacy could reassert itself. Many African Americans and white allies feared that granting amnesty to former Confederates who took up arms against the Union could enable the planter class to regain power in the South, which would place African Americans in an especially vulnerable position and stymie the goals and achievements of Reconstruction. Thus, most of the delegates, tuned into these realities and distrustful of many Louisiana whites were unpersuaded by Pinchback and company, voted to disenfranchise former Confederates in their new constitution. Though a violation of the most fundamental principle of the Republican Party, as Pinchback rightfully argued, they viewed it as a practical measure to create a foundation for democracy in Louisiana and the Reconstructed South and preserve loyal government to the Union. This issue would soon flare up again, but this time on the national level. Black leaders in the newly Reconstructed Congress would face a flood of proposals to grant amnesty to former Confederates, with some adamantly opposed because they argued that it would be empowering their oppressors but with many others ultimately in support of amnesty in a hopeful exchange for the passage of civil rights legislation.[7]

The next issue African Americans united behind at the Constitutional Convention was public education. Considered the most critical issue next to suffrage, Southern African Americans viewed education as the foundation of freedom, arguing that it was unconditionally necessary to protect Black liberty. During and after the Civil War, formerly enslaved persons demonstrated an "unquenchable thirst for education" and created makeshift schools in communities throughout the South. While the Freedmen's Bureau and Northern benevolent societies supplied assistance, it was often dogged work of Black communities that birthed these schools. By 1870, these Black communities in the South had spent over one million dollars of their own money to "purchase land, build schoolhouses and pay teacher's salaries," which is equivalent to almost 20–23 million dollars today.[8]

In New Orleans, education had advanced faster than anywhere else. This included the proliferation of independent Black schools that took off after the Union occupation in 1862 and in the push for integrated universal public education leading up to the 1867 constitutional convention. In this city of over 10,000 free people of color, African American schools were also more firmly established than in any other community in the South. Highly valuing education and denied access to the local public school system created in the 1840s (though still required to pay taxes to maintain white schools), the city's free community of French-speaking Creole elite and other free African Americans had long been sending their children to private schools established and supported with their wealth (as well as some providing their children with tutors). Formerly enslaved persons, while lacking those roots and experience, had also been creating their schools ever since the occupation, including, ironically (and perhaps with some poetic justice), one located in the former slave market in New Orleans. By the time of the constitutional convention, some of these latter schools had been operating for almost half a decade. Indeed, by the eve of the 1867 convention, the number of free people of color and the emancipated attending New Orleans' schools numbered in the thousands.[9]

Black delegates helping to forge the new progressive constitution in Louisiana not only wanted accessible public schools, however. Incredibly visionary for the times, they also advocated for enforced integration. They understood that separate would never mean equal and that their children would always be treated as inferior within a segregated educational system. During the summer convention held that past June, which was the preliminary to the November constitutional convention, Black delegates, including Pinchback, succeeded in urging the Republican platform to promise to "enforce the opening of all schools from the highest to the lowest . . . to all children." The white New Orleans school board was also responding begrudgingly to Black leaders' advocacy for integrated schools. These schools were also getting support from the city's white mayor, Edward Heath, including creating a committee in early September to gauge Black sentiment regarding "mixed schools." The fiery white editor of *The New Orleans Tribune*, Jean-Charles Houzeau, a white man who was still being identified as Black, kept the drumbeat rolling in the press for integrated public schools in the months leading up to the November constitutional convention: "Separation is not equality. The very assignment of schools to certain children on the ground of color is a distinction violative of the first principles of equality." In another editorial, the *Tribune* asked, "When will the right time come? Is it, perchance, after we have all separated for ten or twenty years the two races in different schools, and when we shall have realized the separation of this nation into two peoples? . . . It will, then, be TOO LATE." Anticipating that Black delegates would push for integrated schools at the November convention, the white New Orleans school board tried to preempt their demands by creating a separate Black public school system in hopes of preserving the "racial homogeneity of their white institutions." By the eve of the convention, the city gained control of twenty-two Black schools, many of which had been Freedmen's Bureau schools. Moreover, some radical Republicans, who were expected to support integrated schools, urged local African Americans to accept the Black schools which, they maintained, were in their best interests. However, the *Tribune* reflected the sentiment of many Black leaders when it responded that "a nation cannot have unity and strength unless all children be educated in the same schools." The paper also anticipated that segregated Black schools would become inferior to white ones and urged Black delegates to vote as a bloc for integrated public schools.[10]

This all provided intense momentum for making the controversial issue of establishing public schools for all children regardless of "race, color or previous condition of servitude" a priority during the convention proceedings. Most local whites vehemently opposed integrated schools, believing that it implied the unacceptable taboo of social equality. *The New Orleans Times* shrieked the dreaded trigger word "amalgamation" from its pages and declared Republican efforts the "Congo Convention." Nevertheless, Louisiana was the only Southern state, except for South Carolina, to push incessantly for enforced integration, with all the other states leaving the issue open without overtly acting upon it.[11]

This did not mean that all Black Louisiana families, including Black educators, welcomed the possibility of integration without concern and anxiety. Many were troubled by the prospect that white teachers would abuse their children and encounter hostility from white students. According to the committee report that gauged attitudes towards integrated schools, some Black educators were reluctant to support integrated schools. William Finney, the Black principal of Soule' Chapel School, reflected the concern among many that "mixing the Colored and White in the same schools will excite prejudices and create ill-feeling and dissension between the races." They clearly understood the larger issues Black leaders were making, regarding the rights of children to attend any school regardless of race, and how segregation reinforced Black inferiority. But they believed that because of the present reality of intense racism, it would be in the "best interests of all classes that separate schools should be established for white and colored children. . . ."[12]

It may be an overstatement to say that Black leaders and white allies ignored the concerns of many of their constituents who saw access to education as more important than integration. But they certainly decided to proceed with school integration despite the expressed anxiety of families

Edmonia Highgate tombstone.

and educators not to mention the resistance of white conservatives. Many believed it to be a necessary step to prevent inequality from taking root and that it would eventually become a norm in the educational system. As one young Black educator named Edmonia G. Highgate acknowledged, "mixing the races now may create difficulties and injure the cause of education for the time being," but she believed it would succeed in the long run. One of the fiercest advocates for integrated schools, Highgate was from Syracuse, New York, where as a teenager she had been an antislavery orator and soon became a celebrated teacher in the freedmen's schools after the Civil War. Once in New Orleans and nearby Lafayette Parish, she was twice shot at in her classroom while teaching. In the wake of so much violence and resistance to integration, Highgate resigned in protest from her teaching position and started a school in Mississippi.[13]

Moving forward, Dr. George Wickliffe, the most ardent white defender of Black equality at the convention, fired off four resolutions supporting integrated public education as soon as the convention business was complete. A white transplant from Cincinnati who worked as a dentist, Wickliffe had once vehemently opposed abolitionism but underwent a Damascus-like conversion that propelled him on the other side of the fence with a newfound commitment to Black political and civil equality. His four resolutions endorsed access for all children "without distinction of race, color or previous condition" to all state-supported public schools, colleges, seminaries, and universities and that "there shall be no separate schools established for any race." Wycliffe's resolutions went to the Committee on Public Education, whose six African Americans and one white member endorsed them.[14]

One of these Black committee members, James H. Ingraham, was a leading voice at the convention for accessible public schools. Ingraham inspired a successful resolution to create at least one public school in every parish throughout the state. A close colleague of Pinchback's, so much of his life mirrored Pinchback's: he was born to an enslaved woman and white plantation owner in Mississippi; he organized a Black company for the First Regiment of the Louisiana Native Guards and was likewise promoted to captain; and he encountered hostility from racist white Union officers and was forced to resign during the purge of Black officers under General Banks. As a delegate from the violent Caddo Parish, Ingraham must have been especially bold. He had to navigate a region plagued by intense white hostility where Republicans risked life and limb to work for Black equality.[15]

Pinchback was also one of the most ardent advocates for integrated public schools. He may have had some input on the proposed integration amendment to the new Louisiana constitution, though there is no direct evidence in the records. It appears that Ingraham was the fire behind school integration at the convention. But a year before in Alabama, Pinchback had made strikingly similar arguments that Thurgood Marshall and his team would make eighty-five years later to the US Supreme Court in *Brown vs. the Board of Education*. Indeed, his central argument against segregated schools anticipated the most striking argument made by Marshall in 1954. Pinchback bellowed to his audience,

> establish separate schools, and you by that very act declare the white children superior of the colored, you teach them to look upon colored children as inferiors, and without enumerating the many disadvantages the color children would labor under, in the way of poor teachers, bad schoolhouses, etc., you prolong if not perpetuate that despicable prejudice that has such deep roots in the whites of America.

These arguments were certainly not original to Pinchback, though he appears to have refined them. As we saw above, *The New Orleans Tribune*, and a chorus of other local African Americans, made similar arguments leading up to the convention and even years earlier. While it is not clear why Pinchback was not more of an overt force for school integration at the convention, he became one of the fiercest advocates of his time for school integration. Soon he would be pushing for integration as an elected leader with more power and leverage, working from the constitutional foundation he helped create to secure integrated schools in law. And when resistance to integrated schools blocked his way, he would, as we will see, march his son to the school doors with a police escort and demand that they enroll him.

On February 4, 1868, after much wrangling and resistance from white conservatives, the Committee on Public Education submitted a final proposal based on Wycliffe's resolutions for a vote. With Pinchback in the ayes, the integration clause, known as Article 135, was adopted as part of the new Louisiana state constitution by a vote of 61 to 12, with all the Black delegates voting in favor. This remarkable human rights achievement, largely the work of visionary African Americans, declared:

> All children of this state between the ages of six and twenty-one shall be admitted to the public schools or other institutions of learning sustained or established by the State in common, without distinction of race, color, or previous condition. There shall be no separate schools or institutions of learning established exclusively for any race by the State of Louisiana.[16]

With the hurdle of integration overcome at the convention, Pinchback soon championed a proposal that would prove even more controversial. Known as Article 13, or the Civil Rights Article, on December 31 he proposed a legal ban on all discrimination in public spaces. As groundbreaking as it was, it was nevertheless intentionally a tame proposal without mentioning race specifically, likely because he wanted to inch it out to gauge its support and opposition. The positive response from his peers was overwhelming and over the next several days delegates would hammer out the language for Article 13, with Pinchback crafting the final revised version approved by a vast majority of delegates:

> All persons shall enjoy equal rights and privileges upon any conveyance of a public character; and all places of business, or of public resort, or for which a license is required by either State, parish, or municipal authority, shall be deemed places of a public character, and shall be opened to the accommodation and patronage of all persons, without distinction or discrimination on account of race or color.[17]

After its adoption in the new state constitution in February, opposition erupted in the press and some whites at the convention. "The success of the proposed radical constitution will entail negro equality on the people of Louisiana *beyond hope*," lamented *The Bossier Banner*. "The most abominable contrivance for ruining white people in order to benefit negroes in the new constitution, so-called." If integrated schools violated the color line for their children, granting African Americans the same rights as whites in public places obliterated the color line by forcing an "unjust and unnatural equality" between Blacks and whites. Article Thirteen struck at the core of the established segregated world in New Orleans, and throughout Louisiana, even though unofficially there were some areas of the city where whites and Blacks had interacted socially for generations. To prevent the article from being circumvented by the courts arguing the sanctity of private property, Pinchback had cleverly added the rider to this article clarifying the "public character" of businesses as ones requiring a state, parish, or municipal license. Since every business and public carrier required such a license, this meant that they all fell under Article Thirteen's constitutional discriminatory ban and could not simply be rationalized as private property that was out of reach of the prohibition, inspiring critics to charge that the "article was so subversive to the rights of property."[18]

The Louisiana delegates signed the final constitutional document on March 7, 1868. They created one of the most egalitarian state constitutions anywhere in the nation at that time. They made sure that they opened their remarkable document in a familiar tone: "All men are created free and equal and have certain inalienable rights; among these are life, liberty, and the pursuit of happiness." This time, it would be Black minds that helped breathe life into this declaration, making it true for the first time in American history. The dogged work that went into the new state constitution spanned from eradicating the oppressive Black Codes of 1865 to making African Americans and Creoles the political and social equals of their white counterparts. It was now ready to be put to the popular vote. Despite vitriolic calls from oppositional newspapers to defeat what one editor described as the "Black Crook Constitution," when it was put to a vote the next month for ratification, 66,152 Louisianans voted for it and 48,739 voted against it, with the African American and Creole vote crucial to securing its passage. Nowhere else existed explicit amendments banning discrimination on public transportation and in all places of public accommodation or that supported integrated public schools. Under this revolutionary new constitution, adult males residing in the state for one year, regardless of color and barring former Confederates, were granted "all political and civil rights." All lawmakers, current and new, were now required to plead an oath of equality before assuming office, affirming, "I do solemnly swear, that I will accept the political and civil equality of all men, and agree not to attempt to deprive any person or persons on account of race, color, or previous condition, of any political or civil right, privilege of immunity enjoyed by any other class of men."[19]

For those who had been oppressed and abused, hope had come to Louisiana in 1868, and it would for a moment in history create a seismic shift in the political and social landscape of the region. With the ink barely dry on this new constitution, Pinchback took little time to relish the unprecedented achievement, quickly positioning himself to become a lawmaker where he could help anchor these revolutionary freedoms in law.

CHAPTER 5

PINCHBACK IN THE LOUISIANA STATE SENATE

A WHIRLWIND CRUSADE TO BRING EQUALITY TO THE DEEP SOUTH

After the Louisiana delegates signed the final constitutional document on March 7, 1868, that ushered in democracy, Pinchback emerged as one of the most prominent figures in Louisiana politics. Racial discrimination had been constitutionally banned in every area of life and Pinchback was seen as one of the forces upsetting the old order, particularly because of Article 13 where the rights of people took precedence over the perceived rights of property. Whispers were already floating around about the possibility of a Governor Pinchback—his name had even been tossed in a hat by Republican leaders as a potential candidate—which he quickly hushed because he believed it was too premature for the budding democracy that had just made a monumental transition from a slave state to a free one. Importantly, he knew he would need to skillfully navigate many more obstacles for anything like that to have any chance. Whether or not he aspired to the highest state office at this time, he would for now set his sights on the state senate representing the Second District of New Orleans, which was one of the most important Senate seats in the state. Just days after the convention concluded, Pinchback threw himself into campaigning for this seat against a white supremacist Democrat named E. L. Jewell. He pounded the pavement, gave speeches, and linked his campaign with the Republican carpetbagger Henry Clay Warmoth, a

Lieutenant Governor Oscar Dunn, one of the most popular leaders in early Reconstructed Louisiana.

dashing twenty-six-year-old Union officer from Illinois who was running for governor and whose immensely popular running mate was Oscar Dunn, a former enslaved person from Louisiana with savvy political skill.

A veteran of the battle of Vicksburg that devasted the Confederacy on the Mississippi River, after the war Warmoth began a law practice in New Orleans focusing on cotton claims and courts-martial decisions. Despite being a detested Northerner, Southern belles were said to be smitten by his good looks and charm. Warmoth quickly became one of the central players in the emerging Republican Party in Louisiana where his advocacy of Black political and civil rights put him in good standing with local African Americans. Confident and ambitious, he worked with delegates at the constitutional convention of 1867–68 to lower the age requirement for governor from thirty to twenty-five in hopes of paving his way to the statehouse.[1]

Warmoth's running mate, Oscar Dunn, was at least twenty years older than the Illinois native. Born to an illiterate free woman of color, he spent his early childhood in bondage until his free father purchased his freedom, along with that of his mother and sister Jane. Though not privileged, he attended school until the age of fourteen, learned a lucrative trade, and became a talented musician under the tutelage of an Italian instructor where he mastered the guitar. Dunn's rise in the Black Masons in New Orleans as a young adult "established the foundation of his political network throughout the state", contributing loyal supporters to his rise in politics. In 1867, he was elected to the New Orleans city council where he proposed that "all children between the ages of 6–18 be eligible to attend public schools . . . without distinction to color," which would be one of the impetuses for its adoption in the forthcoming constitutional convention. By the time he was on the ticket with Warmoth, Dunn was the most prominent Black leader in the city, known if not celebrated for his impeccable honesty in a shady political culture. While much has been made over this stellar reputation, both by his contemporaries and historical accounts, this image of honesty masked a burning ambition to shape his new world and, despite his color, the contrast enabled him to uniquely strategize his rise to power as an irresistible leader of a higher caliber.[2]

Warmoth won the governorship and Dunn made history by becoming the first "colored man to hold a political position of an executive nature." History was also made in Louisiana as the new democratic constitution provided the framework for the election of forty-two African Americans to the state house of representatives, making up almost half of that body, with seven elected to the Senate. But it looked like Pinchback would not be among those Black senators enjoying the victory since he lost to Jewell by a total vote of 3,415 to 3,198. Or so it seemed. Immediately charges of fraud arose and Pinchback pushed the newly inaugurated Warmoth to launch an investigation.[3]

As the investigation got rolling, Pinchback was selected as a delegate to the 1868 Republican National Convention in Chicago that May. This was particularly important because, whereas the Louisiana constitutional convention had brought him into association with local and state Black leaders working diligently for the same goals, the national convention brought him into a larger context where he met and formed connections with African American delegates from other parts of the South and around the nation. For himself and others, it was the first time during early Reconstruction that networking occurred on such a large scale. During the convention proceedings, Pinchback eagerly supported Ulysses Grant for the Republican nomination and would later express pride at having participated in Grant's success at the convention and election to the presidency.[4]

After almost two months of investigating during the summer of 1868, a Senate committee found that "ballot-box stuffing, fraudulent tallying, and the substitution of Democratic tickets from Republican tickets" had been committed by the Democrats in the Second Senatorial District. The committee also charged the Democrats with preventing many African Americans from voting for the Republican ticket through intimidation. With its findings in hand, the committee recommended that Pinchback be seated over Jewell and called on the Senate to uphold its recommendation and pass the resolution admitting him to its chamber. Despite charges from critics that Warmoth and Pinchback had made a shadowy backroom deal to get the office—an election commissioner claimed that he was paid to support charges of that Democrat fraud—the Senate adopted the committee's recommendation to not only to seat Pinchback but to compensate the new senator for back salary from the beginning of the Senate session two months earlier. Pinchback was now the eighth Black senator to take his seat in the Louisiana legislature, but the Jewell dispute began the "aura of controversy" that would hover over him during his political career.[5]

SENATOR PINCHBACK LANDS IN JAIL

The reversal of the election in the Second District so angered a political enemy by the name of S. C. Morgan, that a few days after Pinchback was admitted he accosted the new senator on the street. While the details are not clear, a gunfight erupted between the two men after which they were arrested and taken to "the First District lock-up." *The New Orleans Crescent*, a Democrat paper opposed to the Republicans and Reconstruction, offered an interesting and curious description of "the two hot-blooded belligerents." Clearly favoring Morgan, the paper stressed that Pinchback bore "unmistakable evidence of his negro origin," but described Morgan more favorably as a mulatto who could be easily "taken for white," even though most observers of the time also described Pinchback as one who could be mistaken for white, or not Black. It seems in this case the *Crescent* had strategically passed Morgan into the white world, while anchoring their enemy Pinchback in the Black world, evidently to emphasize the larger battle in New Orleans between Black equality and white supremacy. From a modern perspective, color or race historically is perceived as unalterably frozen in their respective categories. But color could be a fluid thing in this time and place, where passing (or being passed) one way or another occurred not infrequently for personal and professional advantage and maximum effect at the moment.[6]

Pinchback was immediately released from jail, likely with assistance from Warmoth, and was on the Senate floor the next day, while Morgan remained behind bars, infuriating Democrats. With news traveling lightning-fast for a time before modern technology, morning articles were already appearing in conservative papers like the *Crescent* critical of Pinchback, questioning his fitness for office and harshly critical of him in general. What Pinchback did in response was brazen for any newly elected official, doubly so for a newly elected Black official. Fuming in a moment fraught with tension, he took the Senate floor and angrily refuted the slander of the conservative press, explaining to his fellow lawmakers that Morgan had been sent to murder him and to the shock of his listeners, threatened to reduce the city of New Orleans "to ashes" if the Democrats continued to bully and harass him. When pandemonium broke out in the chamber among offended white Democrats, Pinchback offered an apology but reiterated that he stood by his words. Despite criticism from the conservative press that his speech "was the ravings of a self-deceived man," and the rawness of a fiery young leader who had not yet learned to temper and channel his anger, as he would as time went on, one thing was clear: the new Senator Pinchback was a force to be reckoned with and would not roll over for his enemies or be cowed by white supremacy.[7]

FIRST SENATE SESSION (1868): LEGALIZING BLACK AND INTERRACIAL COMMON LAW MARRIAGES

After his two back-to-back battles with Jewell and Morgan, not to mention his inflammatory speech on the Senate floor, friends advised Pinchback to keep a low profile for the remainder of the first legislative session. For a newly elected legislator, he had overnight set New Orleans ablaze with controversy, and time was needed for the fire to burn down so that it did not scorch the Republican Party. His opponents for a long time would recall his audacity in "threatening New Orleans with a torch." Reluctantly, the stormy Pinchback complied, remaining quiet and relatively inactive for the rest of the year with one exception: while unobtrusively voting for legislation that was favorable to African Americans (some of which he inspired at the constitutional convention) and supporting executive legislation that was in the interests of Governor Warmoth, Pinchback promoted in the Senate a House bill known as Act 210. This bill, already a constitutional protection he had helped inspire at the convention, made all cohabitation, or common-law marriages, legitimate and legal if the couples appeared before a notary public. This meant that all cohabitations that had begun in bondage where legal marriages were forbidden would now be recognized as legitimate by the state.[8]

Under slavery, marriage or the Black family had no legal basis and thus, from that standpoint, no existence. In 1866, the Freedmen's Bureau sent an order to allow couples cohabitating to contract legal marriages. General

Absalom Baird, commanding Union forces stationed in New Orleans at the time, "issued a proclamation" that offered African American couples the opportunity to have "a civil or religious wedding with a license." While there was some response to these calls, something more was needed. Black delegates and their white allies had pushed vigorously for a constitutional amendment during the 1867–68 convention to legalize Black common-law marriages and legitimize children born in these unions, but it failed to pass. Act 210 went even further in a way that made it revolutionary. Not only would common-law marriages between Black couples be recognized, but interracial common law marriages were also made legal under this act. Even more, Act 210 explicitly overturned the longstanding Article Ninety-Five of the civil code making interracial marriage illegal. This had been a hotly controversial issue with much of the white community. In the 1864 legislature dominated by whites, a proposal to overturn this article and legalize Black-white marriages was soundly defeated by a vote of 57 to 5. But now Black lawmakers were in the halls of power, arguing that "every man had a right to choose his own mate, regardless of custom or law to the contrary." And there was nowhere else in the country where interracial relationships and unions were more conspicuous than in the Crescent City where support was widespread. In his book *Black New Orleans*, John Blassingame writes that "the population was so mixed that it was virtually impossible in many cases to assign individuals to either group." This included the established Creole population of mixed French and African ancestry, and Anglo-Africans who were biracial, generally of English or Irish and African heritage. Many Black and white couples had been cohabitating since antebellum times. Some had married during the Union occupation when formerly enslaved couples were encouraged to get married—despite Article 95 nullifying all such marriages. While most of these interracial unions were white males and Black females, some involved the even greater taboo of Black males and white females. These couples often risked everything to be together, including family ostracism and social isolation, and sometimes restricted economic opportunities.[9]

Act 210 struck at the core of Pinchback's racial identity and the mistreatment that befell his mother, which is why he got actively behind it during his time of silence. One of the reasons his family had to eventually flee from a privileged life in Mississippi to an impoverished one in Cincinnati after his father's death was because his parents' interracial relationship was illegitimate in the eyes of the law in the South. Without his father's protection, they were reduced to property. There was no legal basis protecting the integrity and rights of their family, as well as no safeguards protecting their freedom and ensuring their inheritance, leaving them vulnerable to being enslaved by his father's white North Carolina relatives, which forced them to flee into destitution.

There may have also been a more pressing reason for Pinchback to push so hard for legalizing interracial and common law marriage in Act 210, one that might solve the mystery of the later marriage date for him and Nina. The couple would obtain their marriage license on May 19, 1869, almost six months after the passage of Act 210, and nearly a decade after they had started their lives and family together. If Nina's racial ambiguity was a problem, particularly if she had presented as a white woman, the laws against interracial marriage may have deterred them from legally marrying. It is possible that Pinchback was motivated to create this law so they could be legally married and go on with their lives as a family with all the state-recognized rights and protections.[10]

Pinchback helped eradicate part of the racist edifice that had caused his mother Eliza and family such grief and hardship, and one that possibly prohibited his marriage to Nina, persuading enough of the white majority to push Act 210 through in the Senate. This feat garnered praise for the new state senator among the local Black population since it was the first legal sanction of Black marriages and interracial unions, and it importantly legitimized their children. State-sanctioned marriage was seen as a "powerfully important aspect of freedom and acceptance into civil society" and part of the larger body of civil and political rights that African Americans cherished.[11]

SECOND SENATE SESSION (1869): MAKING RACIAL DISCRIMINATION ILLEGAL

Beginning with the second legislative session in January 1869, Pinchback considered the time of his peer-encouraged silence ended. Following a short legislative recess, he took on his senatorial duties with focus and vigor, working to enforce, in his own words, the "the articles of our constitution which contain everything that is dear to us." Here he sponsored several successful bills and supported others that made it through. One was a bill to creatively reduce the debt in New Orleans by releasing funds for public services and improving the city's economic well-being. Pinchback also proposed a law to make the current law on vagrancy much harsher. Passed in 1865 as part of the Black Codes that established severe penalties for those charged with vagrancy, the Black code vagrancy ordinances were designed to repress and control the mobility—political, physical, economic, and social—of the newly emancipated under the thumb of white supremacy. Vagrancy laws were used to keep African Americans as a cheap source of labor on plantations, and "to get things back as near to slavery as possible." With the vagrancy bill before the Senate, Pinchback threw an obstacle in its path by severely criticizing its definition of vagrant and garnered enough support to prevent its passage. He worked with other legislators to create another version of the bill that said an arrested vagrant could not be simply detained indefinitely or committed to a workhouse without recourse and that they had a right to trial. This revision struck at the unaccountable power of racial profiling aimed at forcing African Americans into a form of quasi-slavery. This bill was passed by the House and Senate and signed by Governor Warmoth.[12]

The most controversial bill of this session was Pinchback's work to enforce Article 13 of the state constitution, which specified that all persons, regardless of race or color, are entitled to equal rights and privileges on any public conveyance or business licensed by the state. Earlier that summer, while Pinchback was in limbo for his Senate seat, Robert Isabelle, a Black member of the Louisiana House of Representatives who was serving as the temporary chairman, had introduced a bill to enforce this article which was sometimes referred to as the Civil Rights Bill or as some of the oppositional press called it, "the civil equality bill." A free man of color in New Orleans before the Civil War, Isabelle had been one of the earliest commissioned Black officers and had served with Pinchback in the Louisiana Native Guards. Once while riding a train in his officer's uniform, Isabelle was accosted by a group of whites who cursed and assaulted him for sitting in the white section, not long after which he boldly used his authority to personally—and successfully—arrest them, declaring that "colored men have rights that white men are bound to respect." For Isabelle, access to public spaces free of discrimination was a deeply personal issue.[13]

With Pinchback's discreet assistance, Isabelle's house bill added teeth, defining discrimination in places of public accommodation as a criminal offense in which violators "could be fined as much as five hundred dollars or jailed for as long as one year." It also included a provision giving priority to cases challenging public discrimination in the courts, which would speed up these cases and make it easier and safer for plaintiffs to have their cases heard. Despite resistance from white supremacists, the House passed the bill by 50 to 14, followed by the Senate almost three weeks later by a vote of 15 to 7, with the newly seated but quiescent Pinchback voting for its passage. Governor Warmoth, however, vetoed the bill and raked legislators over the coals for trying to force social equality. Reflecting the typical white privilege that insulated even progressive whites from imagining what it was like to live with no rights or protections, Warmoth argued that racial prejudice would only be overcome by time. Pinchback bristled at this reasoning, arguing that racial prejudice was so ingrained in white thinking and behavior that "if left to time, time will never come." He complained that he could not even get a drink from the lowliest saloon because of his color. It was thus imperative, he argued, that racial discrimination be "regulated by law."[14]

In response to Warmoth's veto, Black lawmakers organized counterstrategies. They were motivated more than ever after John Willis Menard of New Orleans, the first African American elected to Congress during Reconstruction, was denied his seat and refused entry. As this racially motivated injustice unfolded, it added more fuel for Pinchback and other African American state legislators to push on with their frontal attack against de jure white supremacy in Louisiana. In their next version of Article 13, which had strong support from Lieutenant Governor Dunn, Pinchback stipulated that all future business licenses must include in their issuances that "the place of business or public resort shall be open . . . to all persons without distinction or discrimination on account of race or color." He wrote that those found guilty of violating this law were liable for civil damages and/or the revocation of their licenses, while skillfully excluding any language making discrimination a criminal offense so as not to invite another Warmoth veto.[15]

On February 4, 1869, Pinchback made an eloquent appeal for Article 13 on the floor of the Louisiana State Senate. Newspapers described his tone as "emphatic" and his gestures animated. While his remarks were directed at one state legislative body, and though he was only a new state senator without much of a reputation outside of Louisiana, he believed that in the struggle to make Article 13 into law, he was working more broadly, indeed for "nearly six millions of (Black) people in this country," in addition to "at least ninety thousand (Black) voters in the state of Louisiana." Almost six years before the 1875 federal Civil Rights Act which prohibited racial discrimination in public places and transportation, the potential repercussions from Louisiana's Article 13, he believed, were enormous, and could ripple out across the South, inspiring African Americans and their white allies to sweep away the barriers of public discrimination.[16]

Near the beginning of his speech, acknowledging his racist colleagues who opposed the law, Pinchback explained, "If I were a white man, speaking for the rights of white men, I would have no unwilling ear in this Senate, or in these United States." Stressing white hypocrisy, he continued by saying that white Americans, whatever their heritage, never face the "daily occurrences of outrage" that African Americans do, whose discrimination is encouraged and applauded by the press. He then moved to counter the oft-repeated claim that discrimination cannot be legislated away because whites will need time "to get over their prejudices." Pinchback declared that "if left to time, the time will never come." Reflecting his fervent belief that absolute equality was necessary to protect all rights, he continued, "Unless this matter is regulated by law, we will not only fail to have these privileges, but we may look to have our rights, one by one, taken away from us."[17]

Pinchback challenged the repeated assertion that "Southern whites . . . are the best friends of the colored people," making it clear that he was not playing games: "But if they cannot lay aside their prejudices and grant us full equality before the law, I shall doubt their sincerity, no matter where they come from . . . neither North, South, East, or West, if he professes to be my friend, let him give his aid when I most need it; or let him shut his mouth from the cry of, 'I am your best friend.'" In several places of his speech, he invoked the Golden Rule, declaring to his less-tolerant peers that if they failed to support equality for the most downtrodden, then they were violating this biblical precept and thus would be more than political hypocrites; they would be making a mockery of their faith. He tried to push them to imaginatively step into the shoes of African Americans and feel what it was like for a Black man to be "humiliated, insulted, grossly insulted." He continued: "Oh, sir, how I have wished that the white men who are inclined to oppose this measure and to impose upon the colored man the wrongs and insults we have to endure, could in one single instance take our place and have our feelings. Were this possible our cause would need no defenders."[18]

Pinchback then described a recent incident when he was "refused accommodation" at a public establishment and how it impacted him emotionally to be treated in such a degrading way. He continued, "This was the more galling when I looked around and said to myself, 'What, I, a State Senator—maker of the laws—cannot get accommodation in a *public* saloon.'" Wrapping up his speech, he cleverly demolished the "social equality" argument that the white opposition claimed Article 13 would enforce:

> We are told . . . that it seeks to force upon the white race social equality with Black—"social equality," that bugbear of politics, that cry of the demagogue . . . Do you tell me that all white men who ride in cars and upon steamboats are socially equal? Why, sir, you can find the thief, the vagabond, the harlot all congregated there; and do gentlemen recognize them as socially their equals because they are found upon the same conveyances? . . . If it be, then I will drop my argument at once.[19]

Concluding, Pinchback declared that Article 13 "is an act of justice, of complete justice, and I cannot see how any man who is disposed to be honest and just can oppose the measure."[20]

Pinchback's version of the Civil Rights Act passed the Senate by a large margin on February 9. When it was sent back to the House for approval, Isabelle tried once again to add more teeth to the Act by including that those who discriminated against African Americans would be subject to additional penalties "exemplary as well as actual," which meant that they could lose their business licenses as well as pay a fine. Isabelle also added that cases charging a violation of the Civil Rights Act would take precedence in both the "inferior and superior courts." When it came back to the Senate, Pinchback, who fought hard for the changes, could not get it passed with the amendment because his peers rejected giving these cases preference in the courts. However, he managed to persuade fellow senators, most of them white, to uphold "exemplary" damages and sent this latest version back to the House. Following House approval, the bill was sent to Warmoth with pressure to sign it into law.[21]

During the debates and strategizing for this bill, the conservative press was ablaze, declaring that not only were Blacks forcing themselves upon white people but that whites had a political and natural right to discriminate; they called on Governor Warmoth to veto it. Pinchback responded that the last thing African Americans desired was to be in the company of disagreeable whites and stressed on many occasions that the Civil Rights Act was about assuring equal access to public accommodations for anyone, not social equality. But, of course, he knew the act implicitly conferred upon Blacks an equal status with whites. African Americans rightly saw this law as a "symbolic blow against all racial injustice" and would not give up. The defunct *New Orleans Tribune*, which had been the mouthpiece for Black equality from the Civil War through the constitutional convention of 1868, was inspired to resurrect its presses in support of the Civil Rights Act, declaring that they must unite to "throw off a tremendous load which has been our inheritance for centuries." This time things would not be easy for Governor Warmoth. Because Pinchback had made public discrimination a civil rather than criminal offense, Warmoth could not veto it on constitutional grounds. Moreover, another veto would alienate many more Republicans, and the governor did not yet have enough support from white conservatives to stabilize his power without Black Republicans. Reluctantly, on February 23, 1869, Warmoth signed the new Civil Rights Act, or Article 13, believing, as he later wrote in his memoirs, that it was a "dead letter" because "Public sentiment was strongly opposed to it."[22]

Black power in Louisiana, under the leadership of Pinchback in the Senate and Isabelle in the House, and with support from the popular Oscar Dunn, significantly contributed to pushing through at the local level one of the most visionary pieces of civil rights legislation in the Deep South. African Americans still had to tread carefully because whites would disregard the law and sometimes respond violently. Soon after the passage of Article 13, *The New-Orleans Commercial Bulletin* spoke for many whites when it issued a warning on its front page: "Will any negro, or gang of negroes, attempt to exercise the privilege it confers? If they do it will be at their peril . . . ." Many were forced to ride in the smoking cars near the "soot-spewing engines," barred from sleeping cars, and forcibly ejected from designated white sections of trains and steamers. African American women were humiliated by being "forced to sleep on the deck of coastal steamships," where they were "subjected to uncouth whites," rather than in the privacy and safety of cabins. Black lawmakers also faced discrimination and were "denied the comforts of traveling accorded to all other people." That April, Oscar Dunn himself was refused accommodations in the white section of a train on a trip to Washington to meet with President Grant, and after some resistance, he was forced to ride in the poorly equipped "colored car." In such a climate, African Americans often did not challenge their mistreatment. They either could not get justice in courts dominated by white conservatives, or they could not afford legal representation for civil cases that could go on for a long time. But sometimes African Americans did successfully challenge businesses that discriminated against them under the Civil Rights Act. In one high-profile state supreme court case, the Black sheriff of Orleans Parish, Charles St. Albin (C. S.) Sauvinet was awarded $1,000 in damages and court costs from a white saloon owner who refused him service.[23]

Frustrated by the resistance to the new law, Pinchback once again tried to advocate in the Senate for an amendment to give preference in the courts to violations under this act. Speeding up the process for hearing cases meant less cost and time for Black plaintiffs and a better chance of getting justice. Working in tandem from the House side was Octave Belot, a prosperous Creole who was himself the victim of discrimination and violence for trying to exercise his political rights in the fall elections of 1868. Belot persuaded many whites to support the Pinchback amendment in the House, which passed by a vote of 49 to 8. With so much support, Warmoth reluctantly approved this newest version, signing it into law in 1870. Feeling emboldened and trying to build on their success, Pinchback tried to resurrect the criminal offense part of Article 13 and make another attempt to push it through. He also advocated during this time in an editorial for "a federal enactment to give us our rights in public places and conveyances," more than four years before the federal Civil Rights Act was passed in 1875 that would do just that. Warmoth sat on the newest version until finally returning it with his veto in

1871, arguing again that he would not support enforcing civil rights using criminal prosecution. The governor's resistance and vetoes throughout the fight for the Louisiana Civil Rights Act lost him the support of influential Black members of his party. One of the leading Republican forces in New Orleans, Oscar Dunn, broke away from Warmoth and took many African Americans with him, precipitating a split that would soon manifest in two hostile Republican parties vying for dominance.[24]

Under no illusion that the law was anywhere close to enough, African American legislators and business leaders also used power to create alternative ways to navigate discrimination on public conveyances. One was to pressure railroad companies to include prohibitions against racial discrimination in their charters, some of which had been formed with Black collaboration. If they violated this prohibition, not only would they be liable for civil damages, but they could face the penalty of having their charters revoked and would not be able to operate. In the summer of 1871, Pinchback would test this charter prohibition with one railroad company. After his wife Nina was barred from entering a first-class Pullman berth on the Jackson Railroad, Pinchback threatened to sue the company and have their charter revoked. In response, the Jackson Railroad announced that it would honor all first-class tickets purchased by Black patrons, which set a precedent for other railroad companies that lasted for several years.[25]

African Americans found another way to use power to navigate racial prejudice on public carriers. Between 1868 and 1871, at least a half dozen Black senators and house members secured public funding to create Black-operated ferries in their districts where they could assure safe travel for African Americans. Pinchback secured the passage of an act establishing the Mississippi River Packet Company to "procure and maintain one or more steamboats to run or navigate the Mississippi River, or its tributaries," with the largest amount of funding for any Black-operated carrier allocated in the amount of $25,000. It is often repeated that Pinchback and his board of incorporators pocketed money from this venture, which soon failed. This is not only difficult to verify, but there is no accessible evidence that they ever received the funding in the first place. During this time, waterways were competing fiercely with the growing dominance of railroads. If his venture failed to take off or succeed, it was likely not only due to mismanagement or fraud, if that was the case, but because the railroads were increasingly dominating the transport industry at the expense of steamboats.[26]

In April 1869, President Grant offered Pinchback an appointment as Register of the Land Office of New Orleans, which drew the bitter consternation of the white supremacist oppositional press, like the *Louisiana Democrat*, which criticized Grant for appointing "black and greasy negroes to office from Louisiana." Curiously, the president offered Pinchback this position just as he and Black lawmakers, along with white allies, were creating a democratic revolution in Louisiana. He had only been a senator for a little over six months, and to expect him to resign in the middle of this revolution for a low-level appointment was unrealistic. It makes one wonder if Grant had received pressure to try to get this savvy, charismatic Black man out of the legislature, away from the mechanisms of law, and where he would not have so much influence over the minds and hearts of men and in shaping the new world. Perhaps some were eager to get Pinchback out of the way, maybe reaching as high as Washington, because he was seen to cause the fractures beginning to show in the state Republican Party and they believed he could compromise Grant taking hold of the state in the next election. But the senator declined Grant's offer. He would never willingly relinquish his hold on power. Pinchback would stay in the Senate where he knew he could continue to make an impact and where he knew he had a chance to advance to higher office. The blame for any fractures, in his view—and in that of most other Black lawmakers—lay at the feet of Warmoth.[27]

PINCHBACK THE BUSINESSMAN AND NEWSPAPER OWNER

Later in the year, during the fall of 1869, Pinchback embarked on two ventures. He and his Senate colleague, C. C. (Caesar) Antoine, with whom he had served in the Native Guards and at the constitutional convention (and whom he may have known from their steamboat days), formed an investment, lending, and real estate firm called "Pinchback and Antoine, Commission Merchants." The son of a Black father and West Indian mother, Antoine was born free in New Orleans and commissioned a captain in the Union army. He had lost his young son, Joseph, during the New Orleans anti-Black riots in 1866, motivating this small, dark-skinned, debonair man to beat back white supremacy during Reconstruction with intellect and vision. (In addition to serving as a state senator, Antoine succeeded Pinchback's gubernatorial term as Louisiana's lieutenant governor.) Pinchback and Antoine's firm appears to have been successful with cotton as the principal commodity, often trading and moving cotton for both white and Black clientele.[28]

Importantly for his vision of Black equality, Pinchback also became the joint owner that year of a newspaper, *The Lousianian*, a four-page semiweekly whose masthead declared that it was "owned, edited and managed by colored men." One of his chief partners was Antoine, and their business office

Caesar Antoine, the third Black Lieutenant Governor of Louisiana.

at 114 Carondelet Street did double duty as a newspaper and printing office. Pinchback also brought on board fellow legislators James Ingraham and George Y. Kelso, who worked doggedly to make Black equality a reality. He hired as his chief editor William J. Brown, a fierce civil rights advocate who would become the first Black superintendent of education in Louisiana, one of the very few superintendents during Reconstruction. In his first editorial, Brown declared that the goals of *The Louisianian* included "the security and enjoyment of broad civil liberty, the absolute equality of all men before the law, and an impartial distribution of honor and patronage to all who merit them." Under Pinchback's leadership, *The Louisianian* was the most potent equal rights paper in Louisiana and employed agents to take it to a wider audience from Chicago to Washington, DC.[29]

In *The Louisianian*'s pages, Pinchback announced that "we will agitate, and agitate, and struggle for the enjoyments of our rights at all times, under all circumstances and at every hazard." For several years *The Louisianian* would also be the official mouthpiece of the state Republican Party and would print news from national women's suffrage conventions. *The Louisianian* led the way in advocating Black and Republican interests and would provide a space where future Black journalists, leaders, and newspaper owners would cut their teeth and gain crucial experience.[30]

| P. B. S. PINCHBACK, | C. C. ANTOINE. |
| New Orleans, La. | Shreveport, La. |

PINCHBACK & ANTOINE,
COMMISSION MERCHANTS,
114 Carondelet Street, New Orleans.

Liberal advances made on consignments, and prompt attention given to Buying, Selling and Leasing of Farms, Paying of Taxes, Collecting Rents, etc., etc.

[o20 1y]

C. C. Antoine and P. B. S. Pinchback Business Advertisement.

Front page of *The Louisianian*.

THIRD SENATE SESSION (1870): HOLDING BACK WHITE SUPREMACY

During the third legislative session that began in January 1870, Warmoth introduced four acts to the legislature that would give him wide-ranging powers to protect Republican voters and thus his power. African American lawmakers, increasingly at odds with the governor, nevertheless believed granting the governor expanded powers offered the best possibility of protecting the Black vote. Despite the protection of voting rights at the state and federal levels, and the recent passage of a bill making it a finable offense for planters and other white employers to discharge or intimidate their Black employees because of political beliefs, something more was needed. White Democrats had demonstrated that they would "use large scale collective violence" in their attempts to regain power and restore white supremacy. This was perhaps the most extreme in Louisiana, where an army investigator found that "in most parts of the State a systematic series of outrages, robberies, and murders . . . were committed with the avowed intention of intimidating, and thus forcing, them to abstain from voting."[31]

One of the largest racial massacres during Reconstruction that came to symbolize how far Democrats would go to violently obstruct the Black vote occurred in St. Landry Parish, located in the south-central part of Louisiana. During two weeks of terror and violence leading up to the election of 1868, it is estimated that 250 African Americans were killed, with many more wounded; others were displaced after being forced to flee their homes. Consequently, Democrats won in St. Landry Parish as they did across the state where violence and intimidation were used, handing Grant a defeat and his Democratic rival, Horatio Seymour, a victory in Louisiana. Terrorism directed at African Americans was so widespread in the 1868 presidential election that, according to testimony in a congressional investigation, "twenty-one parishes, casting 28, 814 votes for the Republican state ticket, gave General Grant only 501 votes." St. Landry was one of seven parishes that did not even record a single vote for Grant, despite having an African American population of over 11,000.[32]

During the third legislative session, Pinchback argued that curtailing the violence and intimidation of Black voters required giving unprecedented powers to Warmoth. Importantly, these powers would enable Warmoth to clear the polls of armed white Democrats and protect the integrity of the Black vote with Republican oversight. No "lover or worshipper" of Warmoth, Pinchback knew that the governor was not one to trust in the long term but believed it was in the interests of African Americans to grant him executive overreach to protect the Black vote. Pinchback had no illusions that these acts would eliminate efforts to obstruct the Black vote. Democrats in St. Landry had so terrorized their Black citizens into silent acceptance of racial hierarchy that they would maintain a grip on power in their parish throughout Reconstruction. But Pinchback and other Black Republicans believed that investing Warmoth with these far-reaching powers would mitigate enough of these problems to increase Black voting and rights and turn the tide towards Republican victory in the next national election. Though Democrat senators strenuously opposed the passage of these acts through a filibuster, Pinchback garnered enough support to grant Warmoth expanded executive powers by a vote of 20 to 12.[33]

NEW ORLEANS PUBLIC SCHOOLS:
"[A] TRULY REMARKABLE EXPERIMENT IN INTERRACIAL COEXISTENCE"

Beginning in the summer of 1868, Pinchback and his fellow Black legislators went to work to secure constitutional reforms in law, guaranteeing equal access to public education. The first thing they did was to conduct a quick study on the history and condition of the school system. They concluded that the old school system "has proved to be a failure and should be discontinued." The proliferation of officially supported Black schools began shortly after the Union occupation in 1862; local African Americans created schools that rapidly expanded after General Nathaniel Banks created, at their urging, a board of education in 1864. By the end of that year, city schools boasted over three thousand Black students. However, in 1865, as white supremacy took back power after the occupation ended and before Reconstruction began, the new state superintendent of education, James Lusher, proved openly hostile toward Black education. Believing that education should only "vindicate the honor and supremacy of the Caucasian race," he quickly began to dismantle the thriving Black school system. African Americans responded by organizing private church schools supported by the local Black community until they could press again for public schools.[34]

Replacing Lusher that year was Thomas Conway, a new superintendent with a different orientation. Elected by the power of the Black vote on the state ticket with Warmoth and Oscar Dunn, Conway, a white Union officer from Maine, was committed to "free, universal, desegregated public education." After serving as a chaplain for a Black Union regiment, Conway became a top official for the Freedmen's Bureau in Louisiana where he worked to advance fair labor practices for the freedmen. In his new capacity as state school superintendent, he advocated "organized public school administration and competent school board directors." With his support, the new Black lawmakers and their white allies embarked on an intense campaign to build the most ambitious public school system in New Orleans and throughout Louisiana. In line with Conway's recommendations, legislators helped draft a bill that essentially stacked the new public school system with Republicans who supported its goals. As Black lawmakers and their white allies hammered out a new educational system, they managed in the meantime to quickly push through a bill in September 1868, granting free transportation to all school children on all public conveyances during school hours.[35]

SCHOOL INTEGRATION IN THE 1870S

The most controversial and heated issue involving public schools was the battle to integrate New Orleans schools. The push for integrated public education had begun to stir as early as 1862 during the Union occupation of New Orleans, with some attempts to make it a reality, and continued through the 1867–68 constitutional convention when "every public facility, specifically including schools, was declared open to every person regardless of race." After Black lawmakers came to power in the summer of 1868, they were frustrated that conservative whites in the city were still committed to preserving segregated schools. Charles Sauvinet, an alderman in New Orleans, had enrolled his light-skinned daughter in an all-white city school that April to test the recent provision in the new constitution forbidding segregated schools. When conservative whites discovered that she and other girls of mixed heritage had been admitted, they strenuously protested. The girls were soon after ejected and transferred to a Black school, with the then-white Democratic school board mandating that all Black children found in white schools would be immediately transferred "to the school to which they properly belong." Thus, white leaders had no intention of abiding by the new state constitution regarding integration and were determined to maintain segregated schools.[36]

As Black lawmakers and their white allies hashed out the details for a new public school system, the demands of some local Black citizens for the right of their children to attend any school grew louder and their actions became bolder. The earlier reluctance of local African Americans to send their children to integrated schools during the constitutional convention debates seemed to give way to a confidence that the children should not be denied entry to a school because of their color. Some began to use confrontation tactics by taking their children to white schools to demand enrollment, arguing that segregated public schools were not "giving satisfaction to all ... without regard to 'race, color or previous condition.'" These encounters sometimes led to violent clashes.[37]

With these demands as the backdrop, Black legislators drafted a provision forbidding segregated schools to be included in the new state law for public schools. In the House, Robert Isabelle believed that Black and white children in the same public schools were the one thing that could ameliorate racial prejudice: "I want to see the children of the state educated together. I want to see them play together ... to study together and when they grow up to be men, they will love each other ...." In the Senate, Pinchback argued that separate schools would not be equal and that Black schools would suffer from resources inferior to their white counterparts. Segregated schools would also cause white children "to look upon colored children as inferiors," he explained, and would perpetuate Black inferiority within the larger society. Facing bitter resistance from conservative whites, Black legislators drafted a provision stating that any administrator or instructor who "should refuse into any school any child ... who shall be lawfully entitled to admission" would be subject to a fine of one hundred to five hundred dollars and up to six months imprisonment. By March 1869, they had achieved a miracle for the times: Act No. 121, the Education Act, became law, opening public schools to all children, Black and white, and bringing into existence the most comprehensive and progressive public school system the state—or nation—had ever seen. It was one that would not be seen again in the South for over ninety years.[38]

Meanwhile, the New Orleans School Board, controlled by white Democrats, used their power to obstruct integration. In response, the legislature, led vociferously by Pinchback and Isabelle, authorized Conway to appoint new Republican school boards in each ward that would supersede the ones controlled by Democrats. Conway thus managed to create a rival network of "ward" school boards in the city made up of Black and white members who supported integration while diverting all state funds to this rival board, which essentially stripped the Democratic school board of its power. This move was soon upheld in the courts when Judge Henry C. Dibble, an Indiana transplant committed to Reconstruction, ruled in favor of the new school boards and their right to distribute state funds for the city's public schools. As the power of the school board shifted to the Republicans, Pinchback gave speeches advocating for integrated schools, along with equal access to public accommodations.[39]

With Republicans in control of the school boards, integration began to quietly take place by early 1871 across the city as African Americans enrolled their children in what had been all-white schools. Lieutenant Governor

Oscar Dunn quickly enrolled his three daughters at the Madison School for Girls. The *Daily Picayune*, a fierce critic of Reconstruction and Black equality, seemed almost resigned in tone when it told readers on January 12, 1871, that "the mixing of the public schools has silently and gradually been going on ever since the Ward Boards assumed control." While the integration of New Orleans public schools would never be complete, by the spring of 1874—seventy years before the Supreme Court ruling in *Brown vs. Board of Education*—"between five hundred and one thousand black children and several thousand white pupils were enrolled in no fewer than nineteen mixed New Orleans public schools." This accounted for one-third to one-half of the city's schools. At a time when integrated schools were not common anywhere in the nation, "New Orleans public schools developed into a truly remarkable experiment in interracial coexistence."[40]

Of course, resistance and hostility still appeared. With school integration taking place on an unprecedented scale, most white parents answered the call in the *Daily Picayune* and other Louisiana papers "to take their children out of the public schools." Some enrolled their children in private schools, many of which were religious institutions whose numbers flourished during this time as alternatives to public schools. Other parents simply let their children go without school rather than attend integrated ones. For the latter, the *Daily Picayune* opined that they "will at least escape the contamination of that impurity." In rural areas throughout Louisiana, where whites had greater power over their Black minority populations and more opportunities for using unaccountable terror, white opposition to integrated schools was almost universal and very few schools experienced integration. There was much more success in New Orleans. But even there, some public schools attempted to refuse African Americans entry, with educators and students obstructing their way, sometimes using threats and violence.[41]

Pinchback would become notorious for using power to confront one of these resistant white schools. Shortly after becoming lieutenant governor in 1871, he took his son Napoleon to an all-white school and demanded that they enroll him. Taking no chances, he brought a police escort and pressured the school principal to admit Napoleon. The conservative press was livid, castigating Pinchback for using his power to force Blacks upon whites and into spaces where they were not wanted. Like his threat as a new senator to reduce the city of New Orleans to ashes, this bold act would stick in the craw of whites as much as anything he would say or do. For years, conservative whites would remember Pinchback using direct action backed by state power to integrate a white school, which was likely one of the reasons the US Senate would refuse him entry into their chamber though duly elected.

Even well into the twentieth century, Louisiana public school literature would use the episode to denounce the disgraceful integration experiment that was doomed to failure, while praising the more "natural" system of segregation that had by that time become the norm.[42]

PINCHBACK'S FINAL LEGISLATIVE SESSION: SECOND SENATE TERM (1871)

Throughout their time in the Louisiana legislature, African American lawmakers would promote and support the centralization of power in the hands of favorable state and local leaders to mitigate discrimination. With white allies, they worked to channel this power to advance their interests politically, economically, and socially. Here we can see African Americans pioneering what would become a common strategy of promoting and supporting more centralized authority and programs, generally on the federal level, for procuring and protecting their rights and advancing their interests against recalcitrant and violent Southern states and communities.

EXCESSIVE BLACK SPENDING AND CORRUPTION IN THE LEGISLATURE?

In reconstructed Louisiana, African American lawmakers did not promote the excessive or irresponsible spending of which they have sometimes been accused. Even during the 1871 legislative session, which has been called "one of the most extravagant of Warmoth's administration," Black leaders supported mostly modest expenditures for the poor, sick, and widowed, along with internal improvements, with white members generally promoting more extravagant spending bills—particularly white Democrats. This was a spending legislature only because by that time enough tax revenue had come from tax legislation passed in the 1868–70 session to begin to address the desperately needed internal problems, such as crumbling infrastructure. The spending measures promoted by African Americans were often focused and carefully considered. Even a bill authored by African Americans to alleviate suffering for those in need was rejected by some of its authors after whites tacked on weighty items for "various objects and purposes ... unworthy of any state aid," in the words of the Black state senator James Ingraham.[43]

Pinchback has been accused of promoting excessive spending and funneling it into his own pockets. In one of the most thorough treatments of his political career to date, Agnes Grosz writes in her 1943 thesis that the 1871 legislative session "was characterized by wholesale plundering in which

Pinchback conspicuously shared." She claims it "was common knowledge that many legislators were well paid for their votes on certain legislation." According to Grosz, Pinchback introduced six bills during this session, "the majority calling on the extravagant expenditure of public money." Grosz then goes on to situate Pinchback within a context of scandal and corruption, which has been recycled by writers ever since and is a throwback to the times when his political enemies tried to discredit him. This is not an attempt to deny that Pinchback benefited from his position as senator and beyond. He likely profited from his power on different occasions, as did many legislators in Louisiana, where political racketeering was more common within the political culture. Indeed, corruption was a vibrant part of the political culture of the times on all levels, particularly in Congress, where the buying of votes seemed commonplace. Pinchback admitted in one interview that his position in the state Senate gave him a vantage point to see what investments might be beneficial, which almost certainly included purchasing stock that he knew would become valuable when the legislature passed state-backed bonds for public works projects.[44]

While Grosz maintains that Pinchback was one of many legislators who did use power for financial gain, she offers no hard factual data but writes that it "was said" or "it was gossiped" (many other writers, as well, blur rumor and fact in their treatments of Pinchback[45]). Grosz relies largely on a congressional investigation by a House committee conducted in 1871–72, in which the testimony is based on much hearsay from questionable sources, and very little attention is given to Pinchback. What testimony was leveled against him claimed he was the head of a "ring" in the Senate composed of eleven radical senators whose purpose was to profit from legislation, which smacks of an attempt to ridicule and discredit lawmakers working for Black equality.[46]

The extravagant spending bills that Grosz says Pinchback sponsored during his last year in the Senate are questionable. One was a bill authorizing the secretary of state to purchase two thousand copies of the *Louisiana Magistrate and Parish Officers' Guide*. Annually published at state expense, this guide provided revised and new state forms and instructions for public officials and business owners. Only a modest expenditure, it would have benefited Pinchback if *The Louisianian* secured the contract to print it. Another was a bill to establish the Levee Shed Company to create and maintain warehouses "on the banks or levees on the Mississippi River in front of the city of New Orleans" to store and protect waterway commerce. Originating in the House, Pinchback was its sponsor in the Senate. While the bill authorized a whopping $1,400,000 in state bonds, Governor Warmoth refused to issue these bonds, and the company never got off the ground. Things were improving, but the interest on state and city bonds since the war was still in default, and the state was just beginning to emerge from bankruptcy. Other than investors giving money to the company, money which was later reportedly returned when Warmoth refused to comply with state bonds, it seems difficult to see how Pinchback profited here, much less how this could be considered an extravagant expenditure when the purse strings were never loosened. The third bill that Pinchback sponsored and allegedly profited from was revising the act creating the Mississippi River Packet Company, which sought a $25,000 appropriation. While he and the others have been charged with making a "handsome profit," it appears they never received this appropriation or got the company off the ground. The final bill in which Pinchback allegedly skimmed a profit occurred during Pinchback's last session and sought to incorporate the Lake Shore Building Association. However, it appears this one also never got off the ground, and nothing can be found about this association other than that it was proposed as a bill.[47] But even if these bills were not successful, we can never be sure that Pinchback did not receive some kind of bribe or kickback for trying to push them through.

Whether he intended to line his pockets with some of these bills cannot be said with certainty. He may have sought to profit in some fashion, particularly with speculation that he admitted to. During his career, he amassed a substantial fortune as a public servant. He acknowledged at one point that he did "not possess all the honesty in my State" but qualified that by saying that most politicians of his day were far worse, particularly those who were leveling charges against him. A "prominent lobbyist" and a "steamboat man" told the House investigative committee in 1872 that Pinchback was among a handful of men "paid to vote for the Jackson railroad bill," although there is no accessible evidence to validate this claim.[48]

But Pinchback got the money from somewhere to colaunch an investment and lending firm and start a jointly owned newspaper so early in his political career. He had no inherited wealth and was not working long enough in the city to have adequate savings to provide him with the resources to start the businesses (unless he had substantial savings from his steamboat days). While he was known to have a penchant for gambling, and by some accounts won more than he lost, that likely cannot account for money enough to launch two business ventures. It is possible that he and C. C. Antoine obtained loans, but for Pinchback, at least, it seems difficult to imagine that he would have had enough collateral at this time to borrow. It seems quite probable he may have had money from speculation ventures.

The most often repeated "scandalous" charge against Pinchback involves his role as a park commissioner. According to this story, he and the other park commissioners acquired land for a public park on behalf of New Orleans. The details are unclear and seem inconsistent, but ostensibly the commissioners profited handsomely from the deal at the city's expense. In the one source that charges the Republican government with corruption, a journalist presents the corrupt park deal as fact and that corruption on the part of Pinchback was "common street talk" but offers no proof to validate this hearsay.[49] The only indication that Pinchback may have benefited in some fashion is that his later split with Antoine is said to have revolved around Antoine being pushed out of profiting from the public park deal.

What can be said with certainty is that most of the above bills, along with several others during this second session, were geared towards boosting the economy and creating infrastructure, which was still dreadful. The levees, canals, and roads were in poor shape, suffering from neglect since the war. There were only limited telegraph services, no cotton mills or industries in New Orleans, and only a few warehouses. Clean drinking water and sanitation were a problem, and yellow fever outbreaks, known as the "Saffron Scourge," were common, the deadliest in history taking thousands of lives in 1878.[50] Thus, with at least some tax revenue, public works and other measures aimed at improving the general and economic well-being were seen as a "crying need" in Louisiana, even if there were cases of corruption surrounding some of these bills. Pinchback's bill for building and constructing warehouses by way of the proposed Levee Shed Company, which called for one of the largest expenditures during this time, was seen by many as important for the economic well-being of the city and state since warehouses were almost nonexistent at that time along the New Orleans part of the Mississippi.

The allegations leveled at Pinchback provided ammunition for his political enemies to attempt to discredit him for his entire active political career. Repeated and reprinted with such frequency, not only was a dark cloud of suspicion cast on Pinchback during his lifetime, but it has hovered over him ever since, discrediting him as a legitimate political leader and thinker to the point that most historians and commentators—and not only historians of the old school of racist historiography—have kept their distance, rarely attempting to delve into his life and work. The few that have, such as Agnes Grosz, have repeated Pinchback's corruption as factual, without any rigorous exploration into the charges of scandal and dishonesty leveled against him.

It had been a revolutionary four years that reconfigured the political and social landscape and transformed life as everyone had once known it. Pinchback worked with African Americans and white allies to unfold human rights in Louisiana by securing them in the new constitution and anchoring them by law in the state legislature. Through remarkable vision, strategy, and skill, he and his colleagues dismantled de jure racial hierarchy and white privilege and, in its place, ushered in greater fulfillment of inclusive democracy.

They may have moved the mountains of their times, but Pinchback and his allies' struggle against white resistance was far from over. As they fought a war against white supremacist Democrats in Louisiana, by the summer of 1871, another battle was emerging within their party that would soon split it into two factions, presenting Pinchback with dangerous challenges that threatened his political viability. As danger can also do, however, these challenges offered him opportunities that could take him to new heights if he could carefully straddle the divide with skill and balance.

CHAPTER 6

"WHY, DAMN IT, EVERYBODY IS DEMORALIZED DOWN HERE"

THE STRUGGLE FOR LOUISIANA LIEUTENANT GOVERNOR

Governor Warmoth was struggling to hold onto power in Louisiana. By late 1871, forces seeking his impeachment gathered like a looming storm. His recently deceased lieutenant governor, Oscar Dunn, an immensely qualified and popular Black leader, had called for Warmoth's impeachment before his untimely death that November. Dunn and his supporters had become increasingly dismayed over the governor's growing resistance towards civil rights and his habit of catering to white supremacy, which precipitated a split between Black and white Republicans. An earlier advocate of Black suffrage, Warmoth had risen to power on the Black vote, carrying thirty "black parishes" to win the election. However, as Louisiana's chief executive, he failed to enforce important civil rights provisions of the 1868 state constitution and vetoed antidiscrimination legislation. All this angered Dunn as well as New Orleans African Americans. Revealing a lack of commitment to protecting their rights, Warmoth claimed that racial prejudice would only give way gradually and that forcing Black rights upon whites would delay the rights' arrival. His opponents vehemently and quite correctly, disagreed, believing that such a gradualist argument contradicted the rationale behind Reconstruction, which was to implement legislation to protect the freedmen and prevent discrimination. Without the "iron hand" of the state, they argued, white supremacy would oppress African Americans indefinitely.[1]

With his popular critic, Oscar Dunn, now out of the picture, the teetering governor hoped to make a last-ditch effort to save his job, scrambling to prevent his political opponent, George Carter, the house speaker and Dunn ally, from stepping into the lieutenant governor's office. A former Confederate officer, Carter was what many white Southerners contemptuously referred to as a "scalawag," or Southerner turned traitor to advance his interests. Despite their caricatures that persist to this day, scalawags were a combination of Southerners who genuinely wanted to assist their region in its transition during Reconstruction, as well as men who were motivated by self-interest, not unlike most other politicians of the day. Carter became part of the coalition that joined with Black Republicans and white allies who had grown discontented with how Warmoth appeased white Democrats and stymied the safeguards of Reconstruction. Warmoth understood that with Carter as lieutenant governor, it would only be a matter of time before his opposition mustered the votes to impeach him. Carter was a leader of the Custom House faction, named after the building, where a group of Republicans had organized under Dunn to oppose Warmoth and take control of the party machinery. The Warmoth supporters, with Pinchback among them, became known as the Turner Hall faction, also named after a building where they met to maintain their hold on the party machinery. This party divide in New Orleans was occurring against the larger backdrop of factionalism unfolding in the South between Black and white Republicans, and over competing perspectives on office holding and personal rivalries. Taking advantage of the shock and disorientation—and dashed hopes—in the wake of Dunn's unexpected death, the governor moved quickly to put Pinchback into the empty seat.[2]

Warmoth believed that with Pinchback as lieutenant governor, his opponents would be less likely to seek impeachment since the state senator would be viewed as a worse alternative. This was a reversal of sorts in the world of American politics. Most top-spot contenders or politicians choose a running mate who will be viewed positively and whose strengths and popular appeal will enhance their image. Warmoth intentionally selected a man to fill the number two spot that he hoped would be viewed so negatively that his own tarnished image would be improved by comparison and thus his power protected. But as events would tell, this was a miscalculation. He wrongly believed that his opponents shared his irrepressible "distaste" for the "freelance and dangerous" state senator, as he described him, and he sorely underestimated Pinchback's shrewdness at this time. Nor did siding with the governor automatically make Pinchback an enemy of everyone in the Custom House faction, particularly among Black Republicans. While

Governor Henry Clay Warmoth, Pinchback's friend and rival. From the Henry Clay Warmoth Papers #752, Southern Historical Collection, Wilson Special Collections Library, University of North Carolina at Chapel Hill.

he appeared loyal to administration forces by backing Warmoth over the opposition when the Republican Party split, he had more in common politically with those who went to the Custom House side. Several had worked with Pinchback in making civil rights the cause célèbre in the Louisiana legislature. They had supported him as a US senatorial prospect in March 1871, even over the popular Dunn, though Warmoth ultimately blocked it. They also knew he had "arrayed himself against" Warmoth for resisting antidiscrimination legislation and refused to kowtow to the governor when he failed to act on behalf of African Americans. Warmoth complained about this in his memoirs, describing Pinchback as a "restless, ambitious man" who "had to be reckoned with at all times." The opposition was unhappy with the alliance, but to be sure they recognized a world of difference between Pinchback and Warmoth. The Custom House faction still preferred one of their own to step in as lieutenant governor. And they would struggle against Warmoth to get their selection into that vacant office over Pinchback. But for many, this had more to do with hopes of winning the power struggle in the divided Republican Party and the leverage they believed it would give them to impeach Warmoth than ardent opposition to Pinchback.[3]

This all begs the question: how do we explain Pinchback's support of a leader who was becoming known for his racism? Indeed, Warmoth had opposed almost everything Pinchback was fighting for. During his tenure as governor, "he vetoed two civil rights bills, resisted integration of public schools, and refused to enforce the equal accommodations provision of the state constitution." Before the opening of the legislative session in January 1871, he had collaborated with white supremacist Democrats to get several party members into key chair committee positions in the Republican-controlled Senate. Warmoth also actively thwarted Pinchback's first attempt to be considered for the US Senate in March, backing a white Democrat instead who held African Americans in disdain. By all appearances, the governor seemed the political enemy of Pinchback if there were ever one.[4]

Pinchback was an astute strategist, however. From the time he arrived back in New Orleans after the Civil War when he organized the Fourth Ward Republican Club—and likely before that—he was strategizing his path to power. While it is not clear how far his sights were set during those early days, he was certainly maneuvering his way to the constitutional convention of 1868, where he would be a force for transforming his world into an egalitarian society and, probably saw beyond that too, at least to the state legislature. As the Republican Party began what would become its irrevocable split between Warmoth/Turner Hall and Dunn/Carter/Custom House forces by the summer of 1871, Pinchback maintained delicate neutrality, assessing the political terrain closely, before finally committing to Warmoth as the force likely to prevail in the struggle. Pinchback's decision to stay aligned with the increasingly unpopular Warmoth, rather than the Radical Republicans with whom he shared much more in common, certainly came with political risk. Embattled and unstable, Warmoth still had the organizational advantage as the recognized Republican authority in the state. He had even significantly expanded his authority to become the most powerful governor in Louisiana history to that point. Pinchback also likely moved away from the Radical Republicans because of their allegiance to Dunn—he could not supplant the popular politician—but most importantly he believed that maintaining an alliance with Warmoth for the time being was the safest move for his political viability. The Custom House was for now a splinter group with no official power. As Pinchback shared later, he would "drive along" with Warmoth until he "could get a convenient jumping-off place."[5]

Almost immediately Pinchback began to paddle closer to that oppositional ship by distancing himself from the governor. Shortly after committing to Warmoth, he attempted to assuage his critics by stepping away from the governor while softly defending his allegiance to the administration. At the

Warmoth Republican convention in August, Pinchback declared that he was first a "people's man" and that he only recently began "sustaining Governor Warmoth personally." He continued by skillfully playing both sides of the fence to maintain trust with the opposition: "When Governor Warmoth did what I didn't approve, I always took occasion to tell him . . . but is that a just reason why as a citizen I should oppose the administration of which he is the head?"[6]

THE STRUGGLE FOR LIEUTENANT GOVERNOR

On November 24, 1871, the governor issued a proclamation, calling the state Senate into an extra session without calling the House. This unusual action was done ostensibly to address pressing state affairs, such as investigating state officers' books and accounts. The real motivation was to fill the lieutenant governor vacancy. The opposition in the House was livid because without the opportunity to convene, they could not begin impeachment proceedings against the governor. They were furious that Warmoth was intentionally preventing them from acting. However, he defended his action as constitutional before finally convening the extra session of the state Senate on December 6.[7]

Yet even with the House out of the picture, it was not a given that Warmoth-Pinchback would triumph. The Senate was divided almost equally between administration and antiadministration senators. The strength of the Warmoth group would be tested on the first vote to elect a temporary presiding officer before electing a lieutenant governor. If this vote went in favor of Pinchback, the Warmoth supporters believed it would be a good indication that he could be elected lieutenant governor, though there was no guarantee; there would still be a few more hurdles to make it over. When the count was taken, Pinchback was elected presiding chairman by only one vote, 17 to 16, far too close for comfort.[8]

With opposition and supporters looking on, the new chairman stood and gave his acceptance speech. It was a short speech but one loaded with meaning. Pinchback clearly understood what he had to do. The vote had been extremely close. The opposition was also still disheartened by the loss of the popular Oscar Dunn, whose death meant the loss of their more immediate political hopes. Now on the path as Dunn's replacement, Pinchback was attuned to their reverence and the tenacious local rumor that as Dunn's rival, he had less than friendly feelings for their hero. It was alleged, for example, that Pinchback had threatened Dunn with revealing potentially damaging information weeks before his death. Rumors were also circulating that he may have had something to do with Dunn's demise. A close Dunn ally and respected Black leader, T. Chester Morris, went so far as to accuse Pinchback of his death. Moreover, the Dunn camp had strongly opposed Warmoth's efforts to replace Dunn with Pinchback. In such a tense climate, Pinchback knew he must make his move at that moment with the utmost sensitivity to gain their trust and mitigate opposition. Thus, the central theme of his brief acceptance speech would not be about himself, but rather a hagiographical nod to Dunn.[9]

Speaking in what had become by this time his calm and composed style compared to the firebrand who threatened to burn down the city, Pinchback had grown as a leader and person. He thanked his colleagues for "the compliment" of electing him as "temporary presiding officer." Acknowledging concerns of the opposition to this extra session of the Senate, he then went straight to Dunn, declaring him as the best of the American political tradition of "our founding fathers." Though he was "reared in a community that was prejudiced against his race," denied his education, and surrounded by the "baneful influences" of "slavery," he overcame all these obstacles to rise in the world of Louisiana politics. Pinchback stressed that Dunn was unique in that he even gained respect among racist whites and the "opposition press." He stressed that he was not trying to take Dunn's place. Indeed, he implied, nobody could take that "great and good" man's place. Pinchback continued: "I am led to believe that Oscar J. Dunn, in the history of our country, stands today without a peer, not only in America but in the civilized world." He ended his explicit remarks about Dunn by emphatically denying any "hostility toward him." He was "a man toward whom every feeling of my heart went out in sympathy," declared Pinchback.[10]

Pinchback ended by portraying himself as a reformer committed to the future of reform as advocated by the Republican Party. These last remarks were more strategic and intentional than they first appeared. The Warmoth wing was strongly viewed as a conservative force stymieing the reform that Dunn and the Custom House advocated. He was paradoxically committing himself to the "radical" reformers as he was trying to rise to power as the conservative Warmoth's lieutenant governor. Pinchback did not mention Dunn explicitly in his final remarks. But the message he intended was clear: Dunn was considered a great reformer and Pinchback, by invoking his commitment to reform, wanted his hearers to know that he was committed to carrying on that tradition regardless of his alliance with Warmoth.[11]

While he portrayed himself as Dunn's heir, privately he rejected any notion that Dunn was his equal. Three months into his lieutenant governorship, when a newspaper reporter from *The New Orleans Times* remarked that he was "the inheritor of the mantle which fell from the shoulders of Lt.

Gov. Dunn," Pinchback made it clear that he was his own man: "I stand on my own merits," he stressed. He continued: "[M]y own greater exertions and achievements on behalf of the colored people give me a wider influence, and I think greater popularity." For now, however, he would keep his real feelings to himself and play second fiddle to the legacy of Dunn as the moment required him to do.[12]

Immediately following applause, Senator John Ray, a Pinchback ally, called for "the election of a President to act as Lieutenant-Governor." From there everything moved at lightning speed. Senator Blackman interrupted with a protest, repeating the Custom House grievance that the Senate session was unconstitutional, followed by Senator Ingraham who supported Blackman's protest. Then Senator McMillen stood, defending the Senate session as "legally correct," after which he nominated P. B. S. Pinchback to fill the vacancy. Senator Ingraham responded quickly by nominating Senator Theodore Coupland, a white native Alabaman who was a Warmoth enemy.[13]

With two candidates now vying for lieutenant governor, the roll call vote began. The tension was thick as each senator was called for his vote. The name of Coupland rang out repeatedly and was interspersed with a few voices for Pinchback. Indeed, seven of the first ten senators voted for Coupland, including his once friend and ally, C. C. Antoine. The two had recently broken friendship and ended their business partnership of the investment firm and the newspaper ostensibly because Pinchback had pushed Antoine out of the public park deal, which, according to rumor, Pinchback profited from. He would fume for months about Antoine's refusal to support him, calling it "a positive crime." As the roll call continued without support for his former friend, the tide began to shift as the name Pinchback rang out more and more.[14]

Anticipating a close vote, it appears Warmoth decided to take no chances. Opposition forces accused him of making a deal with a Custom House senator, John Lewis, to purchase his vote. Pinchback had met Lewis during their steamboat days and the two had been close allies in the struggle for civil rights in the Senate. The charge was that sometime before the Senate met on December 6, Warmoth had offered Lewis an extremely lucrative bribe of fifteen thousand dollars if he would vote for Pinchback. Incredibly, this amount in 1871 would be equivalent to over $370,000 today. Some accounts maintain that Lewis was also promised twenty thousand in state bonds. The alleged deal was that the money (and bonds) would be delivered to Lewis through a third party after Pinchback had been elected and confirmed as lieutenant governor. However, according to this story, Warmoth reneged after Lewis kept his end of the bargain. Despite attempts to get his money, Lewis allegedly never received a cent, only a copy of the written agreement in the box that was to contain the money. Warmoth denied any part in bribing Lewis, maintaining that all he needed to persuade anyone was his "presence, cheerful conversation, and pleasant manners." One gets the feeling in reading his testimony that he is hamming it up and confident that he can outsmart his inquisitors. Pinchback would soon tell an interviewer while he was not "aware of such arrangements," considering the "bribery and corruption that had been indulged in to such an extent," he "would not be surprised at anything." Whether he offered a bribe or not, Warmoth was obsessed with holding on to his power. Offering a fake exaggerated bribe, or even an actual bribe, in hopes that he could deflect impeachment would not have been out of character for him. As historian Joe Gray Taylor explains, Warmoth "did not deny being corrupt in the common sense of the word. Once, indeed, he confirmed it." Perhaps the truth of this story is somewhere in the middle, with Warmoth using persuasion that may have contained a lucrative verbal promise of some sort.[15]

Whatever truth there is to the Warmoth bribery story, Lewis voted that day for Pinchback, to the dismay of his fellow Custom House senators. And his vote made the difference: Pinchback defeated Coupland 18 to 16. Had Lewis voted for Coupland, the vote would have been a tie, and they would have had to begin the process all over again, a prospect that the Warmoth men wanted to avoid since it could result in their defeat. When opposition protested with charges of bribery, Warmoth responded brashly, "I can assure you that my own persuasive words . . . were sufficient to convert Mr. Lewis."[16]

Immediately following Warmoth's cocky denial of wrongdoing, his senators were quick to call for an adjournment until the next day to prevent further discussion that could call their victory into question. But just before he adjourned the heated session as presiding officer, Pinchback stood and gave a short acceptance speech. This time, his recent efforts to distance himself from Warmoth while inching towards the Custom House now began to sound like a more definitive break. Standing as the second most powerful man in the state, Pinchback made it clear that he was not a Warmoth man, but his own man, an independent leader: "I am not . . . nor will I ever be willing to become the suppliant tool of Henry C. Warmoth, nor anybody else."[17]

The opposition was not ready to surrender without a fight. Pinchback's election still had to be confirmed in early January. In the weeks prior, a desperate Custom House struggled to overturn the Senate session that had elected Pinchback. Their goal was to gain the support of the legislature, elect one of their own Custom House leaders as lieutenant governor, impeach Warmoth, and finally get their man into the governor's seat. Attacks against Warmoth grew ever more virulent. When lieutenant governor–elect

Pinchback called the Senate to order on January 1, 1872, for his confirmation, fewer than half answered the roll call for attendance with the rest missing. The same thing happened the next day. Without a quorum or the minimum number of senators required to be present to vote on confirmation, Pinchback was in limbo.[18]

Unwanted controversy of another kind stirred for Pinchback as he struggled for confirmation. On New Year's Day, Pinchback was present during a violent altercation in the city that left one man shot. There are conflicting accounts of what transpired, but the gist of the story is that he was out with a group of friends attending a social gathering when they encountered T. Chester Morris. Morris had been a military officer and Black war correspondent during the last year of the Civil War for the Philadelphia Press and a close supporter of the late lieutenant governor, Oscar Dunn. According to reports, a scuffle broke out between Jeffrey Canonge (or P. Z. Canonge by some accounts) and Morris, which ended with the latter wounded by gunshot. Oppositional papers implicated Pinchback in the violence, who was known to have been at odds with Morris ever since he accused Pinchback of Oscar Dunn's death. Friendly papers denied that Pinchback was in any way responsible for what transpired, which he reinforced in his own narrative of events, stating that he tried to defuse the hostility and left the premises before a shot was fired. While Pinchback was charged, the charge was later dropped. Morris quickly recovered from his wound and Canonge was released on bail. It appears that Pinchback had nothing to do with the shooting, but that did not stop his political enemies from using this violent episode to try to discredit him as an unhinged leader.[19]

The Morris shooting controversy may have been one more spoke in the wheel that inspired the opposition to keep rolling on or, in their next move, sailing on. Pinchback and Warmoth soon learned why so many senators were absent during the Senate votes—and they were furious. It revolved around one of those dramatic, comical stories in New Orleans politics during Reconstruction where one side tried to get the advantage over the other through chicanery. It began when a plan was hatched where fourteen anti-Warmoth senators hid in an upstairs room of the Custom House during the first day of the Senate confirmation session. When the streets were clear around midnight, the senators were escorted out of the building under the cover of darkness and ushered to the dock to an awaiting federal ship named *Wilderness*. They were snuck aboard the boat, and for the next week, they sailed around the Mississippi, preventing a quorum vote from being reached in the Senate. Making this story even more comical, S.B. Packard, a Custom House kingpin, frequently boarded the *Wilderness* with a supply of food,

Mechanics Institute as it appeared in the 1860s, the sight of the audacious fight between two Republican factions and where the struggle for lieutenant governor unfolded.

champagne, and cigars for the stowaway senators, reminding the pampered passengers that they were "making a great sacrifice for the good of the state."[20]

As AWOL senators cruised around the river and lived it up, Pinchback and Warmoth complained directly to President Grant, who responded by ordering the *Wilderness* and its passengers back to New Orleans immediately. When the boat docked, however, the Louisiana senators were nowhere to be found. They had disembarked in Mississippi and were now stowed away in a hotel, still wining and dining.[21]

As the House prepared to begin its scheduled session at the Mechanics Institute building with the senators still in hiding, the Custom House tried to lobby enough votes for impeachment, and it looked at first like they had enough strength to succeed. But Warmoth and Pinchback had been working for several weeks to entice opposition members over to their side. While it's not clear how much success they had, Warmoth attempted to show his strength on the third day of the legislative session by swearing in scores of extra deputies to appear at the House and act as a force of intimidation to the opposition. House Speaker Carter responded by calling in federal troops to combat what he claimed was the threat of revolution and to protect the Custom House representatives from the Warmoth police. Things got heated. With the police and soldiers jostling for turf, surrounded by growing crowds of anxious citizens also armed with weapons, the Custom House grabbed the advantage by convincing federal marshals to push through the crowd and arrest Warmoth and Pinchback, along with eighteen representatives and four senators for allegedly depriving them of their right to assemble.[22]

The Custom House had managed to pull off a coup d'état by having detained a sitting governor, his lieutenant governor–elect, and their crucial legislative allies. The Warmoth men that remained in the chamber were intimidated when a swarm of "thugs and Ku Klux" men poured into the room to support Carter "with their hands upon their weapons" and soon they could hear crowds outside changing, "Hang Warmoth! Hang Warmoth!" For a moment, the chaos gave the Carter men full advantage: control backed by threat force. And to observers, it looked like it was over and that the Custom House had won the battle, in clear sight of winning the war. But Pinchback and company soon made bail and rushed back to the institute. When they arrived, they discovered that Carter had gone even further by removing additional Warmoth senators and replacing them with his men. With their grip on power seemingly gone, the recently bailed men stood around in the lobby of the Mechanics Institute, outraged at their turn of fortune as the closed Carter-controlled legislature finished its business for the day. However, political and strategic advantage in New Orleans could swivel as quickly one way as the other, even when all looked dire. With his political career teetering at times on that swivel, Warmoth, relentless and bold if nothing else, told them that he had a plan and to hang tight in the area.[23]

As the Custom House proceeded to their destinations, Warmoth used his powers as governor to call an extra session. He notified the Custom House legislators by messengers of the extra session, but before they could get back, which was the plan, the nearby Warmoth men, acting as quickly and as dubiously as Carter did with his enemies detained, called the session to order and voted to remove Carter as speaker and replace him with one of their men. This body also offered a strong vote of confidence in Warmoth as governor. Before any Custom House men could get back—indeed, before many of them received the message to return—Warmoth had regained momentum and advantage under his power and authority as the sitting governor. The legislature was now securely his—for the moment.[24]

Carter and the Custom House tried to resist this downturn of affairs but to no avail. Desperate, the now exiled faction created a parallel legislative base of operations at a nearby liquor saloon with a wood-planked walkway and swivel doors, another one of those comical scenes that could only occur in the strange universe of New Orleans politics. Though they had put up a good coup d'état fight, they were bested by the savvy Warmoth and the tactical Pinchback who finally had enough votes to regain a quorum in the

Senate to call a vote. Despite several calls for citizens to take up arms and overthrow the Warmoth government, which resulted in a failed uprising that fell apart against the greater force mustered by Warmoth, on January 20, 1872, when the vote was finally taken, Pinchback broke a tie by voting for himself and assured his confirmation to the second highest office in the state. While he admitted that his voting may not have been "absolutely constitutional," he reasoned that he was still a senator and thus could vote however he wished, including on his own behalf. Pinchback added on the icing of defense by claiming that he did so to advance the best interests of the Republican Party. Simmering with resentment, the opposition had no choice but to accept their defeat and coyly return to the Warmoth legislature until they could figure out their next step.[25]

The struggle for lieutenant governor—sometimes audacious and borderline unethical—had been intense. Pinchback had achieved the second highest office by the skin of his teeth, just as he skirted charges of involvement in a public shooting and as chaos threatened anarchy in the Crescent City. The fact that he and Warmoth bounced back so quickly after being detained, pushed through angry crowds, huffing and puffing in the streets outside the Mechanics Institute, and outmaneuvered infuriated opposition without a scratch, speaks not only to their courage but to their remarkable skill at navigating treacherous political terrain by whatever means necessary. Both sides had used something akin to the Machiavellian "foul, iron or poison" to win the war. It had been a bizarre drama of intrigue that Louisianans complained about but tolerated and even followed enthusiastically. Drama and corruption in Louisiana were in some sense a norm in every era: "however much they deplored shady political profit-taking," writes Joe Gray Taylor, they "admired the politician who took his cut with skill, aplomb, a smile, and a wink." None other than Frederick Douglass wrote in a rather blasé tone around this time that "the moral atmosphere in New Orleans has never been noted for its purity and freedom from vice."[26]

Years before Reconstruction, corruption had evolved into theater, including larger-than-life personalities and scandalous power struggles. One scholar of Louisiana politics described this theater as "speculative, devious, personal, exuberant, and highly professional." He continued, "The objective was to win, and in no other state were the devices employed to win—stratagems, deals, oratory—so studied and so admired by the populace."[27] The instability after the Civil War, along with the severely ruptured ruling Republican Party during Reconstruction, made the soil even more fertile for the outrageous "political shenanigans" and drama that continued its normalization in the political culture. Oscar Dunn's repeated portrayal during this time as an untainted anomaly in New Orleans politics only underscores this norm. With all considered, Warmoth may have had some justification when he responded to charges leveled at him: "Why, damn it, everybody is demoralized down here. Corruption is the fashion."[28]

CHAPTER 7

LIEUTENANT GOVERNOR PINCHBACK AND THE RACE TO SAVE THE REPUBLICAN PARTY

With his victory, Pinchback became a history maker, one of only six Black lieutenant governors during Reconstruction. The third one elected in succession during this time, Pinchback now officially stepped into the shoes of Oscar Dunn, the first African American lieutenant governor in US history, who had served from 1868 until he died in 1871. The second Black lieutenant governor was Alonzo Ransier of South Carolina from 1870 to 1872. Ransier served in the state legislature in 1869 and later was elected to Congress where he fought tenaciously for civil rights. The fourth one after Pinchback was Richard Gleaves in South Carolina, who followed Ransier and served as lieutenant governor from 1872 to 1876. Gleaves was the educated son of a Haitian father and English mother in Philadelphia and helped establish South Carolina's multiracial Republican Party and presided over its state convention in 1867. Pinchback's former business partner and ally, Caesar Antoine, was his successor as the fifth Black lieutenant governor, representing Louisiana from 1873 to 1877. Antoine had served in the Louisiana Native Guards with Pinchback and worked with him in shaping perhaps the most equalitarian state constitution of Reconstruction. The sixth lieutenant governor was Alexander K. Davis of Mississippi, who served from 1873 to1876. Davis seems to be the most overlooked Black lieutenant governor of Reconstruction, perhaps because of his impeachment by white supremacists bent on driving him from office. However, he was one of the most progressive leaders in Mississippi fighting for civil rights, working doggedly to create a multiracial democracy.[1]

Revealing even more diversity during the rise of Black leadership in the 1860s and '70s, there were two other minority lieutenant governors, both Hispanic: Pablo de la Guerra served as lieutenant governor of California for one year, from 1861 to 1862, and Romualdo Pacheco was the California lieutenant governor from 1871 to 1875 (elected almost the same day as Pinchback), followed by a short term as governor for over nine months—the only Hispanic governor in California's history.[2]

While it is not clear where they had lived earlier, shortly before becoming lieutenant governor, Pinchback, Nina, and the children moved into a two-story home on Derbigny Street, not far from the French Quarter. This home would become famous for the many lively socials the Pinchbacks would host for friends and colleagues from all walks of life: rich, poor, and in between. One visiting reporter described it as "highly respectable, it not elegant" with a "fine Brussels carpet" and "black hair cloth set of furniture" and "windows ... draped with handsome curtains." The reporter described the "numerous pictures ... selected with both taste and discrimination" and pointed out one wall with a "profusion of photographs" of "colored statesmen."[3]

In Louisiana, as in most other states, lieutenant governors served three main functions: they presided over the Senate, filled in for the governor during absences, and perhaps most importantly, voted to break ties in the Senate. Some unofficial responsibilities included acting as the governor's spokesman and campaigning for state and national politicians. It would be this latter function that would consume most of Pinchback's time as lieutenant governor.

Pinchback stayed true to his promise that he would be his own man and not the tool of Governor Warmoth. Using his new position of power to his advantage, he pushed even harder to get his son, Pinckney Napoleon, into a white school, although Warmoth vehemently opposed forcing integration. More than eighty years before six-year-old Ruby Bridges was famously escorted by federal marshals to her New Orleans elementary school, Pinchback accompanied Pinckney Napoleon, who was about Ruby's age, with a police escort to a white city school and forced it to enroll him. This public effort intensified the hostility of white conservatives, who all along despised Pinchback with a passion because of his Black heritage and his bold defiance of white supremacy. They hurled insults at him daily from their editorial pages, including from newspapers aligned with the more conservative forces in the Custom House, such as *The New Orleans Times* and *The National Republican*. Furious that Warmoth had beaten them just when it seemed their victory was assured, and with the triumphant Pinchback now symbolic of their failure to defeat the governor, they launched attacks against the new lieutenant governor. These attacks were more vicious than ever, reviving with bloodlust every charge that had been leveled against him since even before becoming a public official, including his violent altercation years earlier with his brother-in-law and even his penchant for gambling. With "malignant and relentless persecution," they did everything they could to smear his reputation and compromise his power and authority in the public eye.[4]

Louisiana politics was a complex morass of hypercompetitive and conflicting interests, driven by the ambitions of politicians and journalists—some scoundrels, some visionaries, and some both—it was not a game for the faint of heart. Mudslinging in New Orleans during Reconstruction was as ugly and messy as we see today. But slander was business as usual. For Pinchback, it was an endless struggle to navigate this political and cultural morass, doubly so for an African American who faced racism from whites in his party as well as from Democrats. The new Black lieutenant governor was demonstrating an unwavering focus and sharp political skills that were unmatched by most of his peers. Once easily offended by personal and political attacks, sometimes with a spring-action temper, he was developing a thicker skin to withstand and deflect destructive criticism as well as a talent to duck the punches coming at him from all directions. With foresight and willingness to take risks, he could assess the best steps for achieving his future political goals. Pinchback may have contributed to the morass he had to swim in, but he used power in this unscrupulous world to push his vision of democratic equality. As historian Philip Dray stressed, despite, what he believed, was "the substantial basis for the scandalous gossip that shadowed him," there was "no one more sincere or eloquent than Pinchback in his life-long crusade for equal rights."[5]

BLACK BY CHOICE AND OPPORTUNITY?

The rumors of scandal and the rise to power may explain his grandson's struggle with his Pinchback's work and legacy. Toomer felt that his grandfather, who raised him, had a domineering personality that contrasted with the more sensitive writer who could feel overwhelmed by the "headstrong" Pinchback. In one breath Jean Toomer declared that Pinchback was a "dashing commanding figure," a tower among his people, and a dominating presence in his household. In another, Toomer questioned whether his grandfather was Black, stating that he was a white man passing for Black, and he cast doubt on the authenticity of Pinchback's commitment to African

Americans: "I doubt that he saw himself bearing a mission to secure and maintain the rights of the freedmen," wrote Toomer. He was not an "idealist and liberator" or a "reformer" or "primarily a fighter for a general human cause." Toomer believed that his grandfather had the makings to be a truly great man but was handicapped by ego and was primarily an opportunist: "More than anything else Pinchback saw himself as a winner of a dangerous game. He liked to play the game. He liked to win. Thus, the opportunity to play the game of political chess in Louisiana was the chance his personal ambition had been waiting for."[6]

Pinchback undoubtedly enjoyed the game of politics. Most politicians who entered politics did so, and still do so to this day, in part to pursue their ambitions for power and prestige and usually because of the opportunity to compete in the political arena. However much this was true of Pinchback, he was no different from most of his peers, particularly in Louisiana. The "objective to . . . win" in Louisiana politics, as historian T. Harry Williams explains, was more of a regional cultural and political norm, rather than an individual personality trait. This did not mean that Pinchback embraced a Black identity (when he could have passed for white) only to elevate himself during this unusual time. He was driven in part to right the racist wrongs done to his family, particularly the humiliation of his mother, and his clashes with ugly racism as a military officer and in society in general. With unprecedented opportunities opening for African Americans during Reconstruction, particularly to positions of political power, he saw Black identity as an asset to shaping this new world of Black equality, which it was, temporarily, for many of the thousands of African Americans assuming power at local, state, and national levels.[7]

Toomer was partly incorrect about Pinchback being in it only for vainglorious reasons, though he undoubtedly took pride in his work and accomplishments and strove to win. As a politician, he consistently advocated for Black equality, often maintaining his commitment even when it became politically inexpedient. An opportunist, and perhaps an adventurer in the political arena for the game alone, would likely compromise important positions to stay in the game and assure his viability. Pinchback's alliance with Warmoth may seem like an example of such a compromise, but for Pinchback, it was a means to an end while playing the game without compromising Black equality. His "mission," in contrast to Toomer's assessment, was to secure freedom for his people, to anchor their rights in the fabric of law and amendments with hopes that they would be unmovable. Shortly after becoming lieutenant governor, Pinchback declared publicly his commitment to Black political and civil rights: "I have a duty . . . to the black people of Louisiana—a duty to the children I will leave behind me when I am laid beneath the sod—and when I fail to perform that duty, I hope that I will cease to live." That summer he would stress in a speech, reprinted in newspapers, "I am infamous because from the very day of the constitutional convention met in this city, I have championed the cause of the down-trodden colored people." While the degree to which Pinchback pushed needed economic opportunities for the "down-trodden" is uncertain, he unquestionably advocated for political and civil rights. His trajectory in fighting for those rights remained consistent, revealed in his dogged work for civil rights, in his confrontation of racism, and in his speeches and correspondence. Indeed, his refusal to compromise on Black political and civil rights was one of the factors that would contribute to his being barred from the US Senate and lead to his forced exile in the political wilderness. Even the wavering Toomer expressed proudly that his grandfather was "a fighter of political and civil rights," which seemed to contradict his more loaded assessment that he was in it for the game above all else. Pinchback's craftiness and deceptions, if we may call them that, where he took advantage of his offices for financial gain, often went together with expanding rights and freedoms for those who needed them most, unlike Warmoth, who unabashedly sought power for power's sake, and was more than willing to restrict or roll back African American freedom if doing so assured his upward political mobility and hold on power. Pinchback may have compromised the public trust for his own benefit at times, but not for the rights and freedoms of his constituents. Frederick Douglass, with whom Pinchback began to nurture a deep friendship when he was lieutenant governor, believed that "he would as soon cut off his right arm, as to prove false to the cause of the colored people of Louisiana." Pinchback not only identified with his Black heritage but touted with pride the intrinsic worth of African Americans: "[W]e are proud of our manhood . . . and would not lighten or darken the tinge of our skin, not change the color nor current of our blood." And though he was born free and never experienced slavery other than as a privileged youth on a Mississippi plantation, he sometimes implicitly included himself when making references to slaves or slavery. For example, in a speech on equal rights, he explained, "Slavery, depriving us of liberty and making us dependent upon the will of another . . . But we are not slaves now. . . ." Perhaps Pinchback felt as did his contemporary John Hope, the first Black president of Morehouse College and Atlanta University, who in response to being "taken for white" daily, declared, "From the bottom of my heart, as long as the Negro is the sufferer, as long as the white man makes him suffer, I prefer to be with the oppressed rather than be as puny and mean and un-Christ-like as the white man." Importantly, passing for

P. B. S. Pinchback among Black Leaders of Reconstruction. Library of Congress, Prints & Photographs Division, LC-DIG-pga-02252.

white would have meant a severance at some level from his mother, Eliza, a former enslaved person. She was his unbreakable bond to that part of his heritage, and he would always identify with her.[8]

Although Pinchback was now the confirmed twelfth lieutenant governor of Louisiana, which should have moved him beyond the reach of challengers, the jabs kept coming at him. The Custom House was burning from their loss on the local and state levels, so they now tried to move their fight into the national arena. Desperate to invalidate his election, they convinced the US House of Representatives to investigate "the Louisiana situation." Pinchback refused to step into the heat of this spotlight, never appearing in person before the Washington group even though he was only a few blocks away from the proceedings. This was one political game that Pinchback was not going to play—or perhaps play by not playing. Instead, he sent a handwritten message to one of the House investigators denying all accusations of corrupt activities. He also gave a speech to the Senate, refuting every accusation made against him. He skillfully closed by charging his opponents with a level of dishonesty and corruption that made his own pale by comparison: "While I do not claim to possess all the honesty in the State, yet I venture to say that my character would appear as driven snow in comparison with the character of those gentlemen who have seen fit to traduce and defame me in their testimony before the committee."[9] Pinchback's critique was likely not far off the mark.

Soon after his position as lieutenant governor was beyond dispute in 1872, the rift between Pinchback and Warmoth grew wider. The governor publicly denounced President Grant and opposed his reelection in November while the lieutenant governor decided to ride the fence. A reporter tried to prod Pinchback to say whether he supported Grant, but he refused to take the bait, explaining, "I never like to shoot off my gun half-cocked." He had been displeased with the president's reluctance to take a stand against growing white violence in the South, along with rumors that he might not be entirely committed to the Republican Party in Louisiana. But Pinchback had his finger on the pulse of power enough to know that Grant was almost guaranteed to secure the Republican nomination at the Philadelphia convention in June. Remaining in good favor with Grant would thus benefit him, and Pinchback assured the reporter that his "relations" with the president "are at present most friendly." After flirting with the possibility of breaking from his party to support the Liberal Republican candidate Charles Sumner, one of the most ardent supporters of Black equality Washington had ever seen, and resisting direct appeals to support the Democrats, Pinchback drifted back to Grant, who would easily secure the main Republican Party nomination.[10]

One of Pinchback's first duties as lieutenant governor was stepping into the role of acting governor while Warmoth was away. One of these duties revolved around the most defining New Orleans event: the Mardi Gras Festival, or Mardi Gras Carnival as it was then called. With the Louisiana governor traditionally presiding over the opening ceremonies of Mardi Gras, Pinchback presided that year as two definitive features of the festival were inaugurated that have lasted to this day. One was adopting green, gold, and purple as the official colors of Mardi Gras. By some accounts, these colors symbolize justice, faith, and power, seemingly fitting for the life and work of Pinchback. The other feature inaugurated while Pinchback oversaw the opening ceremonies in 1872 was the crowning of Rex as "King of the Carnival," another definitive feature that has lasted to this day; Rex still stages one of the largest Mardi Gras parades.[11]

It is around this time that we find one of the most vivid descriptions of Pinchback on record. This description links his physical appearance with his political activism and reflects Pinchback's mystique for African Americans outside of New Orleans. After staying at the Pinchback residence during a Black convention in New Orleans, Frederick Douglass, enamored by his host and new friend, described his appearance for readers in his Washington-based newspaper, *New National Era*:

> In person, he is about the medium size, symmetrical in form, neat and trim in his apparel, perhaps a little dainty in respect to the latter. He is neither fat nor lean and is of the "makeup" from which we may safely expect sustained, protracted, and energetic action, without weariness. That he is a man of courage his history not less than his appearance fully proves. No man less courageous than himself could have talked and acted in Louisiana as he did during all the war and held his ground as he has.[12]

Pinchback had only been in New Orleans politics for four years. But he was already growing to legendary status nationally, particularly among African Americans. As much as any Black leader of his time, he challenged white supremacy with a daunting boldness and in the process often came out as the winner.

As the new lieutenant governor, Pinchback stepped into a morass of competing political parties in Louisiana. These were the Regular Republicans, Liberal Republicans, Radical Republicans, and Democrats. Although tightly secure within the ranks of the Regular Republicans, Pinchback also maintained a responsive alliance with the Radical Republicans (or Custom House faction) and the Liberal Republicans, who supported Black suffrage but advocated an end to Northern military presence. The Radical Republicans had been gaining strength since the summer of 1871 as some of the most powerful Republicans in the state. Pinchback was invited to speak at their May convention and was greeted with cheers and a band playing "Hail to the Chief." This reveals not only his immense popularity at this time but also the hopes of some Custom House Republicans that he could be the next governor. With such an exuberant reception, Pinchback also hoped that he could unite the factions. As a party man who wanted to keep the Republican machine in Louisiana a permanent force in politics, particularly one that could combat resurgent Democrat white supremacy, he urged reconciliation between all Republican breakaways within the main party. He linked the protection of equality to Republican power. But as a requirement for reconciliation, Packard, the leader of the Radical Republicans, urged Pinchback to repudiate Warmoth publicly. Pinchback refused, believing it would further weaken the Republican Party, and he was not yet ready to make a definitive break. He almost certainly was biding his time. Warmoth was increasingly losing control of the party due to his growing opposition to Black rights and collaboration with Democrats, which Pinchback candidly warned him of, telling him that "all you have politically you owe to the Republican Party and especially the Colored people." While Pinchback reaffirmed his commitment to Warmoth as late as September 1872, he knew privately that the governor would likely not take his advice. Warmoth had been working steadily against the interests of his party and African Americans for a long time. Pinchback saw Warmoth's end rapidly approaching. In the right place to succeed him if an impeachment investigation was launched before the end of his term, Pinchback would maintain delicate neutrality while carefully balancing alliances with divergent and sometimes hostile leaders.[13]

In June, Pinchback was a delegate to the 1872 National Republican Convention in Philadelphia that nominated Grant for a second term. This may have been where he met his future friend and ally, Blanche Kelso Bruce, who would become a US Senator in 1875 and who was in the City of Brotherly Love attending his first national political convention as a delegate representing Mississippi.[14]

Shortly after the national convention, Pinchback was back in New Orleans attending the state Republican convention, where he emerged as the man of the hour. His colleagues recognized him for his "prominent courage, unwavering devotion to Republican principles, and fidelity to the interests of his race and also to the welfare of Louisiana." But while they pledged to Pinchback their "undivided and hearty support in carrying the flag of Republican principles in the coming contest," the convention stopped short of nominating him as the gubernatorial candidate for the November election. Yet many Republican leaders and citizens in Louisiana, particularly African Americans, dreamed of a ticket headed by Pinchback. They had been sorely disappointed when Warmoth blocked their choice of Pinchback to replace the outgoing US Senator, J. S. Harris, after his term expired on March 4, 1871. Hoping to stir momentum for Pinchback's candidacy, these supporters met in their own convention and nominated the Black lieutenant governor as their candidate for governor. While Pinchback silently rode this wave of support, he was waiting to see if the regular and radical Republican factions worked out a compromise that would make William Pitt Kellogg the Republican candidate for governor, which he saw looming over the horizon. He finally withdrew his name for governor and shifted the weight of his Black supporters to Kellogg which he, as well as Kellogg, believed was necessary to assure Republican victory.[15]

An Illinois-born Republican, Kellogg was part of the Custom House faction and had been serving as a US Senator representing Louisiana. As part of the deal to wedge his supporters behind Kellogg, Pinchback secured the slot of congressman-at-large on the ticket. This was a slot that had belonged to John Lewis, who had given the decisive vote to Pinchback for President of the Senate, paving the way for Pinchback to secure the office of lieutenant governor, allegedly under a cloud of bribery. But Lewis released it to Pinchback, commending him for his "spirit of self-sacrifice" for declining to run for governor.[16]

Pinchback collaborated with Republicans to help shape the Kellogg ticket and load it with Black candidates who he believed would help anchor democracy in the state. With a sense of urgency, he used his influence to secure and prolong Reconstruction, believing that "nothing was to be gained by a timorous and time-serving course." While still on shaky terms with C. C. Antoine, he supported his "smart" fellow state senator and former business partner to run for lieutenant governor. Pinchback also worked to get Pierre G. Deslonde named as the candidate for secretary of state, and William G. Brown for superintendent of education. Deslonde was a Black Creole sugar planter who supported universal suffrage during the 1867–68 Louisiana constitutional convention and became a prominent Black rights state legislator. Brown was a native of Trenton, New Jersey, who taught at schools in Washington, DC, and Demerara, Jamaica, before coming to Louisiana to help create access to education for formerly enslaved persons. He was one of Pinchback's colleagues at *The Lousianian*, where he worked as one of its earliest editors until assuming his duties as secretary of education.[17]

With the ticket complete, Lieutenant Governor Pinchback went into full swing campaigning during the late summer and fall of 1872 for the Kellogg state ticket and for the reelection of President Grant and other Republican candidates. He embarked on a speaking campaign throughout towns and rural areas of the state with sizable Black populations and friendly white Republicans, attracting large crowds wherever he spoke. In Tensas Parish, the *North Louisiana Journal* declared that "there never had been so large an audience composed of both black and white citizens, in our town . . . the Republican clubs turned out *en masse* with banners and music." In his speeches, Pinchback encouraged Black voters to be subversive when they feared intimidation and violence from hostile white Democrats. The lieutenant governor urged them to "lie and practice any kind of deception" to navigate around resistance from white employers and keep their intentions from other whites who posed a threat to their freedom of suffrage. His message was essentially to stay silent to stay safe to be empowered. Considering that most of Pinchback's speaking engagements were in rural districts where whites attempted to suppress the Black vote with the greatest impunity, such a strategy of deception likely enabled many African Americans to vote by pulling the wool over the eyes of their white employers and neighbors.[18]

It was not only Black men addressed at Republican political rallies across the state. Many speakers, including Pinchback, often made it a point to address the hundreds of women who attended these rallies. Some even encouraged women and children to participate with men in voting as a community. Black women had a vested interest in supporting the Republican Party against the Democrats, the party of slavery, since still in recent memory were the abuses they endured as enslaved women, such as forced separation from children and other family members, sexual exploitation, and brutal punishments. They served as "enforcers," using tactics to pressure reluctant husbands to vote and participate in the political process. Steven Hahn explains that "[w]omen, the hubs around which kin and community networks ordinarily grew, were particularly well-placed to influence mobilization and discipline . . . they also became so deeply involved in the creation and expression of partisan loyalties that the vote could itself be regarded as something of a household and family property." J. Henri Burch, a Black state legislator who worked with Pinchback, later told a US Senate committee that Republican political meetings were gender integrated. He explained that Black Southern women "have been very active since 1868 in all political movements, and they form a large number in all political assemblages, and they have evidenced a deep interest in all that pertains to politics. . . ."[19]

It is not clear if Nina Pinchback accompanied her husband to the Republican rallies and meetings that he addressed or how active she was in her husband's political rise and in Republican politics in general. There are no accessible direct references of her involvement. However, there is one interesting piece from *The Philadelphia Times* that maintains that after Pinchback was elected to the Senate, there was anxiety among white elites in Washington about Nina's ambition and outspokenness, which could imply that she was known to openly express, if not advocate for, the Republican issues of the day. The journalist even went so far as to claim that Nina may have been one of the reasons for Pinchback's rejection by the US Senate. Had he been a white man, "or even a negro with an unpretentious wife," he likely would have been seated. Perceived as an ambitious Black woman (though white in appearance), she appears to have threatened the sensibilities of many white males in the capital city. Pinchback did become an open supporter of female suffrage and activism, even as other Black men relegated women to the domestic sphere, which could indicate Nina's influence on him since she was likely a suffragette.[20]

"WARMOTH CHASES PINCHBACK": THE GREAT RAIL RACE FOR REFORM

After campaigning vigorously in his home state, Pinchback was soon headed North to campaign for the Republican ticket, and specifically to Maine to campaign for James G. Blaine's reelection to Congress. Blaine was one of the most powerful House Republicans and would soon be a presidential contender. On his way home from campaigning, Pinchback made a layover in New York City at the Fifth Avenue Hotel, headquarters of the Republican National Committee and a hotspot for party powerbrokers. Republican bigshots maintained alternative addresses at the prestigious hotel, keeping posh suites for visits and meetings, including President Grant. Pinchback was accompanied by Henry Corbin, his personal secretary who was also the current editor of *The Lousianian*. An accomplished Black violinist, Corbin would later become the secretary for the New Orleans public schools and tax collector for the city. But for now, he was wholeheartedly committed to the interests of his boss.[21]

Shortly after his arrival, he and his "chum," Louisiana state senator A. B. Harris, bumped into Governor Warmoth, or so the story goes, who was also staying at the hotel. Warmoth invited his lieutenant governor to join him later that night for dinner. The story goes that after Pinchback agreed, he first paid a visit to vice presidential candidate Henry Wilson, a Republican power broker, nominated to replace Grant's first vice president, Schuyler Colfax, who became a liability amidst corruption charges. At this meeting was another power broker, William E. Chandler, secretary of the Republican National Committee, who allegedly asked Pinchback what chance the Republican Party had to carry Louisiana in the upcoming election. According to Pinchback's recounting of the meeting, he responded "none in the world" because Governor Warmoth refused to sign into law "new registration and election laws" passed by the legislature that would prevent fraud. Without these reforms, he believed Black voter turnout would be suppressed and there would be fewer votes for Grant. The governor, Pinchback explained, was protecting his power at the expense of the Republican Party. Chandler then asked Pinchback if he would "undertake the perilous performance" to rush to Louisiana while Warmoth was in New York and use his power as acting governor to sign the new election bills into law before the governor returned home. Pinchback recounted—either his thoughts or from Wilson and Chandler, it is not clear—that at stake was state Republican victory and "possibly that of the Federal government." If that were the case, he would "dare do anything to save it."[22] Deeply committed to state and national Republican politics and Black voting rights, Pinchback agreed to "start at once for Louisiana" on his urgent mission to make his state safe for Republican rule. He was a party man to be sure, but he was willing and ready to violate his commitment to its leader for larger goals and, perhaps, with an eye on power. The problem, however, was that Warmoth was expecting him for dinner. Pinchback and Corbin thus concocted a plan where they would make it appear that Pinchback was still at the hotel, though he would be a no-show for dinner, and whereby Corbin would give an excuse the next morning for Pinchback's absence. Providing the lieutenant governor cover, the National Republican Committee, via Chandler, quickly released a statement that they had enlisted Pinchback to deliver a speech in Pittsburgh. Privately, Chandler assured Pinchback that he would telegraph him regarding any moves made by Warmoth, particularly if it appeared that the latter was heading back to Louisiana early.[23]

At 9:00 p.m. that night, Pinchback boarded a train and headed south. Shifting to Warmoth's account of what happened next, back at the Fifth Avenue Hotel the governor gave his lieutenant governor's dinner absence fleeting thought, assuming that he and Harris were out on the city "living it up" and went to bed without any suspicion. The next morning, he ran into Harris in the lobby and inquired about Pinchback's whereabouts. Harris responded that he had not seen him since they were on the street together the previous afternoon. According to Warmoth, he suddenly had a "flash" of insight that "Pinchback had slipped off to New Orleans . . . to sign those bills his friends thought would be helpful to them."[24]

Warmoth wasted no time getting out of New York City, attempting to get to Louisiana before Pinchback. He used his connections with a railroad executive to "arrange the fastest rail connections possible." Due to two six-hour delays that Pinchback had encountered on his journey, Warmoth was closing the gap on his red-eye locomotive between himself and his lieutenant governor. Despite literally making record speed, traveling so fast that the engine almost gave out, when Warmoth was just North of Memphis, he learned that Pinchback was too far ahead and that he would never catch him, much less surpass him. He feared that all Pinchback needed was just a few minutes to sign the election reform bills into law as acting governor.

Desperate, Warmoth concocted a plan to detain Pinchback at the Canton, Mississippi, depot.[25]

Shifting back to Pinchback, when the train pulled into Canton, he was awakened by a conductor who informed him, "There is a telegram in the telegraph office for you." Believing that it was news from Chandler regarding Warmoth, he quickly made his way off the train where he was escorted to the telegraph office. Once inside, the door closed behind him and was secured. Pinchback immediately understood that he had fallen into Warmoth's trap. With his eyes darting around the room, he saw a window big enough to squeeze through. But by the time he was on the depot platform, the train pulled away. Pinchback could do nothing now but wait for the next train, which he knew was carrying Warmoth. When his train pulled in, Warmoth playfully acted surprised: "Hello, old fellow, what are you doing here?" Accepting that he had been bested in this game of speed and deception, he responded, "I am on my way home . . . and if you have no objection, I will go on with you the balance of the journey." (In Warmoth's version, he portrayed Pinchback in a defeatist tone from the start of the race, claiming that Pinchback told him that he knew he could never beat Warmoth to New Orleans). News of the race had spread quickly as crowds gathered at depots to cheer and jeer as the Warmoth and Pinchback train made its way from Canton to New Orleans. But most were captivated by the speedy competition down the superhighway of the day between the governor and acting governor. *The Donaldsonville (Louisiana) Chief* was one among many papers that printed an irresistible headline: "Fastest Race on Record: Warmoth Chases Pinchback." As for Pinchback, writes historian Philip Dray, "he seems to have weathered what for any other man might have been a fatal humiliation by considering it from a gambler's perspective." Dray continues: "Warmoth, Pinchback conceded, had simply 'taken the big trick', and he did not bother chastising himself for having misplayed the hand." Indeed, Pinchback brushed it off because he knew there would be other moments—bigger moments yet—to play his best hand.[26]

CHAPTER 8

THIRTY-SIX DAYS THAT CHANGED HISTORY

THE FIRST BLACK GOVERNOR

Pinchback had lost the battle but not the war. This sensational Warmoth-Pinchback race down the rails from New York to Louisiana further amplified the already inordinate split between the governor and lieutenant governor. It motivated both leaders to strategize their next moves with urgency. And soon a new race was on. Grant was elected president in November 1872. In the Louisiana governor's race, Republican William Pitt Kellogg and Democrat-Republican Fusionist John McEnery both claimed victory after two returning boards ruled in favor of each candidate. Kellogg had been a Lincoln-appointed Supreme Court chief justice of the Nebraska Territory and then a Union officer in the Civil War. He ended up in New Orleans at the end of the war when Lincoln appointed him as the collector of customs of the port of New Orleans. McEnery was a former Confederate general and unabashed white supremacist who bitterly opposed Reconstruction. The Kellogg men rightly argued that almost all the voting registrars in the parishes had been appointed by Warmoth. Based on testimony from thousands of recent affidavits, they charged the governor's supporters with perpetuating all sorts of frauds to intimidate and deny Black voters, many of which charges were "well-founded," according to a later congressional investigation.[1]

These affidavits were from an investigative committee that developed under the leadership—and literally under the roof—of Pinchback when several Black members of the community came to his house for a brainstorming session. Warmoth responded by signing into law the new election reform bill sitting on his desk, the same reform bill that inspired Pinchback to race back to New Orleans to circumvent his boss's power. In an ironic twist, Warmoth stripped himself of his powers to get the authority he needed. Though limiting his powers over election machinery, the bill enabled the governor to abolish the two previous boards and call for the Senate to appoint a new returning board to evaluate the election results. The Senate was not in session, however, which was the point. Warmoth claimed that in this case, the constitution of 1868 gave him the power to appoint vacancies "during the recess of the Senate," and on December 3 he appointed five men to evaluate the election results. This board was chaired by a Warmoth-McEnery supporter named Gabriel DeFeriet, who quickly declared McEnery the winner even as votes in most parishes were in dispute. He also certified Horace Greeley as the winner in Louisiana, despite Grant's victory (by most accounts), and claimed that a majority of the McEnery Fusionists had been elected to the legislature. Warmoth also strategically maneuvered into place at this time William Elmore, a white supremacist Democrat, as Eight District Court judge, whom he positioned to rule against any challenge to McEnery. The first thing Elmore did was to uphold Warmoth's action abolishing the two boards.[2]

Warmoth was the quintessential strategist who played the game of politics like a champion chess player but may have nevertheless underestimated the will—or reluctance to surrender—of those determined to protect Black political and civil rights while maintaining the integrity of the regular Republican Party. The battle of skill and fortitude was far from over. For Black Republicans, it was becoming ever clearer that maintaining power meant not only protecting their political and civil rights but also protecting Black lives as much as possible from white violence, which a McEnery victory, many feared, would unleash on an even greater scale with even less accountability. Despite Warmoth's order abolishing the previous election boards, the opposing board that had been favorable to Kellogg, known as the Lynch Board, never disbanded. The board loudly maintained that due to the fraud that the Pinchback committee uncovered, and in light of Warmoth's corruption, their man, and not McEnery, was the new governor. As opposition mounted, Warmoth moved quickly to consolidate power, getting together his forces for an extra session of his legislature to meet on December 9 to swear in his men and certify the newest election results that would establish McEnery as governor beyond dispute. As the date drew near, the moment was at hand for Pinchback to find his "jumping-off place" in what was essentially a coup d'état. Working with Packard and the Custom House Republicans, they made a checkmate move, securing approval from Washington to obtain an order from circuit court judge Edward Henry Durell to dispatch federal troops to take control of the Mechanics Institute, where Warmoth and the legislature were to meet. Durell also ruled that they had the authority to "prevent illegal assemblies," which allowed only legislators elected by the Lynch Board to assemble and prohibited McEnery men from interfering. A native of New Hampshire and graduate of Harvard University, Durell had migrated decades before the Civil War to New Orleans, where he became a city council member during the antebellum period. Once Reconstruction was underway, he became an ardent defender of Black political and civil rights and as a judge upheld state and federal laws that forbade racial discrimination, which he believed he was doing in this latest court order.[3]

With the Durell-ordered troops in place, Pinchback and Packard led the Republicans in an open rebellion against the governor and usurped control of the legislature on the same date and in the same place that Warmoth had christened for the transition of power to his anti-Reconstruction allies. Tensions were high as the Warmoth men stirred and grumbled in the hallway and people gathered on the street outside of the Mechanics Institute. With Kellogg declared the victor, the first thing the lieutenant governor did, against the protests of the Warmoth legislators in attendance, was administer the oath of office to new Republican senators and house members certified by the Lynch board. Pinchback then laid his winning hand on the table, a coup d'état that would bring about the defeat of Warmoth and the triumph of the lieutenant governor in his place—and make history. Bringing the chamber to a hush, he announced that he had some disturbing news to share with his fellow Republicans: Warmoth, he went on, in a meeting arranged by C. E. Weed, the owner of *The New Orleans Evening Times*, had visited his home the night before and offered him a $50,000 bribe and an appointment if he would organize the legislature to favor the Warmoth-McEnery forces. As voices murmured and bodies stirred, punctuated by shouts of protests from Warmoth supporters, Pinchback explained that he had refused the offer, for he "was determined to do my duty to my state, party, and race." Whether Pinchback had been bribed cannot be said with certainty. However, Warmoth did visit the lieutenant governor that night to ask him to do his bidding. In the Warmoth papers is a letter from Pinchback dated the following day, where he informs the governor that he is rejecting "the proposition you made to me last night." He concludes, "I am truly sorry for you, but I cannot help you." With that said, Pinchback appears to have led the governor on during the clandestine encounter since he did not immediately reject the offer, but "slept on it." Pinchback probably felt like manna from heaven was being delivered to his doorstep. He likely went along with Warmoth that night, the final ride with the governor, concealing his intention, knowing that the next day he would have the smoking gun and the perfect "jumping off-place" that would make him governor.[4]

The Republicans now had all their ducks in a row. Despite Warmoth stirring the anger and stoking the violence of his most devoted followers with raucous claims of cheating and fraud, on December 9, Pinchback Republicans usurped Warmoth's control of the legislature. They now had the votes and, most importantly, the *raison d'état*, to finally impeach him (though this would be one of six charges drawn up against Warmoth). Wasting no time, the house that very same day voted by an overwhelming majority to impeach Warmoth for "high crimes and misdemeanors in office," and a few minutes later the Senate voted for a court of impeachment to try the governor on the charges, which meant that Warmoth was suspended from office until after the trial. Then Senator Ingraham, one of the most vociferous leaders for Black equality, took the floor and announced that due to the vacancy in the office of the governor the "duties of Lieutenant Governor, Hon. P. B. S. Pinchback, now President of the Senate, will be required in the gubernatorial chair." Immediately cheers and applause erupted in the chamber, drowning out opposition protests shouting, "Usurper, usurper!" The air was electric. A rush of supportive legislators surrounded the lieutenant governor, congratulating him, patting him on the back, and grabbing his hand.[5]

Exuberant supporters ushered Pinchback to the office of George E. Bovee, the Secretary of State, to be sworn in as governor by Supreme Court associate justice J. G. Taliaferro. As Pinchback repeated each word, those standing by, most African American and Creole, removed their hats and stood in silence and reverence of this incredible historical event unfolding in their midst. With his well-wishers still in tow, Governor Pinchback then went to the executive chamber to take his seat at the desk of his new office. Finding the doors locked, his "enthusiastic adherents entered by way of a window and opened them." Finally, he was in the governor's office, seated in his chair as supporters pushed their way into the room and crowded around his desk. They chanted for a celebration to honor the elevation of Pinchback as chief executive of the state. But the governor knew he had to act fast to legitimize and consolidate his power. Declining their offer, he explained that he had to work with a sense of urgency. He only had thirty-six days to serve as the state's chief executive before the expiration of what would have been Warmoth's term on January 13, 1873, when Kellogg would be sworn in, and Pinchback was determined to do as much as humanly possible. His secretary Henry Corbin was there to assist him in keeping the flow of activity going.[6]

Bronze Head P. B. S. Pinchback in the state capitol rotunda, Baton Rouge, Louisiana. Library of Congress, Prints & Photographs Division, photograph by Carol M. Highsmith, LC-DIG-highsm-67782.

With focus and remarkable political instincts, in less than a half hour after being sworn in, Pinchback began taking control of all mechanisms of power and solidifying his control—executive, legislative, judicial, and among the public. This was not only to secure his own power but also to secure and protect the incoming power of the Republican governor-elect, Kellogg, and his legislature. Moreover, it was to keep Reconstruction alive in Louisiana, which would have been seriously compromised had McEnery and his followers taken control of the power base. Pinchback quickly composed a telegram to President Grant, informing him that he had "taken the oath of office" and was now in "possession of the gubernatorial chair." As a "necessary measure of precaution" to the possibility of organized white violence, Governor Pinchback, with an attached note of support from the Louisiana "General Assembly," requested "the protection of the United States Government" and recommended that "orders" be sent to "General Emory" to use his power to quell any disturbances that might arise in response to Pinchback assuming the governor's chair. In a state where whites used terror and violence to quash

Black suffrage and rights, murdering African Americans and destroying property, Pinchback understood that he must preempt the threat of violence directed at him and his administration by calling for an immediate show of federal power to protect his office and power.[7]

As Stephen Packard rushed off to send this telegram, the governor wrote "A Proclamation" to "the People of Louisiana." He believed he needed to establish publicly the legitimacy of his ascension to power. He explained that due to Warmoth's pending impeachment charges and suspension from office, "executive powers and duties" had fallen upon him as the lieutenant governor by "the Constitution and laws of Louisiana." With his name and the secretary of state included at the end, Pinchback dispersed the proclamation to all New Orleans and Louisiana newspapers, many of which printed it the next day.[8]

After retiring for the night and sleeping in his new office, Pinchback was up in the early morning of December 10 and got quickly to work to stabilize his power. In response to a public demonstration by Warmoth and McEnery denouncing the new government, Pinchback penned another telegram to President Grant, explaining that Democrats in New Orleans were inciting violence, even though "a vast majority of citizens" supported his new role as governor. Reflecting this inflammatory rhetoric was a white Creole named Charles Gayarré, who had lost his fortune by supporting the Confederacy during the Civil War but not his fervor for white supremacy. Shortly after Pinchback became governor and the Kellogg legislators were sworn in, Gayarré wrote, "We are completely under the rule of ignorant and filthy negroes scarcely superior to the orang outing" (evidently, he meant "orangutan"). Without coming out and asking this time, Pinchback's message to Grant was clear: more federal troops were requested to be on standby. Also, recognition of his authority and the election of Kellogg as governor-elect and his legislature was needed from Washington. The new governor was not taking any chances—he was determined to serve out his short term to the very end, and he was not going to let his former boss, much less ardent racists like Gayarré and the like, intimidate him or stand in his way.[9]

That same day, Warmoth and McEnery filed a petition in the Eight District Court with one hundred signatures protesting Pinchback's right to the governorship, declaring him "a wrong-doer and trespasser," as well as sending an appeal to Grant, calling on him to recognize McEnery and his legislators as legitimate and Kellogg, Pinchback, and their men as illegal. An injunction was also served on him that day from Judge Elmore, forbidding him to assume the role of governor, claiming that since his term as lieutenant governor was dependent on his election as President of the Senate, when that senatorial term expired on November 4, so did his authority as the second highest executive state official. Despite loaded threats from enemies that he better take heed, Pinchback responded by not responding, giving little energy to this injunction. He would later state that he did not recognize Elmore's right to issue anything; Pinchback did not recognize Elmore as "someone in authority" because Pinchback had stripped Elmore of his supposed authority in the first place. Friendly Republicans backed the new governor, stating that Pinchback was elected to fulfill the remainder of the term left by Dunn after his untimely death, which would not expire until the second Monday of January 1873. This certainly carried merit and was likely the case.[10]

Pinchback continued to focus on consolidating and securing his power. Despite the flurry of threats on his life if he did not step down, including one that came across his desk threatening to stab him in his heart, he was reported as carrying out his duties in these first few days with an "even tenor . . . calm, dignified, but modest withal." After the second telegram to Grant, he sent his first communication to the Louisiana legislature reaffirming his hold on power as the legitimate executive authority. Cleverly, he implied the legitimacy of his authority by calling for a speedy process to hold Warmoth, the ousted and illegitimate authority, accountable for his "high handed frauds alleged to have been perpetrated during the recent general election." He then called for the modification or repeal of all oppressive laws. He ended by strongly encouraging his legislators to craft and pass legislation "with a view to protect the rights and foster the interests of the whole people. . . ." Pinchback had worked doggedly to help make inclusive democracy a reality in the state constitution, then secured these rights in law as a state senator, and now as the chief executive, he was no less committed to using his authority to anchor democratic freedoms in Louisiana and assuring the continuity of the Republican Party.[11]

Hoping to prevent any challenges to his authority, Pinchback quickly suggested a bill on this second day that "protected the rights and fostered the interests" of his power and that of the Republican legislators. This would be the first of ten bills passed by the legislature, all at his urgency, and signed by him during his short term as governor. A powerful move to further strengthen his authority as well as Kellogg's by insulating them from judicial challenges from McEnery forces, the bill mandated that only the attorney general, Alexander Pope Field, or "A. P." as Pinchback called him, had the power "to institute or continue in the name of Louisiana any suit or judicial proceeding." Field had served as Illinois Secretary of State before coming to New Orleans in 1849. (He had preceded Abraham Lincoln's nemesis, Stephen A. Douglas). The bill gave Field the authority to "discontinue any and all proceedings in the Supreme Court of Louisiana instituted by Horatio Nash Ogden," the attorney general recognized by McEnery who had been a Confederate soldier and was now an ardent opponent of Reconstruction. With Pinchback's urging, the legislature passed this bill—one that the new governor likely had ready before the end of his first day—which essentially made Field the only legitimate attorney general and who now had the unquestionable power to nip in the bud any challenges from the Ogden and Warmoth-McEnery forces.[12]

Over the next several days, Warmoth and McEnery continued to issue public proclamations denouncing Pinchback and Kellogg while calling on the public to withhold recognition. Pinchback and Packard, along with Kellogg and Grant's brother-in-law, James Casey, continued to send telegrams to Washington, requesting official recognition from the president and more troops "for the protection of the legislature and gubernatorial office." The United States District Attorney of New Orleans, J. R. Beckwith, also fired off a telegram to Washington, stating that despite being "impeached and suspended," Warmoth continued to resist and threaten the new government, and he urged "prompt action by the (federal) government" to prevent a "collision." Beckwith would soon become notorious after he attracted the hostility of oppositional whites when he made it his crusade to prosecute those accused of killing and terrorizing African Americans in the racial bloodbath known as the Colfax Massacre. Warmoth also fired off telegrams to the president, urging him to refrain from validating Pinchback and Kellogg until matters could be resolved by the state supreme court, unaware that the judicial machinery was now being maneuvered into the hands of his opposition. With the telegraph wires between New Orleans and Washington buzzing, everyone was nervous in the first few days, not least Grant, who was caught in the crossfire of telegrams from both sides. Despite Washington's support of the Kellogg and Pinchback coup d'état on December 9, things were quickly reaching a boiling point between the dueling governments.[13]

As Pinchback and his allies bombarded Grant with requests for assistance and recognition, the new governor sent another message to the Louisiana legislature. Federal recognition was slow in coming, so he needed to continue solidifying his power with the state legislature, encouraging it to adhere to his framework. In this message on December 11, three days into his term, Governor Pinchback urged equal treatment for all citizens "without respect to race or condition of life." He stressed the importance of assuring that "each citizen, upon the basis of exact and equal justice" is guaranteed the "the right of suffrage." In the moment of the greatest turbulence the state had seen since Union forces first occupied New Orleans, he explained that the "semi-revolutionary condition" that had reigned in Louisiana, fueled by the intense split in the Republican Party, must end, and that the political rights of the citizens be stabilized and made secure. For citizens to gain trust in a government that had been charged with corruption, Pinchback urged legislators to work diligently to decrease taxation and the public debt and for more "economical collection and faithful expenditure of the public revenues." He reminded legislators that, though the past election was contentious and bitter, the "people have, with great unanimity, declared in favor of the healthy, liberal, and progressive ideas advocated by the Republican Party." Pinchback concluded in a tone that signaled his status as chief executive: "I beg you, gentlemen, untrammeled by dead issues or living prejudices, to address yourselves to the honorable and responsible work before you, wishing you a happy issue to your labors."[14]

Moving with lightning speed, Pinchback pushed the second bill through the legislature and signed it into law after its quick passage. This one abolished the court presided over by Judge Elmore, who had been hastily put on the bench by Warmoth to thwart Pinchback and Kellogg. Only the day before, Elmore issued the injunction to forbid Pinchback from taking over the reins as governor. Astonishingly, not more than twenty-four hours later, his court and authority had been abolished by Pinchback and the legislature. Exercising his stated legal power to appoint a judge to the new court, which was to be known as the "Superior District Court" with exclusive jurisdiction in New Orleans, Pinchback appointed a pro-Reconstruction judge. He could now say without question that no recognized authority supported Elmore's injunction and that he had no duty to abide by it. Lerone Bennett Jr. described this shrewd action on the part of Pinchback whimsically when he wrote, "in one stroke, he made the court, the troublesome judge, and the injunction disappear into thin air." Of course, this bill and the one before it went much deeper than simply benefiting the new governor. In two short days, he and the legislature had taken control of the local and state judicial machinery, preventing it from becoming a weapon in the hands of their enemies and securing it in the hands of their friends. It was a brilliant strategy that placed Pinchback, Kellogg, and the Republicans in control of all levels of power in Louisiana while leaving Warmoth, McEnery, and their supporters on the sidelines with no authority.[15]

With the sweep of power now complete in the state, Pinchback finally got word from Washington the next day in a telegram from Grant's attorney general, George H. Williams, who officially recognized the Pinchback government while committing federal assistance to uphold it if necessary. The governor immediately issued a proclamation along with Williams's telegram to the papers, eager for all Louisianans to know that the President of the United States officially recognized his authority. In a last-ditch effort, McEnery and his supporters tried to get Washington to hear them out but were met with a tart response from the attorney general, saying that Grant had made up his mind and was going to stick by it. McEnery supporters screamed out their frustration from the pages of their newspapers where, according to *The New Orleans Republican* which reveled in delight at their misfortune, they "boiled and bubbled, frothed and scolded, threatened and bullied all at once." *The Cincinnati Enquirer* took advantage of the defeat with a witty (if not irresistible) pun: "Somebody had said that the Warmoth party in Louisiana gave General Grant a pretty tight pinch in the last election and that now he has given them a Pinch-back."[16]

On December 11, the day that Pinchback reorganized the judicial machinery, a portion of the state militia in New Orleans refused to acknowledge his authority, holing up their armed resistance in one of the city's armories. The new governor responded by removing the militia commander, General Hugh J. Campbell, and replacing him with General James Longstreet. One of Robert E. Lee's most trusted officers, Longstreet now aligned himself with the Republicans in Louisiana and for the most part supported the aims of Reconstruction, urging Southerners to rebuild the South based on greater racial equality. Campbell had served with Pinchback at the constitutional convention and in the state senate where the two had worked for the same goals. But earlier that fall, a rift emerged after he threw his weight to Warmoth and soon after became a leader of the McEnery wing. With his trust in Campbell weakened, Pinchback believed that Longstreet's reputation from having fought for the Confederacy as Lee's trusted general would make the rebels holing up in the armory compliant and foster their surrender. Instead, they declared Longstreet the worst kind of traitor and refused to turn over their arms and ammunition to the new government. Nevertheless, realizing the futility of their resistance after a tense standoff, the rebels finally surrendered three days later, on December 14, and were removed from service. Pinchback had clearly demonstrated his power over armed adversaries as he successfully purged the militia of those loyal to Warmoth and McEnery.[17]

In addition to all three branches of the Louisiana government, along with the federal recognition and support, Pinchback now had complete control of the Louisiana State Militia as well as the city's Metropolitan Police Force, which he had earlier taken control of without any issues. The Metropolitan Police Force had served as an alternative to the state militia when federal law still forbade a militia in 1868. Even with the reinstatement of the militia, it remained an important arm of power for the Reconstruction government in

New Orleans, maintaining its influence as an armed force under the Republicans until the end of their rule in the state in 1877. Under Pinchback, the Metropolitan Police Force would stand ready to protect the integrity of his power if not his very life before transitioning that January under the control of the newly inaugurated Kellogg government. Some accounts maintain that he rejected protection and performed his duties with a determination to take on whoever came his way with a pistol not far from reach. Frederick Douglass remarked that though his "bold words and measures have fixed upon him . . . the smothered wrath of the old *regime* . . . he moves about freely among men ready for any emergency, and with an air of repose which comes of manly courage and conscious safety." Whatever the case, with the new governor's sweep of power complete—a "virtuoso performance," in the worlds of Lerone Bennett Jr.—there was nothing left for his defeated political enemies to do now but acquiesce or retreat. Perhaps this was nowhere more evident than on December 18 when Democratic officeholders presented their commissions not to McEnery or Warmoth but to Governor Pinchback for the required executive signature. The governor had publicly mandated that "all applications for commissions from the city of New Orleans should be made directly" to him for approval. He would later tell Pierre G. Deslonde, the Black Creole planter whom he helped maneuver into the secretary of state spot on the Kellogg ticket, that he did this to force the Democrats to recognize him as governor. He acknowledged that it was a risky move but was immensely pleased to the point of exaggeration when he told Deslonde that "each one of these gentlemen came in person to the office and received his commission from me" and announced, "We bow to the powers that be." *The New Orleans Republican* could not resist having some fun with the sight of white supremacists acknowledging the authority of a Black governor when it printed, "They did not look as though they were 'oppressed' or humiliated but seemed quite jolly."[18]

That same day, December 18, Pinchback pushed through the legislature his third law, an act extending the extra session "to and including the first Monday in January." This would keep his friendly legislature functioning close to the end of his term as governor. Another strategic move on his part, he could now work as optimally as possible to push legislation and make appointments in the short time he reigned as the state's chief executive. With less than a month left at this point, Pinchback would sponsor and approve seven more laws for a total of ten and make over one hundred appointments to state and local offices, most of which appear to have been Republicans who would strengthen and consolidate the party's power on the local and state levels. In short, by the passage of Act No.3, Pinchback used executive and legislative power to fill as quickly as possible positions of power and influence throughout Louisiana with Republicans who supported the goals of Reconstruction, many of whom would remain there after his short term was over. Working "unremittingly and arduously," he kept the legislature buzzing six days a week (except for Christmas and New Year's Day) with a flurry of nomination appointments that he sent their way for consideration and approval, most of which were submitted in bulk, sometimes three times a day, and almost all of which were approved. Despite "all this toil, anxiety, physical and mental tension," *The Louisianian* assured readers that Pinchback "looks as 'fresh as a rose.'"[19]

Pinchback's nominations spanned many offices across the state and contributed to the diffusion of responsive power. Many of these were vacancies in elected offices that the governor had the power to fill by appointment until the next election, and others were strictly appointive offices, with some appointed for life. They included police jurors, who performed and maintained duties associated with the executive and legislative branches of local governments, such as overseeing local budgets and programs for internal improvements; harbor masters in New Orleans, responsible for enforcing the regulations to ensure the safety of navigation and the operation of one of the largest port facilities in the US, which was essential to the economic viability of the region; notary publics, who were appointed for life in what was a more powerful office in nineteenth century Louisiana compared to other states of the time due to their wide-ranging powers, particularly as civil law notaries; justices of the peace, who ruled on minor crimes and most civil cases; constables, who were fully empowered law enforcement officers, with New Orleans having the largest number of Black constables anywhere in the South during Reconstruction; sheriffs, some of whom were Black/Creole, and who were the chief law enforcement officers in what was the most powerful local office with criminal and civil jurisdiction and the power to collect property taxes and license fees; tax collectors, who assisted sheriffs in collecting taxes; judges, who oversaw serious criminal and civil cases, as well as probate cases and appeals from justices of the peace; mayors and councilmen, who were elected officials who oversaw all city departments (though the legislature also directed city affairs during Reconstruction); inspectors of weights for various districts in New Orleans, who enforced weight and volume standards for commodities. Other nominations that Pinchback made and that were approved by his extrasession legislature were parish and ward officers, commissioners of the Metropolitan Police, assessors, and recorders of mortgages.[20]

Pinchback also made several appointments to higher level offices: judge to the newly created and powerful Superior Court of the parish of Orleans (as we saw above); circuit court clerks and recorders; a resident physician at Quarantine Station on the Mississippi River, which would be vital with the historical outbreaks of malaria and the yellow fever epidemic of 1878 that would ravage the Mississippi Valley in 1878; a board member for the Louisiana State Penitentiary; and the register of the state land office. The highest appointment made by Pinchback was to the state supreme court, a native Louisianan who stayed loyal to the Union during the Civil War named Philip Hickey Morgan. His appointment was hotly contested since another man, John H. Kennard, had been appointed by Warmoth a few days before impeachment charges had suspended him from office. Kennard had been a Confederate officer and was more in alignment with Warmoth's drift toward the white Democrats. The case went to the Louisiana Supreme Court, followed by the US Supreme Court, both of which upheld Pinchback's appointment of Morgan to the highest state bench.[21]

The racial makeup and backgrounds of the more than a hundred people Pinchback appointed have been somewhat of a challenge to unravel. Researching many of the names has produced dead ends. However, for others, there is some information, and it is revealing. If we can treat these as a random sample (acknowledging the uncertainty and incompleteness in doing so), we find that Pinchback's appointees appear to encompass Louisiana's racial spectrum during this time. They include African Americans, both former enslaved persons and those who had been free, including Creoles; white Northerners committed to Reconstruction; white Southerners who had either remained loyal to the Union or former Confederates who joined the Republican Party during Reconstruction; and in at least a few cases, white Democrats, though these appear to be very few who were appointed to larger boards or commissions dominated by Republicans, including Black Republicans. For example, John Pierce, who had been enslaved on a plantation in the troublesome Bossier Parish, was appointed police juror in Jefferson Parish and soon became the jury president. Alfred Barber, whom Frederick Douglass praised as one of the ablest local leaders who are of "uninterrupted African descent," had served as a Black captain in the Union Army with Pinchback, as well as in the state senate, was appointed as a harbormaster for the city of New Orleans. George L. Norton from Maine was also appointed as a harbormaster for New Orleans and would receive a national appointment by President Hayes. Two Creoles (apparently categorized as white Creoles), D. A. Thibaut and C. N. Thibaut, were appointed clerk of court and recorder for Plaquemines Parish, respectively. And a former Confederate and Democrat named Alfred Bonnable, described in his eulogy as a "notable character of the old south," was appointed as a police juror but was wedged safely onto a board that included almost all Republicans and whose president was African American.[22]

As 1872 approached its end and the New Year rolled around, the McEnery forces were stirring once again, desperate to find a way to usurp Pinchback and the incoming Kellogg administration. They tried everything from a direct appeal to Grant, to getting the state supreme court to appoint a friendly judge to the New Orleans circuit court, to launching mass appeals to the public in hopes of stirring grassroots support for "the installation of their government." Pinchback responded by issuing a public threat, claiming that by trying to usurp state authority, the McEnery people were "guilty of treason against the State . . . are disturbers of the public peace and must be dealt with as such." More worrisome to Pinchback was that several of his legislators went over to the McEnery side, with rumors that they were being bribed. He took this seriously and urged the legislature to pass the fourth law, this one to protect Republican power, titled, "An Act to Punish the Crime of Bribery." This was a well-aimed, comprehensive law that outlawed bribery to such an extent that it attempted to discourage Republican Party enemies from even thinking about bribing officials, specifically those in the McEnery camp and Republicans who were being approached with bribes. Act No. 4 mandated that those convicted of bribing judges, jurors, legislators, and state officials and officers, whether directly or indirectly, and those accepting bribes, would receive harsh penalties that included steep fines and imprisonment, including hard labor. The law also made it incumbent upon officials approached with bribes to report offenders and made it the "duty of every judge" to give priority to bribery cases. In a political culture where corruption and bribery were common—where such charges were leveled at Pinchback himself—his act was the most comprehensive and direct law that challenged this norm to date. It was a declaration against his enemies, putting them on notice that they were being watched and that they had better refrain from infringing on Republican power with bribery, or the weight of the new law would come down on their heads.[23]

The next day, Pinchback pushed through his fifth law, which extended the period for collecting taxes, giving more time to get essential funds into the state coffers, a procedure which had been delayed due to the election. That same day, he guided through the legislature his sixth law, establishing a joint Senate and House committee to "investigate the conduct of the late election in the State of Louisiana." As mentioned earlier in this chapter, charges of intimidation, violence, and fraud against African Americans during the past election cycle had been pouring in for months, including efforts to prevent Black citizens from registering to vote. In response, an unofficial investigation had been launched by Louisiana African Americans and white allies in the weeks leading up to the 1872 election. Many of the meetings that strategized about the investigation were held at Pinchback's residence, where charges and evidence of obstructing the Black vote were discussed. With Pinchback's leading, a campaign was conducted to encourage African Americans to file affidavits to document specific examples of voter suppression in parishes throughout the state. Shortly after the election, over fifteen hundred affidavits were filed in circuit court and a detailed report written by Black leaders.[24]

Springboarding from this earlier investigation, Pinchback crafted Act No. 6 to give the legislative committee broad powers to call witnesses and to obtain evidence about the election. The act required the election returning board to cooperate with the investigation by making election documents transparent. Not only did these earlier affidavits draw a vivid picture of intimidation, trickery, and violence against African Americans before and during the election, but they also added to these charges an onslaught of more affidavits and other complaints charging Democrats with using numerous tactics to suppress the Black vote. In her early account of Reconstruction in Louisiana (1918), Ella Lonn described interviews she conducted with "several old residents of the state" in which they described one such tactic to suppress the Black vote: white Democrats would usher Black voters from one poll to the next, saying, "'You don't belong in this ward; you must go to Gold-dust,' etc., until the poor Negro had walked away his chance to vote."[25]

Shortly after the New Year, he went back to work and fired off his seventh law to the legislature, one he had worked on during the short holiday break to "suppress riotous and unlawful assemblies." Several days before, the McEnery forces had held a public mass meeting where they noisily expressed harsh opposition to the Pinchback government. With no success through official channels, they issued a public appeal calling on the white masses for help in deposing Pinchback and the incoming Kellogg regime so that McEnery could take his place as their governor. His political enemies were encouraging citizens to commit treason by overthrowing the legitimate state authority, which had been recognized by President Grant and underscored at this time by his attorney general. Moreover, they were trying to usurp state Republican power and bring an end to Reconstruction. In response, Pinchback crafted and ushered through Act No. 7, which broadly defined "unlawful assemblies" as "three or more persons . . . armed" with "dangerous weapons" or "ten or more persons . . . with the intent to disturb the public peace, or to cause a public disturbance." The latter was more directly aimed at the mass meetings of the opposition, putting them on notice that their assemblies would be monitored by law enforcement officials who were now granted expanded powers to police such assemblies and to disperse and/or arrest offenders. Pinchback also made it legally incumbent upon citizens who were present or near riotous assemblies, if so enlisted, to assist the police in seizing and arresting "persons so unlawfully assembled" or be "deemed to be one of the rioters" and "prosecuted and punished accordingly." Also, any officer or militia member who refused to obey an order to suppress such assemblies or arrest offending persons would be "deemed guilty of a crime" and punished. But the ultimate authority to bring out the big guns and use the full force of state power rested with the governor. Pinchback stressed that "the Governor" at any time deemed necessary could use the state militia and any other armed force to disperse unlawful assemblies and arrest violators. He ended by implicitly declaring that cases under this act would be given priority and violators would face swift consequences with virtually no room to bargain.[26]

Pinchback made it clear that Act No. 7 in no way "shall be so construed as to bridge the right of the people to peacefully assemble and to petition the government for a redress of grievances," but he had nonetheless ventured into a sticky area. The wording of his act did not offer a clear or detailed definition of what constituted an unlawful assembly. Police and militia were given broad surveillance and arrest powers, and citizens could be held responsible for being at or near assemblies deemed unlawful. They also had no choice but to participate in suppression if ordered to do so by authorities or face consequences. Act No. 7 was a broad use of state power that came close to violating basic constitutional rights such as freedom of assembly, speech, and movement. In a private memo to the US attorney general, George H. Williams, the defunct attorney general, Henry Ogden, appointed by Warmoth but replaced by Pinchback with A. P. Field (but still referring to himself as the attorney general), wrote that he considered it a threat of "violent interference" against the McEnery assemblage. Williams and Grant did not take the bait. If they intervened it would be on the side of Pinchback, but they were anxious to leave well enough alone unless the McEnery forces tried to use actual force. The act was nevertheless an ingenious use of executive power in a crisis by Pinchback—a power with less than ten days of life left—to try to impede an immediate threat that was pressing in on his authority and threatening to jeopardize the future of Republican power in Louisiana. The next day he clarified in a statement to the press that "no pretended Governor shall be inaugurated, and no pretended General Assembly shall convene and disturb the public peace." He stressed that "the whole force of the state" shall be brought to bear on such "wrong-doers." But Act No. 7 was much broader than his comments implied and nebulous, with a net so large that nothing could slip through. Whether he believed it would be overturned or not, it would be on the books long enough to support the inauguration of Kellogg on January 13, assuring, he hoped, the safe transition of the next administration of Reconstruction in Louisiana.[27]

The next act that Pinchback urged the legislature to pass was one to consolidate his hold on the state militia. As we saw, shortly after Pinchback became governor in December, part of the state militia in New Orleans refused to acknowledge his authority, barricading themselves in one of the city's armories. It took three days and federal intervention to oust and disarm them. Rumors now abounded that other factions in the state militia were sounding their opposition to the Pinchback-Kellogg government. Responding with Act No. 8, the governor was given the explicit legal authority to use all the power at his disposal to disband and disarm those units or militiamen who are "disobedient or insubordinate." He understood the crucial connection between the hold on the militia and the hold on political power. While he and Warmoth had used skill and strategy to achieve Pinchback's victory as lieutenant governor in 1871, it was control of the armed power through the Metropolitan Police Force and state militia that helped Warmoth stabilize his teetering power. If he had lost that, he would have likely lost it all. Understanding this clearly, Pinchback used Act No. 8 as a message to any dissenters in the militia that the governor was the ultimate authority in the state and had control over their destinies and the militia. They could rebel if they so chose, but their boss, Governor Pinchback, followed by Governor Kellogg, would remove them from service with the full force of the state via Act No. 8. In short, he had created for himself and Kellogg a specific law to purge the militia of those who were disloyal and to warn them that any mutiny would not be tolerated and would be futile.[28]

The final two bills that Pinchback urged the legislature to pass were bills that authorized the expenditure of state funds. Act No. 9 mandated an appropriation of $19,500 to pay tax collectors because the original funds had been exhausted. Act No.10 authorized money for the Extra Legislative Session convened on December 9, 1872. It provided for the sale of $75,000 of legislative warrants to cover the expenses during the extra session for legislators, officers, and all other employees who worked in whatever capacity to help keep the legislative machinery functioning.[29]

Three days after this final bill, on January 13, 1873, Pinchback's historical term as a Black governor ended. Kellogg was sworn in as governor and Caesar Antoine became one of the last Black lieutenant governors of Reconstruction. In front of a crowd gathered at the State House for the ceremony, Pinchback delivered his farewell speech. He told his audience that he had taken the reins as governor under "grave" circumstances that "required all the wisdom, discretion and nerve" he could muster. He had performed his duties as chief executive during a tumultuous time while facing the "bitter antagonisms of race" and unexpected opposition from those he thought were friends. He had done his best under the most trying circumstances imaginable, and he would leave the "verdict" of his short term in office to a time "when the passion of the hour has passed." Pinchback lamented the fractured political condition of Louisiana, declaring that its "many embarrassments" had brought national notoriety. With McEnery being inaugurated a few blocks south, where federal troops held in check a mob of whites, Pinchback reminded his audience that "the evils that are among us and the difficulties that surround us are neither imaginary or superficial, but real and grave," and called on the Kellogg administration to "be catholic in its speech and wise and discreet in its action." With that, he surrendered "the office of the governor" to Kellogg.[30]

It had been among the most remarkable thirty-six days in American political history, perhaps without precedent. The historiography of Pinchback's work and time as governor—as well as his political life in general—have cast him as a peripheral figure who was largely ineffectual, barely worthy of mention on the historical timeline of that period. Even the groundbreaking novelist Alice Walker claimed that he "did nothing of substance for the masses of black people."[31] But Pinchback's record speaks differently. With skill and focus, he outmaneuvered opposition to become governor at a time when the Republican Party teetered on the brink of collapse and then moved decisively to stabilize the party after pulling it back from the cliff it was headed over. To make his success possible, he maneuvered among networks and coalitions of Black and white leaders in high offices, including legislators and judges. After securing his power as governor, he quickly created a space by an act to extend the legislative session to function on his behalf through most of his short term so that he could work obsessively to consolidate his control over every aspect of political power in the state and pass on a functioning government to Kellogg. Working with his allies, Pinchback crafted laws and made appointments, almost all of which were crucial to fortifying Republican leverage and prolonging Reconstruction in Louisiana while disempowering political enemies. Pinchback skillfully molded power while facing daily threats to his life from aggressive white supremacists, who threatened to do all manner of violence to his body, while hostile mobs stirred about the streets of New Orleans, and while a desperate parallel government schemed to usurp his power.[32]

For a Black man to rise as chief executive and exercise power so adroitly in a tumultuous racist society that was on the brink of anarchy, and in one where enemies were pressing in on him, may be unprecedented. With remarkable instincts and using a level of skill and strategy that few political

Pinchback Commemorative Coin issued in 1971.

leaders during his time were required to do—or could do—and with an array of like-minded leaders assisting him, Pinchback overwhelmed political rivals, saved the Republicans for the time being, and in the process kept Black equality alive. Even once Reconstruction began to crumble in Louisiana, and as white supremacy took control of the state, the work that Pinchback had done during his short term as governor contributed to keeping Black rights intact until the 1890s.

CHAPTER 9

"THE STAR OF MY HOPE"

PINCHBACK'S FIGHT FOR THE US SENATE

On January 14, 1873, the day after Pinchback's farewell address as governor of Louisiana, the state legislature elected him to the US Senate. Shortly after he had become governor, he was elected Congressman-at-large as well. This was the office on the Republican ticket that state senator John Lewis and the local party had relinquished and rewarded to Pinchback for his work in unifying Republicans in the 1872 elections. His election to the US House of Representatives was being contested by his opponent George A. Sheridan, a native of Massachusetts who had worked as the sheriff in Carroll Parish, Louisiana. Before the election returns were received, Warmoth had hastily declared Sheridan the winner. Three weeks later, Pinchback responded with an official statement from the "State of Louisiana Executive Department" certifying himself the winner with the governor's seal by a margin of just over twenty thousand votes. In short, Pinchback used his executive power as governor to declare himself a congressman-elect, although it was never clear who won the election. But this office was only a backup. Pinchback only halfheartedly fought for the House seat, focusing his energy instead on his fight for the US Senate seat—the one political office he wanted more than any other and called "the star of my hope."[1]

When word of his election to the Senate that day reached his wife Nina, and mother Eliza, they were so jubilant and proud that they scrambled to put together a celebration in his honor at their home in New Orleans. The matriarchs enlisted Pinckney Napoleon, now ten years old, to organize his younger siblings, Bismarck, Walter, and Nina, to help decorate for the party. A steady stream of well-wishers showed up to celebrate this historical moment in Louisiana. Jean Toomer recalled that it was common for his grandfather to host and mix people from all walks of life, Black and white, well-to-do and poor, and thus he did on this night as he cordially invited them all into his home. "He drew people out of their exhaustive categories, and to this extent cracked the categories open ... permitting people to emerge from them and meet and mix in the liberated flow of common life," wrote Toomer admiringly. With a diverse crowd gathered around him, and others coming through his door, Pinchback promised that as a national senator, he would promote peace, good order, and kindly feelings between the races.[2]

The ex-governor relished the opportunity to serve in the Senate. He believed that it would allow him to work for the interests of African Americans in a greater capacity and to satisfy his ambitions for power and prestige. While Hiram Revels of Mississippi had been the first African American to serve a partial term (1870–71), and before Blanche Kelso Bruce's election there in 1874, Pinchback had now been elected for a full six-year term, from 1873–79. In this thrilling moment, anything seemed possible, and rumors began to immediately swirl that this Black miracle man might even be capable of rising to the vice presidency of the United States. Over the next month, several elaborately catered dinners were held in his honor in Washington, DC, and Baltimore. One of these, sponsored by Washington's wealthy Black elite, was at the home of Frederick Douglass, which included a big brass band to serenade the new senator-elect. The exquisite menu included such exotic delicacies as Filet de Boeuf à la Provençale, Poulet à la Florentine, and Pheasants à la Dauphinoise. During another celebratory dinner in Baltimore held at the Douglas Institute and organized by African American leaders, including James Hill, who would soon be serving as Mississippi's secretary of state, Pinchback told those assembled that he took the honor as their "endorsement" of his commitment to "liberty, justice, and equal rights for all mankind."[3]

But soon a dark cloud appeared. Almost two months after Pinchback's election, on March 1, 1873, the competing McEnery faction, claiming victory over the Republican Kellogg in the election that past November, declared that the legislature that had elected Pinchback under Kellogg was illegitimate. Their selection and the legitimate candidate for the US Senate, they maintained, was a Louisiana state senator named William H. McMillen. An Ohio-born Union surgeon, McMillen was still notorious for having once beaten an imprisoned Confederate general so severely with a sword that he caused him irreparable brain damage. Though his native state of Ohio had always been free, McMillen lacked progressive views regarding African

Senator Blanche Kelso Bruce, Pinchback's friend and confidant, who served in the US Senate from 1875–81. Library of Congress, Prints & Photographs Division, LC-DIG-cwpbh-05070.

Americans and aggressively opposed Pinchback's efforts in the state senate to enforce school integration.[4]

Investigations rolled on throughout the year without any decision. When the Senate adjourned in April without deciding one way or the other, a writer for *The Christian Recorder* was so displeased that he declared that Pinchback in "natural genius and sweeping eloquence" was the "superior of half the senators there, and a far better statesman." The writer continued that had Pinchback "been white with such a record behind him, he would have been seated with applause" and worried that they were trying to "chisel Mr. Pinchback right out of his seat."[5]

Adding credibility to the Kellogg government and thus the election of Pinchback as US Senator, on May 22, 1873, President Grant issued a public proclamation declaring that Kellogg and his government "are entitled to hold their offices," and he commanded all citizens of Louisiana to "submit themselves to the laws and constituted authorities." This should have carried more than enough weight to convince senators in Washington that members of the Kellogg state legislature had the constitutional authority to elect Pinchback. Until the ratification of the Seventeenth Amendment in 1913, US Senators were elected by state legislators rather by popular vote.

But even when Grant officially declared the Kellogg regime as the legitimate government in Louisiana, the Senate continued to stall on doing anything.[6]

Then, on December 4, 1873, the Senate appointed a committee to consider Pinchback's and McMillen's credentials and claims to the Senate. The committee soon announced that they were at an impasse "on the question as to whether Mr. Pinchback is, upon his credentials, entitled to be sworn in as a member of this body," with half the senators for and half against. Curiously, no mention was made in this report of McMillen.[7]

The day after the Senate deadlock, on December 16, the Senate continued the Pinchback debate by linking its consideration for his right to serve with the Louisiana Question. Pinchback's election to the US Senate would now depend on whether the Kellogg regime was the legitimate state government, which would determine if the state legislature that elected him was legitimate. Defenders argued that President Grant and the legislature recognized the Kellogg government as the lawful body of the state. They stressed that the Louisiana Supreme Court upheld this legitimacy recently in a ten-page legal brief: "the Supreme Court of Louisiana has decided that the Legislature which elected Senator Pinchback was the legal Legislature, therefore it should be held and treated by the Senate of the United States as such." This all gave Kellogg's right to power a great deal of credibility. Kellogg unquestionably exercised official gubernatorial duties in contrast to McEnery, who failed to act with the same authority. Defenders were quick to point out that his government debated and acted on economic problems and that the legislature under him passed bills and laws, making it undeniably the functional authority of the state.[8]

Following a three-week recess, on January 12, 1874, the US Senate submitted a new proclamation from the Louisiana legislature urging confirmation of Pinchback.[9] But soon another obstacle appeared to prevent the seating of Pinchback. On January 20, his friend and defender, Senator Morton, suddenly jumped ship, declaring that the Black leader had engaged in unethical or illegal conduct, prompting the Senate to investigate the matter. Morton claimed that Pinchback had accepted a bribe to take himself out of running for the US Senate. The story revolving around this incident is confusing and bizarre. It does appear that Emery Ebenezer Norton, not Pinchback, had originally been the Senate Republican choice of Kellogg and some of his peers. Norton had served in the New York legislature and then as a Union soldier, after which he opened a law office in New Orleans where he dabbled in Republican politics. The story has it that party members gave Pinchback a $10,000 bribe, via Kellogg, for him to abandon his campaign for the Senate and instead support the election of Norton. It does appear that Pinchback may have accepted some unspecified amount but paid the money back "the day after the election." Norton was furious and waited for the right moment to get even. Described as "a sulking and bitterly disappointed," low-ranking Republican, he made sure that the version of the incident he wanted to convey was brought to the attention of senators in Washington.[10]

At this point, the Senate decided to table the matter for the rest of the legislative session. Pinchback was angry and exhausted. With nothing else to stay for in Washington, he departed for home in New Orleans until the next session. He desperately missed Nina, his mother, and the children and was eager to be back in the bosom of his family. In Washington, the embattled senator-elect gave the appearance of steely resolve, described by one journalist as wearing a "sardonic smile" that gave the impression to observers that he was confident that he would win the war. Frederick Douglass, an ardent defender of Pinchback's right to serve in the Senate in his newspaper, *The New National Era*, admired Pinchback's tenacity in fighting the battle in Washington. He observed, "There is something that inspires respect in the calm, patient and persistent efforts of Mr. Pinchback to secure his seat." But inside, Pinchback was growing weary, his hope was waning, and he desperately yearned for the one thing that he never had to question: the love and comfort of his family and the understanding from his close friends back in New Orleans.[11]

Pinchback's case would not come up again for another year. As his potential term in the Senate ticked away, he tended to local politics while campaigning vigorously for more civil rights legislation in Louisiana to create stronger safeguards for the rights of African Americans. During this time one of the most troubling events occurred in New Orleans that threatened to undo everything Pinchback and others had worked so hard for. On September 14, 1874, a paramilitary force led by the White League succeeded for a moment in carrying out an armed insurrection in the city to overthrow the Kellogg Republican government. Known as the Battle of Liberty Place, whites opposed to Reconstruction instigated a violent clash that killed and wounded hundreds of people and then attempted to seat the Democrat John McEnery who had lost to Kellogg in the highly contested gubernatorial election of 1872. Taking the upper hand for a moment, the insurrectionists soon retreated in the face of advancing federal troops sent by President Grant to restore order. For Pinchback, it was another worrisome sign that the interracial democracy he helped build was not only vulnerable but that without the federal government's commitment to protecting it, its days were numbered. More than ever, he saw his Senate seat in Washington as a crucial national platform that could be used to highlight violence in the South and protect his state government. If he could get there, he would hold nothing back.[12]

On January 12, 1875, exactly a year from the day the Louisiana legislature had reaffirmed its commitment to Pinchback, it went one step further and again reelected him as US senator so that "all doubt or questioning of the title . . . be entirely silenced." The vote was a loud and clear declaration that he was their choice, and it should have once again been enough to have him seated. After the certificate of his election was presented to the Senate ten days later, the Committee on Privileges and Elections reopened the case. Four of the seven members agreed almost immediately that "the certificate of reelection gave Pinchback a clear *prima-facie* right to a seat." However, after the committee reported its decision to the Senate, opponents protested that this majority of four was not the real majority since several members were absent during the vote. While the burden of the fault should have been on those absent, and the votes of those who were present upheld, as was common, everything once again stalled, and no decision was reached. Pinchback was dumbfounded. It was ever clearer that some senators were determined at all costs to keep him from being seated.[13]

Pinchback still felt that the Norton bribery controversy was the darkest cloud lingering over him, so dark that his once advocate, Senator Morton, had become his adversary and was an impetus for other Radical Republicans to keep their distance. He thus crafted a narrative reviewing the Norton controversy and sent it to the Senate. In it, he admitted that he did accept the money but explained that the Kellogg government owed it to him for providing out-of-pocket expenses for an extra session of the state legislature. Pinchback even attached a copy of a special order he cashed to pay members for this extra session. Further, he explained that he had been relieved from his "obligations in the matter." A week after Pinchback clarified the Norton matter, Senator Morton, apparently satisfied by Pinchback's narrative, changed his tune, and once again defended Pinchback's claim to the Senate. With the powerful Morton now reviving his case and championing his right to serve, the Senate remained in session for almost twenty-one hours during this time, debating every issue relating to Louisiana, Pinchback, Kellogg, and so on, historical and contemporary, relevant and irrelevant, all in an attempt by his opponents to find enough wiggle room to keep Pinchback from taking his seat. Senator Thomas McCreery of Kentucky admitted with racist candor that he "will give that n----r some sleepless nights before he gets his seat." While several senators came out in support of Pinchback, and with his hope that Blanche Kelso Bruce's recent seating as the second African American senator was an encouraging sign, the case was again tabled with no decision.[14]

Then on March 1 Pinchback's hopes were revived when the US House of Representatives passed a resolution recognizing the Kellogg government, followed three weeks later by a vote in the US Senate approving President Grant's actions in Louisiana and recognizing "W. P. Kellogg" as "the executive." Finally, it was unanimous, and the state government that had been trying to send Pinchback to the Senate for more than two years was declared legitimate by the authorities of the land, including the body that had been stalling his confirmation because it claimed that it could not determine if the Kellogg government was the rightful power in Louisiana.[15]

It would seem at this point that the Senate should have acted promptly in admitting Pinchback to its chamber. But, true to their pattern, the Senate defaulted to doing nothing until December. Pinchback was livid. He declared it "unjustly exceptional" that the Senate failed to decide "promptly and definitely," particularly because the president and both branches of Congress had upheld the Kellogg government. Identifying his struggle against the backdrop that Blacks faced daily from a racist culture, he was determined to continue to "press this contest" when the Senate convened again in December, boldly declaring that "there is no retreat."[16]

CENTRAL HIGH SCHOOL AND THE WAR OVER PUBLIC SCHOOL INTEGRATION IN NEW ORLEANS

In the meantime, Pinchback returned to Louisiana where his train was greeted by a "grand ovation" of friends and supporters. Their favorite son, fighting not only for himself but for the freedom of Black Americans, had returned home. After a nightlong celebration, he wasted no time getting back to work again for Black equality. Shortly before his return to Washington back in December, the New Orleans branch of the White League had brought its campaign to abolish integrated schools to a new level. Still emboldened after its failed coup two months earlier to overthrow the state government, and with the drumbeat of resistance pounding away in the pages of *The Picayune* and *Bulletin*, both virulent anti-Pinchback newspapers, it called for terror and violence to circumvent the law by targeting the schools where integration was being carried out. Answering this call to purge their schools of Black students, white students from Central High School used harassment and violence against Black students, including elementary school children. They even entered schools and dragged Black students out into the street. In many instances, Black students fought back, both by trading blows and by challenging enforced segregation. When courageous African American students appeared at Central High School and demanded admission on December 17, they were barred by white students and a ruckus broke out.

Black parents refused to take all this abuse sitting down. Arming themselves, they marched on these schools to protect their children, engaging in "pitched battles" with white students and teachers. New Orleans African Americans were willing to risk their well-being and very lives to maintain their right to equality in education. Alarmed by the violence, the school board closed the city schools on December 20.[17]

Schools reopened in January 1875 amidst relative calm, but opposition continued to grumble and threatened to rise again. The largest protest arose a month later when a Black student named Roxborough, who appears to have been the son of one of Pinchback's friends and supporters, showed up at Central High School with an order from the school board that he be placed in the senior class. Most white seniors walked out, but Roxborough stayed in his seat. What tremendous courage on the part of this young man to demand his right to attend the most segregated, aggressively white school in the city. While it is not known what became of him, we can safely—and sadly—assume that he likely endured much harassment, insult, and ostracism, if not worse.[18]

Threats, attacks, and resistance infuriated Pinchback, who returned to New Orleans determined to send a message to whites that school integration, which he had worked for in the state constitution, as a senator and by his direct-action enrollment of his son Napoleon under police escort, would still be carried out wherever it could be. That February, Congress passed the Civil Rights Bill, stripped first of its original provision for integrated schools, which Pinchback publicly defended as the best they could get at this time while disappointed by the lack of congressional verve. Privately, he felt overwhelmed by it all, particularly with the White League coming an inch from overthrowing the state government and now with its brazen threats against Black school children. He wrote to Frederick Douglass in a desperate tone, "Oh God how I wish I had your knowledge and ability to grapple with difficulties I see on every hand besetting me in this God forsaken section of our country." He continued, "Our people stand in need of some great mind to guide them in this crisis of our history." But Pinchback was more astute than he gave himself credit for in this correspondence to Douglass, and even more crucial, he was a man of action, and that was perhaps what the time and place of that moment of early integration required more than anything. In the pages of *The Louisianian*, he blamed Republicans and the school board for not doing enough to protect the rights and lives of Black students and for allowing such a blatant violation of law and order that past fall. Frustrated also by the hiring of only a small fraction of Black teachers, and these at the Black, nonintegrated schools, Pinchback used his influence to secure the appointment of a Black teacher, E. J. Edmonds, as an instructor of mathematics in an all-white school against stiff opposition (though later he would curiously deny having recommended Edmonds, while still defending him). The school he selected to place Edmonds in was the troublesome Central High School. Described as "brilliant," Edmonds had impeccable credentials, having been college-educated in Paris, and was more qualified than most teachers in the city's school system. Pinchback believed that if the opposition did arise, the absurdity and injustice of racism would be clearer than ever. In short, he hoped that Edmonds would be the right man to initiate integration at ground zero of the city's most resistant public school.[19]

For a while, things went smoothly at Central High School until a group of white boys protested being taught by a Black man and withdrew from school. On that same day, as Edmonds left the school to go home, he was accosted by white seniors who yelled racial epithets at him. Soon a large crowd of African Americans witnessing the commotion from nearby, gathered and came to Edmonds' defense and the white students withdrew. Despite continued white opposition and editorials blasting Pinchback—"let him install one Negro teacher over white boys and he will install fifty more. Let him mix one school and he will mix them all," declared *The Louisiana Bulletin*—he defended Edmonds as the most qualified teacher in the city who had ranked in the top twenty in a college class of more than 200 students. He encouraged Edmonds to go back to Central and not give up. They had to push through the thick wall of racism with determination and break it apart for good, for the future of all children. Edmonds did return to the school with apparently ever more tenacity and boldness, tossing out challenges to his white peers to mathematical duels, and, by several accounts, it appears he resumed his duties with no more episodes.[20]

BACK TO WASHINGTON

With this fresh victory of integrating the faculty at the once impregnable Central High School, Pinchback returned to Washington as the Senate took up his case again. This most recent New Orleans integration controversy, reported by papers nationwide, further incensed some whites opposed to his Senate confirmation. The Norton bribery controversy may have kept some potential allies at a distance. But his ardent effort to integrate schools likely stirred up further antipathy. The most recent controversy involving Central High School reinforced the belief among his most ardent opposition that he was a radical who would stop at nothing short of forcing the "abominable outrage" of integration by placing Black teachers over white children. But it was not only Democrats. For some white senate Republicans from the North, championing the equality-driven Pinchback against the backdrop of weakening commitment to Reconstruction among their constituents, along with the rising power of the Democrats and ever-looming charges of corruption, was seen as a danger to their political viability.[21]

When Congress convened in December 1875, Pinchback's supposed rival for the Senate, W. L. McMillen, who had disappeared from the debate long ago, announced that he was officially dropping out and would no longer be considered for the seat. This should have been another victory in Pinchback's favor, but the Senate still made no moves to confirm him. Less than a month later, on January 12, 1876, after years of Senate stalling, seventy-five members of the Louisiana state legislature decided to elect a Democrat to Pinchback's seat named J. B. Eustis. But this was still theoretically his seat, and almost every event of the past three years had undeniably strengthened the case for his right to serve there. In response to this latest vote in the Louisiana Senate, forty-four state legislators protested the election of the Democrat. But the US Senate had no intentions of seating the Eustis anyway, likely because the Republican-controlled Senate wanted to limit the number of Democrats, even as much as they wanted to keep out Pinchback.[22]

With no shred of contention left in which to challenge the legitimacy of the Kellogg government, the debate now shifted to Pinchback's character; oppositional senators dredged up his past with a combination of fact and fiction. In the words of Pinchback, his enemies "intended to impress the country, and especially Senators, that I was personally a corrupt and dishonorable man." Furious, and as the final vote approached, Pinchback took his case to the country in newspapers like *The New York Herald*, "appealing for support and a righteous judgement." Here he refuted the "defamation" of his character, and presented his life as an American story of "honorable endeavor" from rags to prominence:

> Robbed of a competency in my youth by my father's kindred, half educated and poor, with the disabilities of a proscribed race attaching to and embarrassing me at every step, I have won in honorable endeavor every success I have enjoyed and every post of honor I have held. And referring to my humble origin without shame, I point to a record of which any American citizen might be justly proud.[23]

He would also tell an audience around this time that senators were trying to obstruct him because they "think me a bad man." But he understood this pretext for the powerful racist undercurrent driving his opposition. He continued: "I am bad because I have dared at all times to advocate and insist on exact and equal justice to all mankind. I am bad because having colored blood in my veins I have dared to aspire to the United States Senate . . . ."[24]

With senators for and against, and as opposition continued disparaging Pinchback's character, his friend, Senator Blanche Kelso Bruce stepped forward on March 3 to argue on Pinchback's behalf. Bruce had let his feelings be known that past January during a closed Senate session. To the shock of senators listening to his remarks that day, his mask came off as he lashed out at them with forceful language for stalling on seating Pinchback. Bruce accused senators of betraying the trust of African Americans by their unethical delay in refusing to seat a Black man in their chamber who had been constitutionally elected by the Louisiana state legislature. He threatened to resign from the Senate and return home to his cotton plantation in Bolivar County, Mississippi, where, he stressed, he could make far more money than he could as a senator. He then stunned his colleagues by castigating President Grant for not lifting a finger to help Pinchback, raking him over the coals for being "untruthful, treacherous, and insincere," and he vowed to repeat his criticism of Grant in the open Senate: "I do not want to belong to a body which stultifies itself in this manner, and if and when the Louisiana case is again called, if be not settled, I will resign my seat in a body which presents this spectacle of asinine conduct," Bruce threatened. *The New York Herald* was one of many papers that could not hold back its enthusiasm for the boldness of the new senator when details of the session leaked out, declaring that Bruce "took the floor like a bombshell, and scattered his shot in all directions," and went on to describe his speech as an "extraordinary attack upon the President and his southern policy." But such bold remarks made others nervous, particularly Black leaders in Louisiana such as Lieutenant Governor Caesar Antoine, who along with other leaders sent a signed "dispatch" to Pinchback opposing "Bruce's speech as impolitic and against the true interests of the colored race," reflecting the desire among many Black leaders to pursue Black rights without inflaming white fear and resistance.[25]

Now, in his maiden speech to an open session of the Senate, Bruce stood to defend his friend in the hope of turning the tide in his favor. His tone was softened, and his language was more tempered than in the closed session. Without the longwinded diatribe characteristics of many of his colleagues, Bruce concisely retraced the crucial events of the past three years that supported the Kellogg government and the election of Pinchback to the US Senate, summarizing much of the past arguments in favor of Pinchback. Pinchback was duly elected by a state legislature that had been recognized by every level of national and state power as the legitimate authority in Louisiana, including by the president of the United States. This clearly meant, Bruce stressed, that Pinchback was legally and constitutionally Louisiana's US senator and that it was in "interest of good-will and good government . . . to admit the claimant to his seat."[26]

Bruce ended his speech with a defense of his friend's character, which had been recently ridiculed by opposition reaching for any straw they could to help deprive him of his seat after it failed to do so on political grounds: "As a father, I know him to be affectionate and worthy; as a husband, the idol of a pleasant home and cheerful fireside; as a citizen, loyal, brave, and true. And in his character and success we behold so admirable illustration of the excellence of our republican institutions."[27]

Five days later, on March 8, 1876, following three years of exhausting and repetitive wrangling over whether or not to seat Pinchback, the issue was finally brought to a vote. Pinchback listened on while standing near the Senate chamber door, described in those final moments with a "cool nerve and brave smile on his face" but fidgeting anxiously with his hands. He had been making his presence felt in the Senate chamber, watching the proceedings with intense focus from the gallery daily. Over the past few years, as he moved in and out of Washington, he became a celebrity with the press, fascinated by his striking good looks, fashionable style, and steely resolve.[28]

As the vote was taken, with each Senator rising when his name was called, those for and against ran neck-in-neck. Senator John Logan of Illinois, disgusted that Pinchback had not yet been admitted, declared before his vote that if "this man had been a white man he would have been in here a long time ago." When David Archibald Harvey of Kansas was called, he stood and declared with emotion that a failure to seat Pinchback would be a "final and conclusive concession" to white supremacy. Democrats like McCreery of Kentucky, proud white supremacists as they were, likely would not have disagreed in the least with either senator. Then in the final votes, it became clear that things would not turn out well. The Senate vote concluded with thirty-two to twenty-nine against seating Pinchback in its chamber. Bruce dropped his head. As part of the body that had committed an injustice by voting "nay," he felt too disgusted and ashamed to look back to see if his friend was still standing at the Senate door. But Pinchback was standing there, as if in defiance and would not move until the chamber was empty so that each senator would have to walk past him.[29]

The star of Pinchback's hope, a seat in the US Senate, had finally burned out for good. Pinchback sent a quick telegram home to Nina, asking her to comfort his mother, as he knew she would take his defeat the hardest and be crushed by the news. Born of the lowest caste in the country, Eliza dreamed with her son of reaching this zenith of power in America. Also dashed was the "hope and belief" of thousands of struggling African Americans "that he would be admitted to the seat he claimed, and which was his right." The Senate's refusal to seat Pinchback likely involved several factors. One was that charges of corruption hovered over him, so much so that even an ardent ally like Senator Morton withdrew his support for a moment and, once restoring his support, could do little to clear up the lingering cloud of suspicion over Pinchback. This could explain why some otherwise supportive peers refused to vote, convinced that these charges had some validity. Next, Northern support for Reconstruction was growing ever more tenuous, and Northern Republicans may have feared that it would not be in their interest to vote into the Senate a controversial Black man. Finally, Pinchback had built a political career on the absolute equality between whites and Blacks. His recent effort to enforce school integration by direct action offended the sensibilities of all but the most enlightened whites and may have cost him support among Republicans as well as Democrats. Historian Lerone Bennett Jr. perhaps framed the Senate's refusal to seat Pinchback best in the form of a question that cut to the heart of the matter: "But what was the world's most exclusive club to do with Pinchback, who not only refused to stay in his place but denied by his words and deeds that white or black people had any particular place?"[30]

Pinchback's final defeat in the Senate in 1876 happened just as white supremacy was beginning to regain control of the South. This would be christened by the Hayes-Tilden Compromise in early 1877 which removed federal protection, allowing white power to reestablish its reign. The rejection of Pinchback was shadowed by the rejection of the reconstructed state governments that had made his rise to power possible, and which had attempted the miracle of advancing and protecting Black political and civil rights. However bad things seemed, Frederick Douglass, who had been deeply invested in Pinchback becoming a US Senator and had entertained the same ambition since his days of enslavement, refused to believe that Pinchback would fade away. Five days after the Senate voted to exclude him, Douglass gave a speech in Washington, DC, entitled, "The Country Has Not Heard the Last of P. B. S. Pinchback." In front of a packed audience, he declared, "the hour of his defeat is the hour of his victory." He told them that Pinchback "has met this storm with the firmness of a hero, and the serenity of a martyr. He has shown in defeat the quality of certain success." Hagiography aside, Douglass knew his friend all too well. True to form, once back in New Orleans, Pinchback wasted little time before jumping back into the fray of Republican politics, making waves, and rocking boats, as he struggled for the next two

Pinchback in his middle-aged years. Library of Congress, Prints & Photographs Division, LC-DIG-bellcm-00646.

decades to hold back the rising tide of white supremacy while protecting Black equality. As far as his lost seat in the Senate, and despite the profound disappointment that he would feel for the rest of his life, he told an audience shortly before the final vote: "if I cannot enter the Senate except with bated breath and on bended knees [meaning toning down his advocacy for black rights], I prefer not to enter it at all."[31]

CHAPTER 10

AFTER RECONSTRUCTION

PINCHBACK'S POST-SENATE CAREER AND LIFE

For years, Pinchback would remain bitter over losing his Senate seat. With the reconstructed South falling apart, political opportunities would gradually grow slim for an ambitious if not branded politician like Pinchback—a Black radical in the eyes of his enemies—to aspire in New Orleans, or anywhere in America, for that matter. By 1879, he would tell Bruce that he had come to "loathe and detest the place and almost hate everything in it." His thwarted ambition and denial of mainstream political mobility aside, while leaving him frustrated, did not leave him feeling defeated. He was too much of a firebrand to go gently into the night and drift into obscurity or political impotence, as his friend Frederick Douglass knew all too well after his battle to get his senate seat. He would remain a potent figure in the Republican Party in Louisiana and work with other African Americans to keep that state party viable, which allowed them to channel their energy into support Republican power on the national level. For fifteen more years Pinchback would work strategically in New Orleans to advance African Americans while slowing down the momentum of the rushing tide of white supremacy Sometimes he prospered, and at other times he floundered in order to survive politically and, according to him, struggled at times to stay afloat financially.[1]

Pinchback would go to unusual lengths to protect the gains that African Americans had made in Louisiana during Reconstruction as well as to protect Black lives. In 1877, as the head of the Louisiana Executive Committee of the Republican Party, he shocked many of his fellow Republicans by giving his support to the Democratic candidate for Louisiana governor, Francis Nicholls, if Nicholls would publicly pledge to protect Black political and civil rights and to restrain his fellow party members from committing terror and violence. An astute political pragmatist, Pinchback saw the writing on the wall, which spelled out clearly that the Republicans were both compromising their commitment to Black equality and losing leverage, while the Democrats were rising and growing ever stronger, poised to take over the state's power base. Pinchback was one of the earliest voices advocating political independence in response to a Republican Party that was taking African Americans for granted, foreshadowing African Americans leading and participating in fusion politics with their former enemies in hopes of protecting rights and viability. But these efforts came with great risks, as can be imagined. Nicholls responded by publicly giving the assurances that Pinchback asked for. But his extremely risky bet to protect Black rights was a losing one. While Nicholls appointed some African Americans to low-level offices, and for a while violence was assuaged, his victory was a triumph for the Redeemers, who sought to destroy Republican power and restore white supremacist control of the state.[2]

A few years later, in 1879, with the Nicholls government convening a new constitutional convention to dismantle the racially progressive constitution of 1867–68, Pinchback and thirty-one Republican delegates, most of them African Americans, attended the convention to do what they could to hold back white supremacy. Despite the shift in power to white Democrats, Pinchback and company did not arrive at the convention without some leverage. The Democrats had to contend with the reality that the Republican Party, while on the decline, still had enough power in Louisiana to elect over thirty delegates to the convention. They were also reluctant to press too much against Black rights out of fear of adding fuel to the exodus movement that threatened to drain Black labor from Louisiana. White League intimidation and violence, backed by its commitment to enforcing "a white man's government" in Louisiana and the declining power to protect Black rights, had for several years by this time stirred Black calls and organized efforts to emigrate from the state, as it did for African Americans in other parts of the South. The announcement of the convention itself inspired more calls for a Black exodus throughout Black communities, convincing enough Democrats to step back from the hardliners of their party, including defeating their party's call for a poll tax.[3]

Pinchback advocated for Act 188 to protect Black suffrage and the right to hold office. Of course, with white conservatives taking control of the mechanisms of power in the absence of federal oversight, African Americans would have fewer chances of getting elected to office and their right to vote

Pinchback in his senior years (1911)

in many places would be infringed upon by unchecked white intimidation and violence. However, due to the efforts of Pinchback and the other African American delegates, Black rights were at least tenuously upheld in the new constitution. But gone was the explicit language of the 1867–68 constitution, such as the ban on segregated places of public accommodation, the mandated pledge required of all officeholders to uphold racial equality, and the enjoinder against separate schools or institutions based exclusively on race. Nevertheless, Pinchback hoped that with Black voting and office-holding explicitly guaranteed as part of the new constitution, there was at least a basis for creating stronger protections.[4]

If such optimism seems naïve during this time, keep in mind that this was a period directly after the end of federal commitment to Reconstruction and several years before Jim Crow began to sweep across Louisiana. The Supreme Court's invalidation of the 1875 federal Civil Rights Act was still four years away. No Louisiana segregation statute would appear until 1890 and legal disenfranchisement in the state would not occur until 1898. Here in 1879, state judicial machinery had not yet found ways to circumvent the Fourteenth Amendment that expressly forbade any state to pass laws discriminating against African Americans. In that in-between space of wide expansion and brutal contraction, even many conservative white leaders

Southern University in the 1880s, an HBCU that Pinchback helped found.

were cautious about moving too quickly to eliminate many of the transformations that had been achieved during Reconstruction, lest they provoke a backlash from the federal government and, as we saw above, fuel a Black exodus. Pinchback believed that the federal government would not make such a "fatal blunder" as to "turn the lamb over to the Wolf."[5]

During convention proceedings, Pinchback also spearheaded a commitment to create Southern University to provide postsecondary education to African Americans. Responding to the rising discrimination and overt hostility at University of Louisiana in New Orleans and Louisiana State University in Baton Rouge, Pinchback believed that the best chance African Americans had at securing a postsecondary education was to have another university. He understood that he was inadvertently supporting segregation by mandating a segregated university. But he felt that racist realities in Louisiana, particularly the opposition to integrated schools at the convention, required that he do something to serve the interests of African Americans. The appropriation he achieved for Southern University was almost the same as that allocated for white schools. He worked with others to breathe life into the school and served on its board of trustees. Southern University would eventually birth a large educational system for African Americans with three campuses—Baton Rouge, Shreveport, and New Orleans, with the latter the largest one today known by its acronym SUNO. The original school in Baton Rouge is noted as being a math and science HBCU and today boasts the P. B. S. Pinchback Engineering building.[6]

Despite his declining political agency compared to his work during the zenith of Reconstruction, Pinchback remained popular among African Americans in Louisiana and throughout the nation. One indication of his influence with Black Louisianans during the latter nineteenth century was when a Black baseball team in New Orleans changed its name to the Pinchbacks and was soon fielding one of the best teams in the league to packed-out ballparks up through the Midwest as far as Chicago. Described by one white supremacist newspaper as "a gang of hustlers," the New Orleans Pinchbacks, led by superstar pitcher George Hopkins, were so good that a white championship team agreed to play them even as the color line was being so rigidly drawn in sports at that time. Changing the name of the team to the Pinchbacks was an intentional choice by the owner and the Black players to take on the name of the Black governor who was a living symbol of Black power. Pinchback became an avid baseball fan and attended home games to cheer on the team carrying his name into competition.[7]

In the early 1890s, Pinchback joined other African American leaders to "organize a counterattack" against the hardening of white supremacy in law in Louisiana. One of the most controversial challenges was a newly passed law requiring railroads to provide separate accommodations for white and Black passengers, which legally overturned Pinchback's famous Article 13. Homer Plessy, a Creole shoemaker, was recruited to purchase a first-class ticket in New Orleans and sit in the white section of a train. After he was removed and arrested, his attorneys took his case to the state supreme court where they lost and then to the US Supreme Court which in 1896 upheld that law in its infamous *Plessy v. Ferguson* decision, establishing the famous "separate but equal" doctrine, which meant that the dominant white majority could legally discriminate against African Americans in every area of life.[8]

Shortly before the Plessy case reached the US Supreme Court, Pinchback was finally ready to leave Louisiana for good. It had been a tense and draining experience for him to remain in the city and state where the interracial democracy he helped build continued to crumble beneath his feet. Segregation was spreading throughout the South, Black rights were being trampled upon, and violence and intimidation were rampant. White supremacy was now winning every battle and gnashing its teeth against the Black South, and he had little faith that things could take a turn for the better in the foreseeable future.

> **SPORTSMAN'S PARK.**
> Great Game for Championship of Col-
> ored Clubs of America To-Morrow.
> **NEW ORLEANS PINCHBACKS vs.**
> **WEST ENDS OF ST. LOUIS.**
> PLAY AT 3:30 P. M.
> Admission 25 Cents.

New Orleans Pinchbacks vs. St. Louis West Ends baseball announcement.

New Orleans Pinchback's superstar pitcher, George Hopkins, whom Pinchback would have seen pitch at the games he attended.

After a stint in New York where, by some accounts he worked as a federal marshal, he and Nina relocated to Washington, DC, by 1894 or 1895, joining their close friends, the Bruces, and others. Bismarck and Walter, now in their twenties, accompanied their parents to Washington. The oldest son, Pinckney Jr., was then working as a pharmacist in Philadelphia, and Nina was living with her new husband in a house on Twelfth Street. Perhaps this final move was inevitable. It was the city that had been his second home, where the Black elites had been enticing him to come for years. "The Governor" had been unofficially designated one of their favorite sons, and they honored him every chance they could at high-society events. He was not so much moving to a new place as to a familiar one where he had established deep roots and had forged intimate connections.[9]

Pinchback's Richardson-style house located in Columbia Heights, Washington, DC. This home was built by the leading Black builder in the city, Daniel Murray, and based on a design that Pinchback helped create. Today, this home serves as a safe space for unhoused women and women recovering from addictions. Courtesy of the author.

The Pinchbacks temporarily moved into a home owned by their friend Daniel Murray. There they awaited the construction of their new home, being built by Murray with Pinchback's assistance in creating the design. Murray was the leading Black builder in the city of "houses of a higher order," and it would take him several years to complete the three-story house designed in the then fashionable "castle-like Richardson style" on Bacon Street (today Harvard Street). Situated in the Northern part of Columbia Heights, Jean Toomer would remember it fondly as a nice neighborhood to grow up in with streets full of "low limbs of budding chestnut trees." The Pinchback home was the site of elaborate gatherings where, Toomer recalled, "doors were open to all men of all color; white whites, creoles of whatever group, people of color, black blacks." Regardless of Pinchback's elite status, Toomer continues: "There was not caste or color prejudice in him, no social snobbery ... and I thoroughly admired him for it."[10]

Shortly after Pinchback relocated to Washington, his close friend Frederick Douglass died. In addition to being selected as an honorary pallbearer, Pinchback was asked to give a eulogy for Douglass at the funeral, an honor he would cherish for the rest of his life. The flow and power in this eulogy highlight Pinchback's writing style at its best. Sometimes poetic and generally poignant while telling the story of Douglass's rise and life, he begins by honoring Douglass's mother, Harriet Bailey. She "left him the remembrance of a mother's care, a mother's tenderness, and a mother's love. The wrongs of slavery had failed to crush out the beauty of a mother's love . . . ." Undoubtedly, Pinchback felt this way about his own mother, Eliza, who more than anyone else inspired him in his life and work, and likely had her in mind when he penned these words. He continued by contextualizing Douglass as not only the greatest Black man in American history and one of its greatest orators and thinkers, but also one of the greatest men in American history and even world history, comparable in his ability and intellect with the greats of ancient times. He had confronted and overcame far more challenges than any white leader, stressed Pinchback, who had the benefit of privilege in the form of freedom and ancestry. "Now mark the contrast," he explained. "Here a man nameless, whose lineage began with himself, with many a weary year of the degradation of ignorance, the curse of slavery behind him. Great Father! Could it have been worse! Maybe it was better so. Men's souls need startling things to move them."[11]

In 1896, daughter Nina and her infant son Nathan Pinchback Toomer Jr. moved in with her parents. Nina had lived with her husband, Nathan Toomer, only for a short time, a handsome, debonaire figure of mixed ancestry from Georgia only two years younger than her father who had spent the first two decades of his life enslaved in North Carolina. Three months after they were married, he left Nina and would return fleetingly until finally disappearing altogether, possibly passing forever into the white world. Furious that Toomer had deserted his daughter and grandson, Pinchback demanded that Nina change the baby's name, which she complied by calling him Eugene with no legal change. He would be Eugene Toomer for her, but the grandparents would call him Eugene Pinchback, and to his playmates he would be Pinchy. Alongside his mother, Eugene would grow up mostly in the "tower-like" mansion on Bacon Street, with cooks and maids and a gardener they called Old Willis, who had spent his earlier life in bondage and whom the boy adored. Here Pinchback became his father figure, sheltering him with love and protection from the increasingly racist atmosphere of the nation's capital. Toomer would write that it was not until his senior year in high school that he "came face to face with the race question in a personal way." Changing his name to Jean as a young adult, he would become one of the lights of the Harlem Renaissance whose novel *Cane*, and his complex life and struggle with racial identity, would attract scholars to his writings to this day.[12]

Pinchback's daughter, Nina Pinchback Combs.

Pinchback's son, Walter A. Pinchback, in his military uniform.

In 1898, Pinchback lost one of his best friends when Blanche Kelso Bruce passed away from complications due to diabetes. He served as one of thirty-two pallbearers at the large funeral of white and Black leaders. The two had drifted apart over the last few years, but Pinchback still took the loss of his one-time confidant hard. Later that year, Pinchback became one of the founding members of one of the early civil rights organizations in the country, the National Afro-American Council (NAAC). Created against the backdrop of the spread of Jim Crow throughout the South and the rising tide of violence against African Americans, the spark that ignited the creation of the NAAC was the brutal murder of a Black postmaster and his two-year-old daughter by a white mob who resented his appointment as postmaster in Lake City, South Carolina.[13]

Pinchback would continue to join and lead political, social, and cultural organizations in Washington, DC, perhaps keeping up the tempo as a way of dealing with what must have been terrible grief of having tragically lost his son, Pinckney Jr., a successful pharmacist, to tuberculosis in 1900, followed by another tragic loss when his daughter Nina, Toomer's mother, died unexpectedly after an operation in 1909.[14] During the first decade of the twentieth century, he gave extensive speeches where he presented thoughtful overviews of the spread of Jim Crow and where he touted Black progress and achievement, including setting the record straight about Reconstruction at a time when the school of racist historiography was creating the myth of "Negro domination" and "corruption." His political activism would focus on racism in the South, particularly the Deep South, but by the turn of the century "color prejudice in Washington" was spreading and becoming more overt. African Americans, regardless of status, were encountering segregation or exclusion in public transportation, theaters, restaurants, churches, and hospitals. Racial profiling by police and unequal treatment by the courts was becoming a growing problem.[15]

During this time when Jim Crow permeated everything, many of Washington's Black elite rallied behind Booker T. Washington, who had become the most powerful Black leader in the nation. His message to Blacks to abandon the struggle for their rights while turning within to build materially was for many both a pragmatic strategy of survival and a realistic assessment of a racist America whose doors were now tightly sealed against any notion of interracial participation. It was a message that in part resonated with Pinchback who left the South because of the restoration of white despotic rule that deprived African Americans of their basic political rights. He knew firsthand how invasive and pervasive white supremacy was in the South, and he appreciated the need to explore additional approaches and strategies for

Black empowerment. Pinchback grew close to Washington, advising him on matters in the nation's capital and working with him in securing patronage for African Americans. While he rejected submission to white supremacy, he believed that economic progress was an important factor in protecting Black lives and advancing the status of African Americans.[16]

THROUGH THE GRANDSON'S EYES: PINCHBACK, TOOMER, AND THE LAST DAYS

In his later years, Pinchback appears to have lived mostly on his investments and perhaps speaking fees, supplemented by a series of low- to mid-level government appointments. The latter may have been the result of Washington's influence, particularly after the death of Blanche Kelso Bruce in 1898. In a 1910 article from New York's *Amsterdam News*, the writer noted, "Pinchback has been covered into the Civil Service, by order of President Taft." He had a reported substantial net worth of $90,000 that same year (which would be roughly equivalent to 2.3 million today), but it appears that his wealth began to dwindle considerably sometime during the second decade. According to Toomer, this may have had something to do with Pinchback's penchant for betting on racehorses, though this is difficult to confirm. The financial burden of maintaining a "genteel life" that included a large home, staff, fashionable attire, and vacations may have taken its toll on his finances. He likely lost his government job to a white man during the Woodrow Wilson government's purging of Black federal appointees and civil service employees in 1913 and 1914. Sometime in the mid-teens, the Pinchbacks moved from their lavish home on Bacon Street to an apartment at 1341 U Street, NW. This was due to money problems, but a smaller space was easier to manage and navigate and more suitable for the elderly couple. Even with his dwindling finances, his style and status remained intact. He was "The Governor" among his Washington friends and community, recognizable from afar by his white Vandyke beard, Black diplomatic cutaway coat, a top hat, and a stylish walking stick. Toomer remembered fondly when during his childhood this "dashing commanding figure, the center of the . . . exciting world" would take him to meetings and events around the city, intermingling with men who "made much to-do over me, giving me the feeling that I was a scion of a great family." He recalled nights when he would crawl in bed with his grandfather, who listened on in the darkness as the child talked about his day at school or whatever else was on his mind. Toomer recalled times when he would recite poetry and orations to the delight of Pinchback, who gave his full attention and praise. "No one could speak to me and make me laugh and get me excited the way he did," Toomer wrote. "He made me feel I was having a part in everything."[17]

There is much in Toomer's recollections about the love and affection between him and his grandfather. But he also had a very conflicted relationship with Pinchback. He would describe his protective grandfather as "affectionate and domineering, loving and tyrannical." While some have used this, and other remarks from Toomer, to reflect negatively on Pinchback (one writer described Pinchback as a "tyrannical" patriarch with no context), such dichotomous language describing a parent who loves yet enforces boundaries and creates expectations from which parent and child clash is not unusual, not to mention the domineering patriarch common among elites in the latter nineteenth and early twentieth centuries. Yet as Toomer grew into early adulthood, he often felt at war with his grandfather. Revolving largely around a clash of personalities, Toomer was moving in the direction of a thoughtful, sensitive artist and intellectual, much like his Uncle Bismarck who had a profound influence on him (Pinchback's second child), exhibiting little interest in worldly ambition and even less drive for traditional achievement. This put him at odds with the grandfather who for Toomer incarnated the masculine Victorian quest to rise and shape the world with a focused sense of purpose. In short, the clash seems to have been between masculine and feminine energies, particularly as they were viewed during that time. Consequently, Toomer appears to have developed a sense of inadequacy within the large shadow cast by this "active dominant man." He would admit that "there is no doubt that his image, and the picture and sense of his life, were deeply impressed upon me, later to function as an unconscious ideal for myself, for how I wished to look and be; and also, to serve as standards by means of which I measured men and life." But it was an image and standards that Toomer ultimately rejected for himself, refusing to fulfill even if he could live up to them.[18]

Juggling his admiration for Pinchback's image and life while wanting to come out from under his shadow, he appears to have done so in part by casting doubt upon his grandfather's identity and legacy. Pinchback may not have really been Black, according to Toomer, and only claimed to be so to take advantage of the opportunities presented by Reconstruction to satisfy his ambition to achieve power and status rather than a sincere interest to "secure and maintain the rights" of African Americans. Henry Louis Gates Jr. and Rudolph P. Byrd write that as Toomer struggled with racial identity, his claim that Pinchback "was 'passing for black' was rooted in (his) desire to paint the roots of his family tree white; to do so, he had to stress that Pinchback was the political opportunist par excellence." Thus, Toomer appears to have struggled with the need to escape from the heavy, oppressive shadow of his grandfather so that he could be his own man who could live and define life on his terms and escape from the strict confines, if not the penalties, of being Black. But more than painting the roots of his family tree white, Toomer's conflict with racial identity also had to do with an authentic desire to fit into a more universal understanding and experience of humanity, even if he used race, and more specifically, Black as race, as a discursive concept, only to transcend it. He desired to be a man, an American, and even more than that, a human being who was part of a greater whole. This appears to be what he was striving for most when he embraced Quakerism and its belief in the inherent if not mystical oneness of humanity (his Uncle Pinckney Jr. appears to have embraced Quakerism as a student in Philadelphia and may have had some influence on Toomer). And in that desire, he perhaps more closely merges with Pinchback who had openly railed against the limitations imposed upon him by the white world because of his "colored blood," living in a way that refuted the notion that any race had a particular place and desiring to be treated the same as a white man who could participate fully in life and politics as part of the larger citizenry.[19]

By the late summer of 1920, Pinchback's health was rapidly deteriorating. Despite their challenging relationship, Toomer devoted himself to caregiving for his father figure as his health declined. The conflict still flared, however. He described the aged Pinchback at this time as a "game fighting cock," still arguing with Toomer over the direction of his future. With Nina too elderly to care for both herself and her husband, Toomer took control of all the household responsibilities in the U Street apartment and nursed his grandfather almost around the clock while easing the daily burdens for his grandmother. Uncle Bismarck also got sick around this time, and Toomer found his energies stretched to the limit, going back and forth between homes to take care of his loved ones while accommodating the daily flow of his grandparents' friends and well-wishers who stopped by the house. Under the weight of such a grueling schedule, and at times "feeling dangerously drained of energy," he disciplined himself to write as much as possible, taking every little opportunity he could to give life to his imagination and to nurture his skills as a writer, which he realized at this time was his "true direction in life." Toomer found some relief for a few hours at nights when he would meet with a community of writers in Washington who, like him, would contribute to creating the Harlem Renaissance, such

An original edition of Jean Toomer's celebrated novel, *Cane*, part of which written by Pinchback's bedside.

as Georgia Douglass Johnson, Zora Neale Hurston, Langston Hughes, Alain Locke, and Waldo Frank.[20]

A year into caregiving, the pressure became unbearable. Toomer felt like he was suffocating. He planned for his grandparent's care while he accepted a short-term position as the acting principal of an industrial school in Sparta, Georgia. During this three-month stint, he got to see "the heart of the South," connecting deeply to the ancestral past of his father, Nathan, who connected him to his own, as well as the region where Pinchback was born. While there, he found plenty of "materials, inspiration and the setting" for *Cane*. Toomer returned home that November and found Pinchback, who had grown ever feebler and was not far from death, lingering in a hospital. "His condition there was too pitiable for me to bear," wrote Toomer. "I had my grandfather brought back from the hospital . . . . He touched my heart so strongly that I resolved to care for him until the very end." Toomer tended to his every need, and as the old statesmen "sank very rapidly" throughout December, Toomer wrote by his bedside "Kabnis," the "long semi-dramatic closing-piece of *Cane*," a novel that would become "the most seminal and original work of literature published in the entire Harlem Renaissance." Thus, it was in Pinchback's U Street bedroom where one remarkable life was ending as one of the most distinctive flowers of the Harlem Renaissance blossomed.[21]

"LET ME STATE, SIMPLY, THAT I AM THE GRANDSON OF THE LATE P. B. S. PINCHBACK"

As he wrote "Kabnis" at the bedside of the elderly governor, who slumbered between life and death, the fading Pinchback may have found his way into Toomer's story. As part two of the story opens, Toomer describes a portrait of "a bearded man" hanging prominently in the home of his interracial character Fred Halsey: "Black hair, thick and curly, intensifies the pallor of the high forehead, The eyes are daring. The nose, sharp and regular. The poise suggests a tendency to adventure checked by the necessities of absolute command."[22]

Toomer would use similar descriptions for Pinchback. In his essay "On Being American," he described a photograph of Pinchback that showed "a sturdy fearless man of prominent forehead, bold dark eyes, a black beard, forceful personality." Elsewhere in Toomer's posthumously published autobiographical writings, the patriarch Pinchback is similarly described as the old patriarch looking down from the wall in "Kabnis." While it is beyond the scope of this study to explore Toomer's feelings, views, and motives for writing *Cane*, not to mention all his conflicted views of his family and its racial heritage (Barbara Foley largely accomplishes this in *Jean Toomer: Race, Repression, and Revolution*), his book in general and "Kabnis" in particular seems to reflect his own internal struggle over racial identity. It is a struggle that finds its source in Pinchback's ambiguous racial identity, where Toomer awkwardly tries to appropriate a white identity for his grandfather, interweaving through the life and identity of his father, Nathan, a shadowy figure of mixed-race ancestry who never fully reveals himself to the son so that the son can better understand himself. This self-described "agony of internal tightness, conflict, and chaos" finds its expression if not some sense of relief in the research and writing of *Cane*. Writing his friend and mentor Waldo Frank, Toomer revealed that "Kabnis is me," a Northern, urbane, mixed-race intellectual who is deeply conflicted about his Black ancestry but who is confronted with it when he travels South where no matter how much white ancestry he has, he is still definitively Black. In real life, Toomer describes the confrontation with his Black roots during his trip to "Middle-Georgia," which inspired *Cane* as an awakening and reconnection: "And a deep part of my nature, a part that I had repressed, sprang suddenly to life . . . ."[23]

Toomer finished the first draft of "Kabnis," the ending of *Cane*, the day before his grandfather passed away on December 21, 1921, at eighty-four. In the days and hours before his death, Toomer had reconciled with his grandfather. "In these last days he seemed to know just what I meant him," Toomer wrote. "I knew and realized all he had done for me . . . and all my love and gratitude for the once so forceful and dominant but now so broken and tragic man came to the fore." Gates and Byrd speculate that the "powerful, quasi-mythic encounter at *Kabnis's* conclusion—between the Northern, mulatto . . . and the old, black Father John, the haunting figure of the slave past—was informed by this final, intense encounter and reconciliation between Toomer and Pinchback himself." Perhaps another indication of this reconciliation was that Toomer would later step out as Pinchback's grandson when asked about his racial heritage in a way that implied his—and Pinchback's—Black ancestry. Shortly before the publication of *Cane*, Toomer responded to a writer from the Negro Associated Press who inquired about his racial identity; Toomer responded that he was "body and soul . . . Negroid." He continued: "Let me state, simply, that I am the grandson of the late P. B. S. Pinchback. From this fact, your contention is sustained. 'I have peeped behind the veil.'"[24]

Pinchback's death certificate listed the causes of death as "senile debility" and "interstitial nephritis." The former was a medical term used during this time which implied physical and mental deterioration due to old age, and the latter is a disorder that can lead to kidney failure. Still lovingly watching over his grandfather even in death, Toomer rode with the body by train for burial in New Orleans. Accompanying him was Uncle Walter, Pinchback's youngest and the only child to survive his mother's death in 1928 (in addition to Pinckney Jr.'s death in 1900 and sister Nina in 1909, Bismarck would die in 1924).[25] The train traveled not far from the same route where William Pinchback and Eliza Stewart and family had trekked by horse and wagon back in 1837, past Macon, Georgia, where the future Black governor was born, and on down through the Deep South and into New Orleans. Once back in the city that he had helped raise from the ashes of slavery and war, Pinchback was taken to Metairie Cemetery off Pontchartrain Blvd. Considered one of the most hauntingly beautiful and elaborate cemeteries in New Orleans, then as well as today, many of its tombs are structured like Egyptian pyramids, abandoned British castles, and grandiose mausoleums—just the kind of ostentatious style that Pinchback appreciated when he was alive. Many famous and wealthy people share this eternal resting place, including the very first governor of the state following the Louisiana Purchase, William Claiborne. Here at Metairie, in an elaborate stone mausoleum, Pinchback joined his mother, Eliza, and daughter Nina, Toomer's mother. By some accounts, this was a white cemetery; Pinchback had to fight to purchase the family mausoleum there, and Toomer had to fight to lay his grandfather to rest in the hallowed white ground of Metairie. If this is indeed true, it would be a fitting if not poetic end to the life of a man who had struggled against racial injustice to successfully integrate white spaces during his life, to score

Pinchback Tomb at Metairie Cemetery, New Orleans. Courtesy of the author.

in death one last victory by overcoming racist resistance to integrate another space with his body—the body of the only Black governor—in an eternal resting place that had been reserved for whites only. In death, he may have once again defied and defeated white supremacy.[26]

Pinchback lived a life of intense, unrepentant confidence in his views and abilities while unapologetically experiencing life to the fullest—a gusto to live as fully as possible while going against the grain that could be mistaken for simple pride and arrogance. This may be why the Rev. Francis Grimke, fearing that the end was near, felt compelled to stop the elderly Pinchback on a Washington street in 1916 to save his soul. Sitting quietly at his desk one evening not long after, Pinchback responded to the reverend, scribbling a short note that all was well with his soul.[27]

NOTES

INTRODUCTION

1. *Daily Picuyune* (New Orleans), January 5, 1873.

2. Pinchback speech, Box 81-2, Series H, Folder 56, Pinchback Papers, Moorland-Spingarn Research Center, Howard University.

3. Frederick Douglass remarks from *The Natchitoches Times*, reprinted in The *Opelousas Journal*, February 3, 1872; Roger W. Shugg, *Origins of Class Struggle in Louisiana: A Social History of White Farmers and Laborers During Slavery and After, 1840–1875* (Louisiana State University Press, 1939), 227.

4. For example, Frances Wayne Binning seems to treat it as factual that "Warmoth had given bribes and Pinchback had accepted them . . ." but offers no evidence, in "Henry Clay Warmoth and the Louisiana Reconstruction" (PhD diss., University of North Carolina, 1969), 333. "Pinchback Interviewed . . . Who He Is," reprinted from *The New Orleans Times* March 6, 14, 1872; "n.d. Draft" of Pinchback defense to the Senate, P. B. S. Pinchback Papers, Box 81-1, Series G, Folder 31, Moorland-Spingarn Research Center, Howard University.

5. "The Louisiana Investigation," *New York Herald*, February 9, 1872, p.7; "Pinchback Interviewed . . . Who He Is," *New Orleans Times*, March 6, 14, 1872.

6. Sybil Kein, *Creole: The History and Legacy of Louisiana's Free People of Color* (Louisiana State University Press, 2000), 38–37, fn98.

7. Nicholas Patler, *Jim Crow and the Wilson Administration: Protesting Federal Segregation in the Early Twentieth Century* (University Press of Colorado, 2007), 73; W. E. B. Du Bois, *Black Reconstruction in America, 1860–1880* (Free Press, 1998), 595.

8. In *Essays on the Civil War and Reconstruction* (1897), William Archibald Dunning of Columbia University, a Traditionalist who is considered the pioneer of the school of racist historiography, does not once mention Pinchback. A decade later, in another book on Reconstruction, Dunning manages to squeeze out one reference to "the mulatto Pinchback" as Warmoth's "temporary successor." Dunning had plenty to say critically about the reconstructed governments. Another pioneer of the school of racist historiography, James Ford Rhodes, neglects to mention Pinchback by name in his copious study (1920) but castigates and humiliates the black leaders of Reconstruction—and African Americans in general—as inferior: "Most of them developed no political capacity, and

the few who raised themselves above the mass, did not reach a high order of intelligence." Historians also found a way to fit Pinchback within the myth of Reconstruction as an unscrupulous leader helping to perpetuate an illegitimate government. John Burgess (1907), a colleague of Dunning's at Columbia University, who decried the rule of "uncivilized Negroes over the whites of the South" and believed it was "the white man's mission . . . to hold the reins of political power," deplored the events that led to the "installation of . . . the Negro Pinchback" as governor in 1872 as a "palpable outrage." He had no problem, however, declaring that Pinchback's white political adversaries represented the legitimate authority, though offering no evidence to support his claim. One the last purveyors of racist historiography, E. Merton Coulter (1947), considered Pinchback as "one of the loud-talking and troublesome . . . Negro officeholders" who deserved their reputations as "unscrupulous troublemakers or inane ninnies." Other than a few other disparaging remarks about Pinchback, the leader's vision, skill, and work to remake Louisiana into the image of democracy is ignored in Coulter's almost 400-page study of Reconstruction. See William Archibald Dunning, *Reconstruction Political and Economic, 1865–1877* (Harper Brothers Publishers, 1907), 218; James Ford Rhodes, *History of the United States from the Compromise of 1850 to the McKinley-Bryan Campaign of 1896, Volume VII* (Macmillian & Co., Ltd., 1920), 232–33; John Burgess, *Reconstruction and the Constitution, 1866–1876* (Scribner's, 1907), 218, 270–72; E. Merton Coulter, *The South During Reconstruction, 1865–1877* (Louisiana State University Press, 1947), 134, 143, 144, 352.

9. Eric Foner has stressed that racist historiography "was not just an interpretation of history. It was part of the edifice of the Jim Crow system" and helped to "propagate a racist system in this country." See Foner, *Reconstruction: America's Unfinished Revolution, 1866–1877* (Harper & Row, 1988), xx.

10. Lerone Bennett Jr., *Before the Mayflower: A History of the Negro in America, 1619–1964* (Penguin Books, 1970), 202; James Lowen, *Lies Across America: What Our Historical Sites Get Wrong* (Touchstone, 2000), 213. Public perception was also shaped by "negative portrayals of Black people in literature and on the movie screen," such as the 1915 racist blockbuster film, *Birth of a Nation*.

11. William J. Simmons, *Men of Mark, Eminent, Progressive, and Rising* (Cleveland, 1887) 534–35; Frederick Douglass, "The Country Has Not Heard the Last of P. B. S. Pinchback: An Address Delivered in Washington, D.C., on March 13, 1876," accessed July 12, 2024, https://frederickdouglasspapersproject.com/s/digitaledition/item/18198), (Accessed July 12, 2024; "Frederick Douglass on Louisianans," reprinted from *The New National Era* in *The Louisianian*, May 11, 1872. The scholarship of Carter G. Woodson and his coterie of black historians was not only equal to that produced by white counterparts; in most cases, it was superior in its methodology and depth even as it was ignored or negated. It is not an overstatement to say that Woodson set in motion a paradigm shift that would reconstruct the black image, culture, and contributions, cutting through the blinding force of white distortion to reframe history by placing African Americans at the core of history.

12. For early favorable mentions of Pinchback in the scholarly literature, see Carter G. Woodson and Charles H. Wesley, *The Negro in Our History* (Associated Publishers, 1922), 407; Charles Rousseve, *The Negro in Louisiana* (Xavier University Press, 1937), 107; J. Saunders Redding, *They Came in Chains: Americans From Africa* (Lippincott, 1950),

175; Hilda Mulvey McDaniel, "Francis Tillou Nicholls and the End of Reconstruction," *Louisiana Historical Quarterly* 32 (April, 1949); A. E. Perkins, "Some Negro Officers and Legislators in Louisiana," *Journal of Negro History* 14 (October, 1929), 526.

13. Agnes Smith Grosz, *The Political Career of P. B. S. Pinchback, The Louisiana Historical Quarterly* 27:2 (April 1944), 607; Lerone Bennett Jr., *Before the Mayflower: A History of the Negro in America, 1619-1964* (Penguin Books, 1970), 203, and *Black Power USA: The Human Side of Reconstruction, 1866-1877* (Penguin Books, 1967), 236, 269; James Haskins, *P. B. S. Pinchback: The First Black Governor* (Africa World Press, 1996), 216; Stewart, "Reconstructing Pinchback: The Story of Gov. P. B. S. Pinchback," February 10, 2011, *Ezine Articles*; Joe Gray Taylor, *Louisiana Reconstructed, 1863-1877* (Louisiana State University Press, 1974), 90-91, 138-42, 143, 154-55, 214; Charles Vincent, *Black Legislators in Louisiana During Reconstruction* (Louisiana State University Press, 1976), 9, 16-17, 44-47, 58-60; Ingrid Dineen-Wimberly, *The Allure of Blackness Among Mixed-Race Americans, 1862-1913* (University of Nebraska Press, 2019), 26; Dana Bash and David Fisher, *America's Deadliest Election: The Cautionary Tale of America's Most Violence Election in American History* (Hanover Square Press, 2024), 16.

14. Michele Faith Wallace, "The Good Lynching and *The Birth of A Nation*: Discourses and Aesthetics of Jim Crow," *Critical Journal* 43, no. 1 (Fall 2003), 95.

15. George E. Lankford, ed., *Bearing Witness: Memories of Arkansas Slavery: Narratives From the 1930s WPA Collection* (University of Arkansas Press, 2003), 9; Loewen, *Lies My Teacher Told Me*, 156.

16. John Hope Franklin, *From Slavery to Freedom: A History of Negro Americans* (Knopf, 1969), 316-17; "Constitution Adopted by the State Constitutional Convention of the State of Louisiana, March 7, 1868," *Internet Archive*, accessed July 10, 2024, https://archive.org/details/constitutionadop1868loui/page/n3/mode/2up.

17. Louisiana Constitution of 1974, accessed July 10, 2024, https://senate.la.gov/Documents/LAConstitution.pdf.

18. Kein, *Creole: The History and Legacy of Louisiana's Free People of Color*, 38-37, fn98.

19. Toomer Papers, Series II, Box 18, Folder 492 and 493, Beinecke Rare Book and Manuscript Library, Yale University.

CHAPTER I: PINCHBACK'S EARLY YEARS

1. "William Pinchback File," Lexington, Mississippi Public Library, donated to the library by a local historian, Jimmie Johnson; Jean Toomer Papers, Series II, Box 18, Folder 493, Beinecke Rare Book and Manuscript Library, Yale University; John Chandler Griffin Jr., "Jean Toomer: American Writer (A Biography)" (PhD diss., University of South Carolina, 1976), 8-10; "The Exceptionally Cold Spring of 1837," , accessed August 14, 2024, https://www.netweather.tv/forum/topic/76238-the-exceptionally-cold-spring-of-1837.

2. Jean Toomer Papers, Series II, Box 18, Folder 492, Beinecke Rare Book and Manuscript Library, Yale University; Robert William Fogel, *Without Consent or Contract: The Rise and Fall of American Slavery* (W. W. Norton, 1994), 63-65; L. Beatrice W. Hairston, *A Brief History of Danville, Virginia, 1728-1954* (Deitz Press, 1955), 25. For a good consideration of

this early depression, see Alasdair Roberts, *America's First Great Depression: Economic Crisis and Political Disorder After the Panic of 1837* (Cornell University Press).

3. Stephen Yafa, *Big Cotton: How a Humble Fiber Created Fortunes, Wrecked Civilizations, and Put America on the Map* (Penguin Group, 2005), 174–74; Jean Toomer Papers, Series II, Box 18, Folder 492, Yale University; John M. Barry, *Rising Tide: The Great Mississippi Flood of 1927 and How It Changed America* (Touchstone Books, 1997), 102.

4. William J. Simmons, *Men of Mark: Eminent, Progressive and Rising* (George M. Rewell, 1887), 759; *New Orleans Times*, March 11, 1872; Annette Gordon-Reed, *The Hemingses of Monticello* (W. W. Norton, 2008), 88.

5. "Slaves and Free Persons of Color. An Act Concerning Slaves and Free Persons of Color," North Carolina General Assembly, 1831, FCp326.1 1831, North Carolina Collection, University of North Carolina Chapel Hill; "Tobacco in Caswell County, North Carolina," Caswell County Historical Association, March 20, 2012; Jean Toomer Papers, Series II, Box 18, Folder 492, Yale University; Annette Gordon-Reed, *The Hemingses of Monticello* (W. W. Norton, 2008), 86.

6. Jean Toomer Papers, Series II, Box 17, Folder 485, Yale University; Haskins, *The First Black Governor*, 1–2.

7. "William Pinchback File," Lexington, Mississippi Public Library, donated to the library by a local historian, Jimmie Johnson; Haskins, *The First Black Governor*, 1–2; Jean Toomer Papers, Series II, Box 18, Folder 492 and 493, Yale University.

8. Haskins, *The First Black Governor*, 2; Agnes Grosz, "The Political Career of P. B. S. Pinchback," *The Louisiana Historical Quarterly* 27, no. 2 (April, 1944), 527; Luis-Alejandro Dinnella-Borrego, *The Risen Phoenix: Black Politics in the Post-Civil War South* (University of Virginia Press, 2016), 19–20; Gordon-Reed, *The Hemingses of Monticello*, 126–27, 340, 342.

9. "Biographical Sketch of Hon. P. B. S. Pinchback," undated, in P. B. S. Pinchback Papers, Box 81-1, Moorland-Spingarn Research Center, Howard University; Grosz, "The Political Career of P. B. S. Pinchback," 527. For the names and birthdates of the three older Pinchback children, see https://www.ancestry.com/genealogy/records (Accessed August 1, 2024). There are different dates given for Elizabeth's birth. It seems likely that the earlier date of 1825 is accurate.

10. Jean Toomer Papers, Series II, Box 18, Folder 483 and 485, Yale University.

11. "DEED—William Pinchback, April 7, 1845," Holmes County, Mississippi Deed Records, Book H, pages 5–6, transcribed by Dan Edwards; 1840 Holmes County, Mississippi Census, Transcribed by Don Rubarts and Enumerated by William T. Courts; 1840 US Federal Census, Ancestry.com; Betty Couch Wiltshire, *Holmes County, Mississippi Pioneers* (Heritage Books, 1995), 6; Will D. Campbell, *Providence* (Baylor University Press, 2002), 80, 110; "Pinchback Interviewed . . . Who He Is," reprinted from *The New Orleans Times* in *The Louisianian*, March 14, 1872.

12. Phillip Dray, *Capitol Men: The Epic Story of Reconstruction Through the Lives of the First Black Congressmen* (Houghton Mifflin, 2008), 103; Wiltshire, *Holmes County, Mississippi Pioneers*, 6; Richard Grant, *Dispatches from Pluto: Lost and Found in the Mississippi Delta* (Simon & Schuster, 2015), 1, 7.

13. Haskins, *The Black Governor*. In his consideration of his grandfather, Toomer laments that there is "no record of what befell Pink during his first ten years," Jean Toomer Papers, Box 18, Folder 493, Yale University.

14. "Pinchback's Case," *New York Commercial Advertiser*, February 23, 1875, in Haskins, *The First Black Governor*, 216.

15. Jean Toomer, "The Cane Years," in Darwin Turner, ed., *The Wayward and the Seeking: A Collection of Writings by Jean Toomer* (Howard University Press, 1983).

16. Toomer Papers, Series II, Box 18, Folder 483, Yale University; John Chandler Griffin Jr., "Jean Toomer: American Writer (A Biography)" (PhD diss., University of South Carolina, 1976), 30. Pinchback's outlook may have also been shaped by other oppressed people living in his plantation orbit. Years before the family had arrived in Holmes County, the Choctaw people were forced from that region by a series of dubious treaties that swallowed millions of acres of their land. The largest and final one, the Treaty of Dancing Rabbit Creek, sealed the fate of Choctaw mass removal in 1830, only seven years before the Pinchbacks arrived. Many had lived on the very land that William Pinchback would own, with some still nearby as squatters. See Campbell, *Providence*, 45, 56–58, 65.

17. The description of Pinchback Plantation comes from the writer's visit to Holmes County in August, 2017, and exploration of the landscape where P. B. S. spent his childhood.

18. Charles M. Payne and Adam Green, eds., *Time Longer Than Rope: A Century of African American Activism, 1850–1950* (New York University Press, 2003), 339; Nikki M. Taylor, *Frontiers of Freedom: Cincinnati's Free Black Community, 1802–1868* (The Ohio University Press, 2005), 162–63.

19. William Cheek and Aimee Lee Cheek, "John Mercer Langston: Principle and Politics," in Leon F. Litwack and August Meier, eds., *Black Leaders of the Nineteenth Century* (University of Illinois Press, 1991), 110–14, 118; Stanley Turkel, *Heroes of the American Reconstruction: Profiles of Sixteen Educators, Politicians and Activists* (McFarland, 2005), 81.

20. Haskins, *The First Black Governor*, 7; Family History, Jean Toomer Papers, Box 18, Folder 493, p.7.

21. Pinchback Family History, Toomer Papers, Series Box 18, Folder 493, Yale University; "DEED—William Pinchback." Still on this hill today is a weather-beaten marble slab that reads: "Sacred to the memory of William Pinchback, A native of North Carolina, born April 12, 1775, departed this life Oct. 12, 1848. An honest man is the noblest work of God. Such was he."

22. "Will Abstracts," December 12, 1848, Book 3:102,169, Holmes County Chancery Office, Lexington, Mississippi; "Plea Against William Pinchback by Sister Lydia Holeman," 1850, ancestry.com; Toomer Papers, Series Box 18, Folder 493, Yale University; Simons, *Men of Mark*, 769; *New Orleans Times*, March 11, 1872.

23. "DEED—William Pinchback."

24. Also, Elizabeth was not deceased, since she is later found in census reports under the married name, Elizabeth Nesbit. The two dates we have for Elizabeth's birth are 1825 and 1829. The former date is found in Rita Doncarlos, Rootsweb.com (William Pinchback FGS (rootsweb.com), and the latter is from Ancetry.com (both accessed August 20, 2025).

25. "DEED—William Pinchback."

26. "DEED—William Pinchback"; Willard B. Gatewood, *Black Aristocrats of Color: The Black Elite, 1880–1920* (Indiana University Press, 1990), 164.

27. Toomer writes that William and Eliza had ten children altogether: Elizabeth, Napoleon, Mary, Pinckney, Adeline, Nathaniel, and William. He writes that he had been "told" that three had died and that two brothers (Nathaniel and William) left

home and passed into the white world, see Jean Toomer Papers, Series II, Box 18, Folder 492, Yale University.

28. Jean Toomer Papers, Series II, Box 18, Folder 493, Yale University; Patler, "An Early 'Human Rights' Movement on the Frontier," 105–6, 267. Challenging Toomer's claim that they decided to pass for white in Cincinnati at this early time is the fact that his sister Adeline and her husband Rueben would not definitively declare their white status until early adulthood. See Adeline B. Saffold to P. B. S. Pinchback, April 30, 1863, Jean Toomer Papers, Box 79, Folder 1751, Yale University.

29. Toomer Papers, Series II, Box 18, Folder 493, Yale University; Louisiana *Weekly*, February 15, 1869; Simmons, *Men of Mark*, 760.

30. Thomas E. Buchanan, *Black Life on the Mississippi: Slaves, Free Blacks and the Western Steamboat World* (The University of North Carolina Press, 2004), 8, 10, 13.

31. John C. Willis, *Forgotten Time: The Yazoo-Mississippi Delta After the Civil War* (University Press of Mississippi, 2000), 80–81, 85–85; Buchanan, *Black Life on the Mississippi: Slaves, Free Blacks and the Western Steamboat World*, 8, 10, 13; Mark Twain, *Life on the Mississippi* (Reader's Digest Association, 1987), 98.

32. Gatewood, *Aristocrats of Color: The Black Elite, 1880–1920*, 19; Vincent, *Black Legislators in Louisiana*, 56; Haskins, *The First Black Governor*, 107–9.

33. George Devol, *Forty Years a Gambler on the Mississippi* (Home Book Company, 1887); Ingrid Dineen-Wimberly, *The Allure of Blackness among Mixed-Race Americans, 1862–1916* (University of Nebraska Press, 2019), 9.

34. Devol, *Forty Years*, 9–10, 216; Dray, *Capitol Men*, 104. Jean Toomer has strong doubts about some of Devol's recollections about Pinchback, particularly how Devol quotes Pinchback using a demeaning, subservient dialect. Devol's narrative is likely a mix of fact and fiction. See Devol comments in Jean Toomer Papers, Series II, Box 18, Folder 493, Yale University.

35. Buchanan, *Black Life of the Mississippi*, 76; Jean Toomer Papers, Series II, Box 18, Folder 493, Yale University.

36. Terre Haute may have been on the fringes, but it was a center of African American empowerment. In the mid-1840s, Hiram Revels, an A. M. E. minister who would go on to become the first African American US senator in 1870, started a school for African Americans at Allen Chapel A. M. E. Church in Terre Haute. Like Gilmore in Cincinnati, Revel's school gained renown and attracted black students from as far away as North Carolina. Terre Haute was situated along the most traversed westerly Underground Railroad route in Indiana, known as the "Wabash line," where runaways made their way north from the Kentucky borderland to freedom. By the time Pinchback arrived there in the latter 1850s, this line was highly organized with "stations" and "friendly homes" dotting the south-to-north landscape and busier than ever with the ever-increasing flow of runaways passing through on their journeys to freedom. One of the most active stations assisting runaways on the Wabash line was Allen Chapel A. M. E. Church. See Nicholas Patler, "An Early 'Human Rights' Movement on the Frontier: Building an Underground Railroad Community in Wayne County, Indiana, 1820–1950 (master's thesis, Bethany Theological Seminary, 2015), 264; Gwendolyn Crenshaw, *"Bury Me in a Free Land:" The Abolitionist Movement in Indiana, 1816–1865* (Indianapolis: Indiana Historical Bureau,

1993), 26–30; Cheryl Janifer LaRoche, *The Geography of Resistance: Free Black Communities and the Underground Railroad* (University of Illinois Press, 2014), 64.

37. Mike McCormick, "P. B. S. Pinchback: First Black Governor in the US," *Terre Haute Tribune Star*, February 5, 1995; Jean Toomer Papers, Box 18, Folder 493, Yale University.

38. Haskins, *The First Black Governor*, 17.

39. Cynthia Earl Kerman and Richard Eldridge, *The Lives of Jean Toomer: A Hunger for Wholeness* (Louisiana State University Press, 1987), 17; Buchanan, *Black Life on the Mississippi*, 37.

CHAPTER 2: PINCHBACK JOINS THE STRUGGLE FOR LIBERATION

1. Jean Toomer Papers, Series II, Box 18, Folder 493, Beinecke Rare Book and Manuscript Library, Yale University; "Pinchback Interviewed . . . Who he is," reprinted from *The New Orleans Times* in *The Louisianian*, March 1872; William Simmons, *Men of Mark, Eminent, Progressive, and Rising* (Cleveland, 1887), 760; *Congressional Record, Forty-Fourth Congress, First Session*, 886; Thomas C. Buchanan, *Black Life on the Mississippi: Slaves, Free Blacks and the Western Steamboat Word* (The University of North Carolina Press, 2004), 26, 27.

2. Grosz, "Political Career of P. B. S. Pinchback," 529; New Orleans *Daily Picayune*, May 24, 1862; *New Orleans Times*, March 11, 1872; *Congressional Record, Forty-Fourth Congress, First Session and Special Session*, 887; Phillip Dray, *Capitol Men: The Epic Story of Reconstruction Through the Lives of the First Black Congressmen* (Houghton Mifflin, 2008), 104–5.

3. The "historian of Negro soldiers," Joseph T. Wilson, wrote that an untold number of mixed-heritage soldiers served in white units during the Civil War "who were so light in complexion that their true race connection could not be told." See *The Black Phalanx: A History of the Negro Soldiers in the Wars of 1775–1812, 1861–1865* (New York, 1968), Introduction, 179.

4. Charles Vincent, *Black Legislators in Louisiana During Reconstruction* (Louisiana State University Press, 1976), 9; *Congressional Record, Forty-Fourth, First Session and Special Session*, 887.

5. Early Pencil Sketch, Pinchback Papers. Moorland Spingarn Research Center, Howard University.

6. Brady-Handy Photograph Collection, Library of Congress Prints and Photographs Division, LC-BH826- 3467. There is another early photograph of Pinchback taken by the Carl Giers studio in Nashville, where it appears lighting was used as well, washing out Pinchback's coloring.

7. Arna Bontemps, *One Hundred Years of Negro Freedom* (Dodd, Mead, 1961), 55; "Frederick Douglass on Louisianans," reprinted from the *New National Era* in *The Lousianian*, May 11, 1872.

8. Kerman and Eldridge, *The Lives of Jean Toomer*, xiii, 15, 17; Dray, *Capitol Men*, 103; Brent Staples, "Escape into Whiteness," *New York Times Book Review*, November 24, 2011; W. E. B. Du Bois, *Black Reconstruction in America* (Transaction Publisher, 2012), 418.

9. "Pinchback Interviews . . . Who He Is," *New Orleans Times* interview reprinted in *The Lousianian*, March 14, 1872; Darwin Turner, ed., *The Wayward and the Seeking: A Collection of Writings by Jean Toomer* (Howard University Press, 1980), 23–24.

10. Adeline B. Saffold to P. B. S. Pinchback, April 30, 1863, Jean Toomer Papers, Box 79, Folder 1751, Yale University.

11. Willard B. Gatewood, *Aristocrats of Color: The Black Elite, 1880–1920* (Indiana University Press, 1990), 175; Adeline B. Saffold to P. B. S. Pinchback, April 30, 1863, Toomer Papers, Yale University.

12. Jean Toomer, "Jean Toomer and P. B. S. Pinchback," *New Mexico Sentinel*, 1937, quoted in John Chandler Griffin Jr., "Jean Toomer: American Writer (A Biography)" (Ph.D. diss., University of South Carolina, 1976), 29, 98–100; Pinchback Family Genealogy, US African American Griots (http://sites.rootsweb.com/~aagriots /NC/WmPinchback.htm) (Accessed August 3, 2024).

13. Toomer Papers, Series II, Box 18, Folder 492 and 493; Letter From Mr. Pinchback, *New York Herald*, February 12, 1876, Box 81-2, Series H, Folder 56, Pinchback Papers, Howard University.

14. Vincent, *Black Legislators in Louisiana*, 5; Toomer Papers, Series II, Box 18, Folder 492, Yale University.

15. Jean Toomer Papers, Series II, Box 18, Folder 493, Yale University; Nell Irvin Painter, *Creating Black Americans: African American History and Its Meanings, 1619 to Present* (Oxford University Press, 2007), 119; James G. Hollandsworth Jr., *The Louisiana Native Guards: The Black Military Experience During the Civil War* (Louisiana State University Press, 1995), 12–13.

16. Hollandsworth, *Native Guards*, 11–12; Vincent, *Black Legislators in Louisiana*, 1–3.

17. John W. Blassingame, *Black New Orleans* (University of Chicago Press, 1973), 15; Hollandsworth, *Native Guards*, 1–2.

18. Hollandsworth, *Native Guards*, 1–2.

19. Blassingame, *Black New Orleans*, 11. The true physical wealth of this free black community lied in its real estate, which by 1850 amounted to over two million dollars (which would be roughly equivalent to four billion today). In contrast, the greatest wealth of the region's white planters lay in their slaves, even compared to their land and crops, as it did for most white planters throughout the antebellum South.

20. Wilson, *The Black Phalanx: A History of the Negro Soldiers in the Wars of 1775–1812, 1861–1865*, 195.

21. Butler to Halleck, November 6, 1862, and Halleck to Butler, November 20, 1862, *Official Records of the Union and Confederate Navies in the War of the Rebellion, Vol. 15* (Washington, DC, 1894–1927), 162, 601.

22. "Pinchback Interviews . . . Who He Is," *New Orleans Times* interview reprinted in *The Lousianian*, March 14, 1872; Vincent, *Black Legislators*, 9–10; Hollandsworth, *Native Guards*, 21, 24, 118–24.

23. Edwin S. Redkey, ed., *A Grand Army of Black Men: Letters from African American Soldiers in the Union Army, 1861–1865* (Cambridge University Press, 1992), 140–41; Henry Ian Davis, "For Civilization and Citizenship: Emancipation, Empire, and the Creation and the Creation of the Black-Citizen Soldier Tradition" (PhD diss., Mississippi State University, 2021), 39–40; and Hollandsworth, *Native Guards*, 24.

24. Whitelaw Reid, *After the War: A Tour of the Southern States, 1865–1866* (Cincinnati, 1866), 244.

25. Willard B. Gatewood, *Aristocrats of Color: The Black Elite, 1880–1920* (Indiana University Press), 131, 171.

26. Blassingame, *Black New Orleans*, 43–44; Hollandsworth, *Native Guards*, 43.

27. Hollandsworth, *Native Guards*, 44–45, 71; Douglass M. Hall, "Public Education in Louisiana During the War Between the States With Special Reference to New Orleans" (master's thesis, Louisiana State University, 1940), 67–68; Jean-Charles Houzeau, *My Passage at the New Orleans Tribune: A Memoir of the Civil War Era* (Louisiana State University Press, 1984), 19.

28. Adeline B. Saffold to P. B. S. Pinchback, July 16, 1863, and P. B. S. Pinchback to Adeline B. Saffold, August 20, 1863, Jean Toomer Papers, Box 79, Folder 1751, Yale University; Biographical sketch in *Semi-Weekly Louisianan* (New Orleans), July 6, 1871; Captain P. B. S. Pinchback to Major General N. P. Banks, March 2, 1863, in Ira Berlin et al., eds., *Freedom: A Documentary History of Emancipation, 1861–1867*, Series II (Cambridge University Press, 1982), 321–23.

29. Reprints of Pinchback/Bank's personal correspondence in *Congressional Record, Forty-Fourth Congress, First Session and Special Session*, 887. The dates listed with them appear to be incorrect, however.

30. Jean Toomer Papers, Series II, Box 18, Folder 493, Yale University; Undated draft of speech, titled, "On the Negro in the Civil War," P. B. S. Pinchback Papers, Moorland-Spingarn Research Collection, Howard University.

31. *New Orleans Times*, November 6, 1863.

32. Roger A. Fisher, "A Pioneer Protest: The New Orleans Streetcar Controversy of 1867," *Journal of Negro History* 53:3 (July 1968), 219, Fisher, *The Segregation Struggle in Louisiana, 1862–1877* (University of Illinois Press, 1974), 22–41; Nicholas Patler, "The Startling Career of P. B. S. Pinchback: A Whirlwind Crusade to Bring Equality to Reconstructed Louisiana," *Before Obama: A Reappraisal of Black Reconstruction Era Politicians* (Praeger Publishing, 2012), 216; Douglas R. Egerton, *The Wars of Reconstruction: The Brief, Violent History of America's Most Progressive Era* (Bloomsbury Press, 2014) 274–75; Dray, *Capitol Men*, 105–6; Suzanne-Juliette Mobley, "Streetcar Protest 1867," *New Orleans Historical*, accessed June 10, 2023, https://neworleanshistorical.org/items/show/1433.

33. P. B. S. Pinchback Speech on State Constitution Amendments, Box 81-2, Series G, Folder 43 and 44, Pinchback Papers, Howard University.

CHAPTER 3: PINCHBACK, NINA, AND THE RISE IN THE NEW ORLEANS REPUBLICAN PARTY

1. Jean Toomer Papers, Series II, Box 18, Folder 493, Yale University; Darwin T. Turner, ed., *The Wayward and the Seeking: A Collection of Writings by Jean Toomer* (Howard University Press, 1980), 23; Cynthia Earl Kerman and Richard Eldridge, *The Lives of Jean Toomer: A Hunger for Wholeness* (Louisiana State University Press, 1987), 17.

2. Jean Toomer Papers, Series II, Box 18, Folder 493, Yale University; Arna Bontemps, *One Hundred Years of Negro Freedom* (Dodd, Meade, 1961), 35–36; Turner, ed., *The Wayward and the Seeking*, 23; Kerman and Eldridge, *The Lives of Jean Toomer*, 17.

3. Jean Toomer Papers, Series II, Box 18, Folder 493, Yale University; Gatewood, *Aristocrats of Color*, 42; John Chandler Griffin Jr., "Jean Toomer: American Writer (A Biography)" (PhD diss., University of South Carolina, 1976), 12; Jean Toomer Papers, Series II, Box 18, Folder 492, Yale University; Rudolph P. Byrd and Henry Louis Gates Jr., "Afterword," in Jean Toomer, *Cane* (Liveright Press, 2011), 231. Byrd and Gates enlisted genealogist Megan Smolenyak to explore the racial identity of the Pinchback family in public documents, including census records.

4. In *A Chosen Exile: A History of Racial Passing in American Life*, Allyson White writes that compared to the antebellum period, many "light-skinned blacks" during Reconstruction chose not to pass when they could have because they embraced unfolding "possibilities for social, economic, and political freedom that the Reconstruction Era promised to bring," 74–75. This decisive choice not to pass, or to pass as black, is dealt with extensively Ingrid Dineen-Wimberly's excellent book, *The Allure of Blackness Among Mixed-Race Americans*.

5. Pinchback/Hawthorn Marriage License, May 19, 1869, VEC 678,261, Louisiana Division, New Orleans Public Library; Jean Toomer Papers, Series II, Box 18, Folder 493, Yale University.

6. Darwin Turner, ed., *The Wayward and the Seeking: A Collection of Writings by Jean Toomer* (Howard University Press, 1983), 23.

7. Jean Toomer Papers, Series II, Box 18, Folder 493, Yale University; Turner, ed., *The Wayward and the Seeking*, 23.

8. Pinchback Family History, Jean Toomer Papers, Box 18, Folder 418, pp.7–8, Yale University; Jean-Charles Houzea, *My Passage at the New Orleans Tribune: A Memoir of the Civil War Era* (Louisiana State University Press, 1984), 19, 24, 34, 36; Robert A. Fischer, *The Segregation Struggle in Louisiana, 1862–77* (University of Illinois Press, 1974), 40–41; Charles Vincent, *Black Legislators in Louisiana During Reconstruction* (Louisiana State University Press, 1976), 16–17; Stephen Hahn, *A Nation Under Our Feet: Black Political Struggles in the Rural South From Slavery to the Great Migration* (Harvard University Press, 2005) 165.

9. Jean Toomer Papers, Series II, Box 18, Folder 493, Yale University.

10. "National Lincoln Association: A Call for a Convention," Mobile, Alabama, P. B. S. Pinchback Papers, Box 81-1, Series E, Folder 24, and "P. B. S. Pinchback Speech," Montgomery, Alabama, Box 81-1, Series G, Moorland-Spingarn Research Center, Howard University; Douglas R. Egerton, *The Wars of Reconstruction: The Brief, Violent History of America's Most Progressive Era* (Bloomsbury Press, 2014), 190–92, 204; Eric Foner, *Reconstruction*, 110, 112; *New Orleans Republican*, April 12, 1872; Hahn, *A Nation Under Our Feet*, 221, 233; Haskins, *The First Black Governor*, 39.

11. Steven Hahn, *A Nation Under Our Feet*, 104; Herman Belz, "Origins of Negro Suffrage During the Civil War," *Southern Studies* 17:2 (Summer 1978), 115, 117, 118, 122, 123; Foner, *Reconstruction*, 117–23, 183, 189.

12. Fatima Shaik, Caryn Cossé Bell, and Libby Neidenbach, "Much More Than Music: Economy Hall and the Struggle for Civil Rights," *The Historic New Orleans Collection's 2021 Symposium*, New Orleans, Louisiana, March 5–7, 2021; Foner, *Reconstruction*, 189–90, 262–63; Donald E. Reynolds, "The New Orleans Race Riot of 1866," *Louisiana History: The Journal of the Louisiana Historical Association* 5:1 (Winter 1964), 13–14.

13. Fischer, *The Segregation Struggle in Louisiana*, 42. Foner, *Reconstruction*, 277, 278; Reynolds, "The New Orleans Race Riot of 1866," 15.

14. Howard Jones, "Biographical Sketches of Members of the 1868 Louisiana State Senate," *Louisiana History* 19.1 (Winter, 1978), 69.

15. "Biographical Sketch of Hon. P. B. S. Pinchback," undated, in P. B. S. Pinchback Papers, Box 81-1, Moorland-Spingarn Research Center, Howard University; Richard Campanella, "Culture Wars, Ethnic Rivalry, and New Orleans Messy Municipality Era," *Times-Picayune*, March 11, 2016.

16. Haskins, *The First Black Governor*, 50.

17. Agnes Grosz, "The Political Career of P. B. S. Pinchback," 532; Central Executive Committee Republican Party Resolutions, Box 81-1, Series C, Folder 13, and Draft of Pinchback Speech to the Louisiana Republican convention, June 19, 1867, Box 81-1, Series G, Folder 33, P. B. S. Pinchback Papers, Moorland-Spingarn Research Center, Howard University; Joe Gray Taylor, *Louisiana Reconstructed, 1863–1877* (Louisiana State University Press, 1974), 138–42, 143; Vincent, *Black Legislators in Louisiana*, 44–47.

18. *Alexandria (LA) Democrat*, October 2, 1867, in Vincent, *Black Legislators in Louisiana*, 47.

19. Vincent, *Black Legislators in Louisiana*, 46–47; Taylor, *Louisiana Reconstructed*, 146–47.

CHAPTER 4: PINCHBACK AND THE LOUISIANA CONSTITUTIONAL CONVENTION

1. Fatima Shaik, Caryn Cossé Bell, and Libby Neidenbach, "Much More Than Music: Economy Hall and the Struggle for Civil Rights," *The Historic New Orleans Collection's 2021 Symposium*, New Orleans, Louisiana, March 5–7, 2021; Jean-Charles Houzeau, *My Passage at the New Orleans Tribune: A Memoir of the Civil War Era*, ed., David C. Rankin (Louisiana State University Press, 1984), 143; *Official Journal of the Convention for Framing a Constitution for the State of Louisiana* (J. D. Roudanez, 1867–1868), 9.

2. Joe Gray Taylor, *Louisiana Reconstructed, 1863–1877* (Louisiana State University Press, 1974), 144–45, 148; Herman Belz, "Origins of Negro Suffrage During the Civil War," *Southern Studies* 17:2 (Summer, 1978), 117; Charles Vincent, "Negro Leadership and Programs in the Louisiana Constitutional Convention of 1868," *Louisiana History: The Journal of the Louisiana Historical Association* 10:4 (Autumn, 1969), 342, 343–49; Eric Foner, *Reconstruction: America's Unfinished Revolution, 1863–1877* (Harper & Row, 1989), 319; Steven Hahn, *A Nation Under Our Feet: Black Political Struggles in the Rural South from Slavery to the Great Migration* (Harvard University Press, 2003), 232.

3. *Official Journal of the Convention for Framing a Constitution for the State of Louisiana*, 5; "Distinguished Guests: Gov. Pinchback, of Louisiana, and Senator Bruce of Mississippi: Their Speeches at Corinthian Hall Last Night," *Atchison (KS) Daily Champion*, July 21, 1877; "Pinchback Interviews . . . Who He Is," *New Orleans Times* interview reprinted in *Louisianian*, March 1872; Alrutheus Taylor, "Negro Congressmen a Generation Later," *The Journal of Negro History* 7:2 (April 1922), 156.

4. "Pinchback Interviews . . . Who He Is," *New Orleans Times*, March 6, 1872; Richard L. Hume and Jerry B. Gough, *Blacks, Carpetbaggers, and Scalawags: The Constitutional Conventions of Radical Reconstruction* (Louisiana State University Press, 2000), 163, 180, 186, 188. As far as Black lawmakers in Louisiana, most came with some sort of

distinction—political, military, economic, education, and/or family background, including many former enslaved persons. See Vincent, *Black Legislators*, 71–77, 113–22.

5. *Official Journal of the Convention*, 22, 24.

6. *New Orleans Tribune*, March 15, 1868; Foner, *Reconstruction*, 324; Charles Vincent, *Black Legislators in Louisiana During Reconstruction* (Louisiana State University Press, 1976), 58–60, 122; Luis-Alejandro Dinnella-Borrego, *The Risen Phoenix: Black Politics in the Post-Civil War South* (University of Virginia Press, 2016), 54–55, 83–85; Douglas R. Egerton, *The Wars of Reconstruction: The Brief, Violent History of America's Most Progressive Era* (Bloomsbury Press, 2014), 254; Nicholas Patler, "The Startling Career of P. B. S. Pinchback: A Whirlwind Crusade to Bring Equality to Reconstructed Louisiana," in Matthew Lynch, ed., *Before Obama: A Reappraisal of Black Reconstruction Era Politicians* (Praeger Publishing, 2012), 218; James Haskins, *The First Black Governor: Pinckney Benton Steward Pinchback* (Africa World Press, 1996), 60; Taylor, "Negro Congressmen a Generation Later," 142–44.

7. *Official Journal of the Convention*, 22, 24; Foner, *Reconstruction*, 324; James Haskins, *The First Black Governor: Pinckney Benton Steward Pinchback* (Africa World Press, 1996), 60; Luis-Alejandro Dinnella-Borrego, *The Risen Phoenix*, 83–85; Taylor, "Negro Congressmen a Generation Later," 82, 142–44. The only exemption to Article 98 was if former rebels would swear an oath in favor of Radical Reconstruction, which most would never do.

8. Foner, *Reconstruction*, 96, 98. Estimated amounts in today dollars comes from MeasuringWorth.com.

9. Betty Porter, "The History of Negro Education in Louisiana," *Louisiana Historical Quarterly* 25 (July, 1942), 731; J. Morgan Kousser, "Before Plessy, Before Brown: The Development of the Law of Racial Integration in Louisiana and Kansas," *Social Science Working Paper* 681, California Institute of Technology, October 1988, 219.

10. Donald E. Devore, "Race Relations and Community Development: The Education of Blacks in New Orleans, 1962–1960 (PhD diss., Louisiana State University, 1989), 19–22; *New Orleans Tribune*, May 12, 1867, June 18, 1867, July 9, 24 and 31, 1867, October 29, 1867; Roger A. Fischer, *The Segregation Struggle in Louisiana, 1862–1877* (University of Illinois Press, 1974), 44–45.

11. Vincent, *Black Legislators in Louisiana*, 60.

12. Devore, "Race Relations and Community Development, 20.

13. Devore, "Race Relations and Community Development," 21–22; Robert Searing, "A Light in the Darkness: The Extraordinary Life of Edmonia Highgate," accessed November 23, 2024, https://www.syracuse.com/living/2023/02/a-light-in-the-darkness-the-extraordinary-life-of-edmonia-highgate.html.

14. *Official Journal of the Convention*, 11, 17, 60–61, 201.

15. Carin Peller-Semmens, "Unreconstructed: Slavery and Emancipation in Louisiana's Red River, 1820–1880" (PhD diss., University of Sussex), 154–55.

16. *Official Journal of the Convention*, 60–61; Francis Newton Thorpe, ed., *The Federal and State Constitutions, Colonial Charters, and Other Organic Laws of the States, Territories, and Colonies Now or Heretofore Forming the United States of America* (G.P.O., 1909), III, 1465.

17. *Official Journal of the Convention*, 121, 124, 125, 128, 242, 243; *New Orleans Republican*, February 28, 1868; Thorpe, *Federal and State Constitutions*, 1450.

18. *The Bossier Banner*, March 21, 1868; *Official Journal of the Convention*, 125, 242, 243, 291.

19. New Orleans *Republican*, March 18, 1868; Donald W. Davis, "Ratification of the Constitution of 1868—Record of Votes," *Louisiana History: The Journal of the Louisiana Historical Association* 6:3 (Summer, 1965), 302; "Constitution of the State of Louisiana," *New Orleans Republican*, April 15, 1868; "Black Crook Constitution," quoted from *The New Orleans Times* in *The Weekly Echo*, Lake Charles, LA, April 18, 1868.

CHAPTER 5: PINCHBACK IN THE LOUISIANA STATE SENATE

1. Richard Nelson Current, *Those Terrible Carpetbaggers* (Oxford University Press, 1988), 6–12; Teddy Bill Tunnell, "Henry Clay Warmoth and the Politics of Coalition," (master's thesis, North Texas State University, 1966), 4; Philip Dray, *Capitol Men: The Epic Story of Reconstruction through the Lives of the First Black Congressmen* (Houghton Mifflin, 2008), 106, 111.

2. Brian Mitchell, "Oscar J. Dunn: A Case Study in Race & Politics in Reconstruction Louisiana" (PhD diss., University of New Orleans, 2011), 35–38, 46.

3. Louisiana Senate Journal, 1868, 138; Howard Jones, "Biographical Sketches of Members of the 1868 Louisiana State Senate," *Louisiana History* 19:1 (Winter 1978), 69.

4. Agnes Smith Grosz, "The Political Career of Pinckney Benton Stewart Pinchback," *The Louisiana Historical Quarterly* 27:2 (April 1944), 537–38.

5. *Louisiana Senate Journal*, 1868, 138, 139–43; Jones, "Biographical Sketches," 68, 70; Frances Wayne Binning, "Henry Clay Warmoth and the Louisiana Reconstruction" (PhD diss., University of North Carolina, 1969), 124–25. The others, who together with Pinchback would form a Black brain trust, were Ceasar Antoine, John Randall, Alexander François, George Y. Kelso, Julien J. Monette, Curtis Pollard, and Robert Poindexter.

6. *New Orleans Crescent*, September 2, 1869; Taylor, *Louisiana Reconstructed*, 161.

7. *New Orleans Crescent*, September 2 and 4, 1868; *Daily Picayune* (New Orleans), September 3 and 4, 1868; Taylor, *Louisiana Reconstructed*, 163.

8. "From New Orleans," *The South-Western* (Shreveport, LA), January 13, 1869; "Acts of the State of Louisiana (A. L. Lee State Printer, 1868), 279.

9. *Acts of the State of Louisiana* (A. L. Lee State Printer, 1868), 279; J. D. Thomas, *Law of Slavery in the State of Louisiana*; Blassingame, *Black New Orleans*, 201–10; Taylor, *Louisiana Reconstructed*, 437.

10. The State of Louisiana, Parish of Orleans—City of New Orleans, Marriage License, May 19, 1869.

11. *Louisiana Senate Journal*, 1868, 231; *Louisiana Acts*, 1868, Act No. 210, 210, 278–80; Charles Gayarre, *Reports of Cases Argued and Determined in the Supreme Court of Louisiana, Volume 25* (New Orleans: Republican Office, 1873) 621; *Southern Reporter, Volume Containing All the Decisions of the Supreme Courts of Alabama, Louisiana, Florida, Mississippi, Volume 42* (West Publishing Co., 1907), 471; *Journal of the Proceedings of the Convention for Framing a Constitution*, 16, 48, 192, 198, 206–7; Katherine M. Franke,

"Becoming a Citizen: Reconstruction Era Regulation of African American Marriages," *Yale Journal of Law and the Humanities* 11:2 (Summer 1999), 251–58, 307–9.

12. *Louisiana Senate Journal*, 1869, 37, 82, 149, 228, 230, 234; 1870, 40, 47, 173; Acts of 1869, No. 87, 87–89; 1871, No. 99, 11–13; Haskins, *The First Black Governor*, 72; Foner, *Reconstruction*, 198, 199.

13. Vincent, *Black Legislators in Louisiana*, 95; "From New Orleans," *The South-Western* (Shreveport, LA), January 13, 1869; *New Orleans Crescent*, February 5, 1869; Fischer, *The Segregation Struggle in Louisiana*, 67–68; Germaine Reed, "Race Legislation in Louisiana, 1864–1920," *Louisiana History* 6:4 (Autumn 1965), 380.

14. *Louisiana Senate Journal*, 1869, 21, 91, 93, 95, 96, 98, 159; *Louisiana Acts*, 1869, no.38,37; *Louisiana House Journal*, 1869, 131, 136; *New Orleans Crescent*, February 6, 1869; Reed, "Race Legislation in Louisiana, 1864–1920," 380; Haskins, *The First Black Governor*, 72; Edwin Redkey, ed., *A Grand Army of Black Men: Letters From African American Soldiers in the Union Army, 1861–1865* (Cambridge University Press, 1992), 250, 251–56.

15. *Louisiana Senate Journal*, 1869, 21, 91, 93, 95, 96, 98, 159; *Louisiana Acts*, 1869, no.38,37; *Louisiana House Journal*, 1869, 131, 136; Reed, "Race Legislation in Louisiana, 1864–1920," 380; Haskins, *The First Black Governor*, 72; Dana Bash and David Fisher, *America's Deadliest Election: The Cautionary Tale of the Most Violent Election in American History* (Hanover Square Press, 2024), 45; Glen Starks, "The Biography of John Willis Menard, First African American Elected to the US Congress," in Matthew Lynch, ed., *Before Obama: A Reappraisal of Black Reconstruction Era Politicians* (Praeger Publishing, 2012), 230, 231; *Louisianan*, May 18, 1871, February 8 and March 14, 1872.

16. "Speech of Hon. P. B. S. Pinchback: Delivered to the Senate of Louisiana, February 4, 1869, upon the Civil Rights Bill, to be entitled, 'An act to enforce the Thirteenth Article of the Constitution of the State'"; *New Orleans Crescent*, February 5, 1869, and February 6, 1869.

17. "Speech of Hon. P. B. S. Pinchback."
18. "Speech of Hon. P. B. S. Pinchback."
19. "Speech of Hon. P. B. S. Pinchback."
20. "Speech of Hon. P. B. S. Pinchback."

21. *Senate Journal*, 1869, 10, 67, 73, 91, 95–96, 98; *House Journal*, 1869, 20, 41, 55, 159; *New Orleans Tribune*, January 8, 1869; *New Orleans Times*, February 11, 27; March 2, 1869; Vincent, *Black Legislators*, 94–96.

22. *Senate Journal*, 1869, 139, 142; *Senate Acts of 1869*, No. 38,37; *New Orleans Tribune*, February 4, 1869; *New Orleans Crescent*, February 5, 1869; Fischer, *The Segregation Struggle in Louisiana*, 68–69; Warmoth, *War, Politics, and Reconstruction*, 92.

23. *New Orleans Commercial Bulletin*, February 29, 1869; "The Travels of Lynch and Dunn," *Daily Picayune*, April 3, 1869; Peter F. Lau, ed., *From the Grassroots to the Supreme Court: Brown v. Board of Education and American Democracy* (Duke University Press, 2004), 25; Paul H. Gates Jr., "Toward a Common Goal: Jean-Charles Houzeau, P. B. S. Pinchback and New Orleans' Black Press, 1862–1882" (unpublished paper, College of Journalism and Communications, University of Florida, 1993), 13; "C. S. Sauvinet vs. J. A. Walker," Supreme Court of Louisiana, No. 3513 (L'Avenir Job Office). This case is also accessible online. The online version of the Sauvinet case is a version that was donated to Harvard University by Charles Sumner, who certainly followed the case closely and celebrated its verdict https://babel.hathitrust.org/cgi/pt?id=hvd.32044018647792&seq=5&q1=filleul).

24. Brian K. Mitchell, Barrington E. Edwards, and Nick Weldon, "Oscar Dunn and His Radical Vision for Louisiana," Conference Presentation, *The Historic New Orleans Collection's 2021 Symposium*, New Orleans, Louisiana, March 5–7, 2021; *Louisiana House Journal*, 1870, 80, 106, 211–12, 215, 327, and *Extra Session*, 346; *House Acts of 1870*, Extra Session, No. 39,93; *Louisiana Senate Journal*, 1870, 186, 191, 202–3, 278, 327, and 1871, 4–5; *Senate Debates*, 1870, 807–8; *Louisianan*, January 19, 1871; Fischer, *Segregation Struggle in Louisiana*, 69–73; Agnes Smith Grosz, "The Political Career of Pinckney Benton Steward Pinchback," *The Louisiana Historical Quarterly* 27:2 (April 1944), 540fn67.

25. Lau, *From the Grassroots to the Supreme Court*, 25.

26. *Acts Passed by the General Assembly of Louisiana, Third Session of the First Legislature* (A. E. Lee, State Printer, 1870), 128–29; Vincent, *Black Legislators*, 80–82.

27. *Louisiana Democrat*, April 21, 1869; *Morning Star and Catholic Messenger* (New Orleans), June 13, 1869; Grosz, "The Political Career of Pinckney Benton Stewart Pinchback," 538.

28. The *South-Western* (Shreveport, LA), November 24, 1869, December 8, 1869; Arna Bontemps, *One Hundred Years of Negro Freedom* (Dodd, Meade, 1961), 42–43; Grosz, "The Political Career," 539fn53.

29. Peter J. Breaux, "William J. Brown and the Development of Education: A Retrospective on the Career of a State Superintendent of Public Education of African Descent in Louisiana" (PhD diss., Florida State University, 2006), 67–70. Pinchback to Bruce, October 26, 1879; November 22, 1879, Bruce Papers, MSRC, Howard University, Bontemps, *One Hundred Years of Negro Freedom*, 42–43; John N. Ingham and Lynne B. Feldman, *African American Business Leaders: A Biographical Dictionary* (Westport, Connecticut: Greenwood Press, 1994), 559; "Take it to a wider audience. . . ." For example, Lewis White was the agent for *The Louisianian* in Chicago, Illinois, where that same year he became one of the city's first African Americans appointed as a mail clerk, which *The Chicago Times* decried as "mongrels" taking away jobs from whites. See Robert L. McCaul, *The Black Struggle for Public Schooling in Nineteenth-Century Illinois* (Southern Illinois University Press, 1987), 98–99.

30. For example, J. Henri Burch, a black lawmaker and educator representing East Baton Rouge Parish, worked for *The Louisianian* after which he started the Baton Rouge *Courier*. See A. E. Perkins, "James Henri Bruch and Oscar James Dunn in Louisiana," *Journal of Negro History* 22 (July 1937), 321; *Louisianan*, April 11, 1872.

31. *Lousiana Acts*, No. 74, 74, 99, 100; *Senate Debates*, 1870, 169–75; *Senate Journal*, 72, 74, 110, 136, 139–40, 150; *House Journal*, 1868, 45, 51, 120; *Daily Picayune*, August 14, 20, 25, 26, 1868: Act No. 54, "Extending Protection to Laborers in the Exercise of Their Privilege of Free Suffrage"; Vincent, *Black Legislators in Louisiana*, 78–79; Matthew Christensen, "The 1868 St. Landry Massacre: Reconstruction's Deadliest Episode of Violence" (master's thesis, University of Wisconsin-Milwaukee, 2012), iii, 1, 31, 61, 62.

32. Christensen, "The 1868 St. Landry Massacre," 1, 31, 61, 62; Blake, Tom, transcriber. "St. Landry Parish: Largest Slaveholders from 1860 Slave Census Schedules and Surname Matches for African Americans on 1870 Census," accessed August 7, 2024, https://freepages.rootsweb.com/~ajac/genealogy/lastlandry.htm; "Political Troubles in Louisiana," House Miscellaneous Documents, Second Session of the Forty-Second Congress, IV, No. 211, 1871–72,284.

33. *Senate Debates*, 1870, 75–76, 169–75, 189–90, 304; *Senate Journal*, 110; Vincent, *Black Legislators*, 79.

34. *House Journal*, 1868, 25, 38, 91, 147, 152; *New Orleans Times*, November 23, 1870; Mishio Yamanaka, "Erasing the Colorline: The Racial Formation of Creoles and the Public School Integration Movement in New Orleans, 1867–1880" (master's thesis, University of North Carolina at Chapel Hill, 2013), 14–16; Louis August Lynn, "A History of Teachers' Institutes of Louisiana, 1870–1921" (Ph. D. diss., Louisiana State University, 1961), 23–24.

35. *House Journal*, 1868, 25, 38, 91, 147, 152; Yamanaka, "Erasing the Colorline," 14–16; Lynn, "A History of Teachers' Institutes of Louisiana," 23–24.

36. Fischer, *The Segregation Struggle in Louisiana*, 111, 112; J. Morgan Kousser, "Before Plessy, Before Brown: The Development of the Law of Racial Integration in Louisiana and Kansas," in Paul Finkleman and Stephen E. Gottlieb, ed., *Toward A Usable Past: Liberty Under State Constitutions* (Athens: University of Georgia Press, 2009).

37. Fischer, *The Segregation Struggle in Louisiana*, 111, 112.

38. Vincent, *Black Legislators*, 91; Gray, *Louisiana Reconstructed*, 471.

39. "The New Orleans Schools" and "Public School Notice," *New Orleans Republican*, December 28, 1870; *The South-Western* (Shreveport, LA), October 19, 1870.

40. Fischer, *The Segregation Struggle*, 110, 114, 119; James E. Blassingame, *Black New Orleans, 1860–1880* (University of Chicago, 1973), 118–19, 120; Walter C. Stern, "How New Orleans Schools Created a Segregated City," May 17, 2018, WWNO interview with Jess Clark; Peter J. Breaux, "William G. Brown and the Development of Education: A Retrospective of the Career of a State Superintendent of Public Education of African Descent in Louisiana," (PhD diss., Florida State University, 2007), 70; Donald E. Devore, "Race Relations and Community Development: The Education of Blacks in New Orleans, 1862–1960" (PhD diss., Louisiana State University, 1989), 40–43.

41. "The Public Schools," The *Daily Picayune*, date undecipherable, Box 81-2, Series H, Folder 51, Pinchback Papers, Howard University; Fischer, *The Segregation Struggle in Louisiana*, 109, 115–18; Devore, "Race Relations," 46, 61–62.

42. Haskin, *The First Black Governor*, 117, 118–19; Fischer, *The Segregation Struggle in Louisiana*, 110; T. H. Harris, "The Story of Public Education in Louisiana" (PhD diss., University of Louisiana, 1924), 31.

43. Vincent, *Black Legislators*, 124–25; Senate Journal, 1871,222; "Political Troubles in Louisiana," House Miscellaneous Documents, Second Session of the Forty-Second Congress, IV, No. 211, 1871–72,284.

44. James W. Illingworth, "Crescent City Radicals: Black Working People and the Civil War in New Orleans" (PhD diss., University of California Santa Cruz, 2015), 382; Ingrid Dineen-Wimberly, *The Allure of Blackness Among Mixed-Race Americans, 1862–1916* (University of Nebraska Press, 2019), 66; "Pinchback Interviewed . . . Who He Is," reprinted from *The New Orleans Times* in *The Louisianian*, March 14, 1872.

45. For one writer who portrays Pinchback as a Machiavellian leader who participated in bribery and corrupt deals admits that it is based on hearsay without any substantive evidence, see Bernard A. Weisberger, "The Carpetbagger," *American Heritage* 25:1 (1973).

46. Grosz, "The Political Career," 543–44; "The Louisiana Investigation," *New York Herald*, February 9, 1872, 3.

47. William J. Simmons, *Men of Mark: Eminent, Progressive and Rising* (George M. Rewell, 1887), 765; Henry Clay Warmoth, *War, Politics, and Reconstruction: Stormy Days in Louisiana* (University of South Carolina Press, 2006), 108; Acts Passed by the General Assembly of Louisiana, 1870, 128–29; Official Journal of the Proceedings of the House of Representatives of the State of Louisiana (New Orleans, A.E. Lee, State Printer), 201; Feldman and Ingham, *African American Business Leaders*, 559–60.

48. ; "The Louisiana Investigation," *New York Herald*, February 9, 1872; "Pinchback Interviewed . . . Who He Is," reprinted from *The New Orleans Times* in *The Louisianian*, March 14, 1872.

49. Grosz, "The Political Career," 543–44; Charles Nordhoff, *The Cotton States in the Spring and Summer of 1875* (D. Appleton, 1876), 62. Charges of corruption would be leveled against Pinchback years later even as his power waned. See, for example, "An Open Letter from Ex-Gov. Pinchback," *Times-Democrat* (New Orleans), April 24, 1884, where Pinchback angrily refutes charges that he had taken a bribe made by a newspaper editor.

50. Jo Ann Carrigan, "The Saffron Scourge: A History of Yellow Fever in Louisiana, 1796–1905" (PhD diss., Louisiana State University, 1961), 155, 179, 184, 478; "The Louisiana Investigation," *New York Herald*, February 9, 1872, 3.

CHAPTER 6: "WHY, DAMN IT, EVERYBODY IS DEMORALIZED DOWN HERE"

1. The (Louisiana) *Opelousas Courier*, February 3, 1872; David Rankin, ed., "Introduction," in Jean-Charles Houzeau, *My Passage at the New Orleans Tribune: A Memoir of the Civil War Era* (Louisiana State University Press, 1984), 55; Joe Gray Taylor, *Louisiana Reconstructed, 1863–1877* (Louisiana State University Press, 1974), 210; Wayne Binning, "Carpetbagger's Triumph: The Louisiana Election of 1868," *Louisiana History* XIV (Winter, 1973), 31–38.

2. Charles Vincent, *Black Legislators in Louisiana During Reconstruction* (Louisiana State University Press, 1976), 133–34; James Haskins, *The Black Governor: Pinckney Benton Stewart Pinchback* (Africa World Press, 1996), 99–100; Justin Behrend, *Reconstructing Democracy: Grassroots Black Politics in the Deep South After the Civil War* (University of Georgia Press, 2015), 148–49, 159–60.

3. Philip Dray, *Capitol Men: The Epic Story of Reconstruction Through the Lives of the First Black Congressmen* (Houghton Mifflin Co., 2008), 118; Henry Clay Warmoth, *War, Politics, and Reconstruction: Stormy Days in Louisiana* (McMillan, 1930), 120; Joe Gray Taylor, *Louisiana Reconstructed*, 214; Will D. Campbell, *Providence* (Baylor University Press, 2002), 90–91; Haskins, *The Black Governor*, 99–100.

4. *New Orleans Tribune*, January 7, 8, 13, 16, 1869; Official Journal of the Proceedings of the House of Representatives of the State of Louisiana, 1868 (A. E. Lee, State Printer, 1868), 246–49; House Journal, 1870, 80, 106, 211–12, 215; Official Journal of the Proceedings of the Senate of the State of Louisiana, 1870 (A.E. Lee, State Printer, 1870), 278; Senate Journal, 1871, 4–5; Ted B. Tunnell, Jr., "Henry Clay Warmoth and the Politics of Coalition" (master's thesis, North Texas State University, 1966), 8–9; Linda English, "'That Is All We Ask For—an Equal Chance': Oscar James Dunn, Louisiana's First Black Governor" in Matthew

Lynch, ed., *Before Obama: A Reappraisal of Black Reconstruction Era Politicians* (Praeger Publishing, 2012), 77.

5. Rankin, ed., "Introduction," 56; Joe Gray Taylor, *Louisiana Reconstructed*, 214; English, "'That Is All We Ask For—an Equal Chance'," 77; Lerone Bennett, Jr., *Black Power USA: The Human Side of Reconstruction, 1866–1877* (Penguin Books, 1967), 280.

6. *Official Report of the Proceedings, Addresses and Resolutions of the Republican State Convention of Louisiana, August 9 & 10, 1871* (New Orleans: Office of the Republican Party, 1871), 7.

7. *New Orleans Republican*, December 7, 1871. In his memoirs, Warmoth claims that he received confirmation from the chief justice of the Louisiana Supreme Court and other legal experts that he had the authority to call the Senate alone to fill the vacancy, see Warmoth, *War, Politics, and Reconstruction*, 119.

8. *New Orleans Republican*, December 7, 1871.

9. Brian Mitchell, "Oscar J. Dunn: A Case Study in Race and Politics in Reconstruction Louisiana" (PhD diss., University of New Orleans, 2011), 203; Brian K. Mitchell, Barrington S. Edwards, and Nick Weldon, *Monumental: Oscar Dunn and His Radical Fight in Reconstruction Louisiana* (New Orleans: The Historic New Orleans Collection 2021), 210, 234.

10. *New Orleans Republican*, December 7, 1871; *New National Era and Citizen*, December 24, 1873.

11. *New Orleans Republican*, December 7, 1871.

12. "Pinchback Interviewed . . . Who He Is," *Louisianian*, March 14, 1872.

13. *New Orleans Republican*, December 7, 1871.

14. *New Orleans Republican*, December 7, 1871; *The Citizen's Guard*, July 23, 1872.

15. *New Orleans Republican*, March 5, 6, 7, 8 and 13, 1871; "Political Troubles in Louisiana," House Miscellaneous Documents, Forty-second Congress, Second Session, IV, No. 211, 1871–72, 553–54; Taylor, *Louisiana Reconstructed*, 220–21, and Taylor, "Henry Clay Warmoth," in Joseph G. Dawson III, ed., *The Louisiana Governors: From Iberville to Edwards* (Louisiana State University Press, 1990), 168; "Pinchback Interviewed . . . Who He Is," *Louisianian*, March 14, 1872.

16. *New Orleans Republican*, December 7, 1871.

17. *New Orleans Republican*, December 7, 1871; *Evening Bulletin* (Philadelphia), reprinted in *The Opelousas Journal*, February 3, 1872.

18. *National Republican*, January 2, 1872; Warmoth, *War, Politics, and Reconstruction*, 125–26; Haskins, *The First Black Governor*, 110.

19. *Weekly Louisianian*, January 4, 1872; *Times-Picayune*, January 21, 1872; Farrell Evans, "America's First Black War Correspondent Reported From the Civil War's Front Lines," History.com, January 3, 2024 (America's First Black War Correspondent Reported from the Civil War's Front Lines | HISTORY) (Accessed August 20, 2024).

20. *New Orleans Republican*, January 4, 14, 1872; Warmoth, *War, Politics, and Reconstruction*, 126.

21. Warmoth, *War, Politics, and Reconstruction*, 126.

22. *Evening Bulletin* (Philadelphia), reprinted in *Opelousas Journal*, February 3, 1872; Dray, *Capitol Men*, 118–19; Warmoth, *War, Politics, and Reconstruction*, 130, 139, 140.

23. Dray, *Capitol Men*, 118–19; Dana Bash and David Fisher, *America's Deadliest Election: The Cautionary Tale of the Most Violent Election in American History* (Hanover Square Press, 2024), 64.

24. Dray, *Capitol Men*, 119; Warmoth, *War, Politics, and Reconstruction*, 134–35.

25. *The Congressional Globe and the Debates and the Proceedings of the Third Session Forty-Second Congress* (Office of the Congressional Globe, 1873), 1128; No.457, 329; Bash and David, *America's*, 65–67; *Deadliest Election* Warmoth, *War, Politics, and Reconstruction*, 141.

26. *The Natchitoches Times*, reprinted in *Opelousas Journal*, February 3, 1872; Taylor, *The Louisiana Governors*, xiv, 221; "Frederick Douglass on Louisianans," reprinted from the *New National Era* in the *Lousianian*, May 1872. The unique political development of corruption in Louisiana began to form into a tradition under early French and Spanish rule, where leaders took the initiative to break the laws of the ruling European home country out of economic necessity.

27. T. Harry Williams, *Huey Long: A Biography* (Penguin, 1969), 183–84.

28. Roger W. Shugg, *Origins of Class Struggle in Louisiana: A Social History of White Farmers and Laborers During Slavery and After, 1840–1875* (Louisiana State University Press, 1939), 227.

CHAPTER 7: LIEUTENANT GOVERNOR PINCHBACK AND THE RACE TO SAVE THE REPUBLICAN PARTY

1. Eric Foner, *Freedom's Lawmakers: A Directory of Black Officeholders During Reconstruction* (Louisiana State University Press, 1996); Buford Satcher, *Blacks in Mississippi Politics, 1865–1900* (University Press of America, 1978), 65–69. Pinchback and his five peers would be the only African Americans to hold that office for almost one hundred years, until 1975 when Mervin Dymally of California and George L. Brown of Colorado became the first black lieutenant governors since Reconstruction.

2. Judson A. Grenier, "'Officialdom': California State Government, 1849–1879," *California History* 8:3/4 (2003).

3. "Pinchback Interviewed . . . Who He Is," *New Orleans Times*, March 6, 1872.

4. T. H. Harris, "The Story of Public Education in Louisiana" (PhD diss., University of Louisiana, 1924), 31; *New Orleans Republican*, January 30, 1872; Haskins, *The First Black Governor*, 117–19

5. Philip Dray, *Capitol Men: The Epic Story of Reconstruction Through the Lives of the First Black Congressmen* (Houghton Mifflin, 2008) 107.

6. Pinchback Family History, Toomer Papers, Box 18, Folder 493, Yale University; Jean Toomer, "Jean Toomer and P. B. S. Pinchback," *New Mexico Sentinel*, 1937, quoted in John Chandler Griffin Jr., "Jean Toomer: American Writer (A Biography)" (PhD diss., University of South Carolina, 1976), 30; Darwin T. Turner, ed., *The Wayward and the Seeking: A Collection of Writings by Jean Toomer* (Howard University Press, 1980), 24–25; Cynthia Earl Kerman and Richard Eldridge, *The Life of Jean Toomer: A Hunger for Wholeness* (Louisiana State University Press, 1987), 18–19.

7. Ingrid Dineen-Wimberly, *The Allure of Blackness Among Mixed-Race Americans, 1862–1916* (University of Nebraska Press, 2019), xx, xxvi, xxviii, 3, 4; T. Harry Williams, *Huey Long: A Biography* (Penguin, 1969), 183–84.

8. Pinchback printed speech, Box 81-1, Series G, Folder 36, and P. B. S. Speech on equal rights, Box 81-1, Series G, Folder 38, Pinchback Papers, Howard University; Pinchback Family History, Toomer Papers, Box 18, Folder 493, Yale University; *New Orleans Republican*, January 30, February 11, 1872; "Frederick Douglass on Louisianans," reprinted from the *National New Era* in *The Lousianian*, May 1872; William B. Gatewood, *Aristocrats of Color: The Black Elite, 1880–1920* (Indiana University Press, 1990), 173; "Said in His Honor: Funeral of Frederick Douglas at Washington," *Rochester Democrat and Chronicle*, February 26, 1895.

9. *Congressional Globe, Forty-Second Congress, Second Session*, 412, 471; *House Misc. Doc., Forty-Second Congress, Second Session*, IV, No. 92, 1–41, and No. 211, 489–90; *New Orleans Republican*, February 11, 1872; Agnes Smith Grosz, "The Political Career of Pinckney Benton Stewart Pinchback," *Louisiana Historical Quarterly* 27:2 (April, 1944), 550–51.

10. "Pinchback Interviewed ... Who He Is," *New Orleans Times*, March 6, 14, 1872; The *Opelousas Journal*, March 23, 1872; *New Orleans Republican*, March 8, 12, 24, 28; April 12, 21, 24, 28; May 30; and August 15, 1872; Grosz, "The Political Career," 551; Haskins, *The First Black Governor*, 144–45. The Liberal Republicans, ironically enough, supported an end to Reconstruction, a strange bedfellow for Sumner to align himself with. The Liberal Republicans would split the Republican Party in the election of 1872, contributing to the downfall of Reconstruction. See Andrew L. Sapp, *The Doom of Reconstruction: The Liberal Republicans in the Civil War Era* (Fordham University Press, 2006).

11. Haskins, *The First Black Governor*, 130.

12. "Frederick Douglass on Louisianans," reprinted from *New National Era* in the *Lousianian*, May 1872.

13. *New Orleans Times*, May 2, 1872; Grosz, "The Political Career," 552; English, "'That Is All We Ask For—an Equal Chance," 77; P. B. S. Pinchback to Henry Warmoth, September 11, 1872, Folder 46, Henry Clay Warmoth Papers, Wilson Library, University of North Carolina.

14. *Proceedings of the National Republican Convention Held at Philadelphia*, June 5–6, 1872 (Gibson Brothers Printers, 1872), Appendix,11.

15. *New Orleans Republican*, June 23, 1872; P. B. S. Pinchback to John Lewis, August 27, 1872, Box 81-1, Series B, Folder 3, Pinchback Papers, Howard University.

16. James Lewis to Hon. P. B. S. Pinchback, August 27, 1872, and P. B. S. Pinchback to Hon. James Lewis, August 27, 1872, P. B. S. Pinchback Papers, Box 81-1, Series B, Folder 3, Howard University.

17. Vincent, *Black Legislators in Lousiana*, 52, 139–40; Haskins, *The Black Governor*, 144–45; Gonzales, "William Pitt Kellogg," 403: *New Orleans Republican*, April 16, 1872.

18. Justin Behrend, *Reconstructing Democracy: Grassroots Black Politics in the Deep South After the Civil War* (University of Georgia Press, 2015), 179–80.

19. Carol Faulkner, *Women's Radical Reconstruction: The Freedmen's Aid Movement* (University of Pennsylvania Press, 2004), 6, 7–8, 67, 152; Hahn, *A Nation Under Our Feet*, 227; Behrend, *Reconstructing Democracy*, 180–81, 191, 199–202; "Report and Testimony of the Select Committee of the United States Senate to Investigate the Causes of the Removal of the Negroes from the Southern States to the Northern States," *Congressional Record*,

Forty-Sixth Congress, Second Session, 1880, Part 2, page 232. Also, for Black women's influence on Reconstruction politics, and policies, and activism, see Kate Masur, "Black Civil Rights Activism During Reconstruction: A National View," *The Historic New Orleans Collection's 2021 Symposium*, New Orleans, Louisiana, March 5–7, 2021.

20. Allyson Hobbs, *A Chosen Exile: A History of Racial Passing in American Life* (Harvard University, 2014). 99–100.

21. P. B. S. Pinchback to Henry Warmoth, September 11, 1872, Folder 46, Warmoth Papers, University of North Carolina; *Congressional Record, Forty-Second Congress, First Session*, Appendix, 433; James M. Trotter, *Music and Some Highly Musical People* (Lee and Shepard Publishers, 1881), 345–46. Trotter mentions Corbin's work with "Governor Pinchback." Trotter was one of the first commissioned Black officers in the Union Army and led a protest for pay equality. He would also become Recorder of Deeds in Washington, DC and was the father of William Monroe Trotter (1872–1934), who would become one of the most engaged civil rights activists of the early twentieth century.

22. Warmoth, *War, Politics, and Reconstruction*, 202; Dray, *Capitol Men*, 128. Philip Dray most recently recounts the story with lively skill; *Official Journal of the Proceedings of the Senate of the State of Louisiana* (A. L. Lee, 1870), 72, 74, 110, 136, 139–40; William J. Simmons, *Men of Mark: Eminent, Progressive and Rising* (George M. Rewell, 1887), 777–79; "Fastest Race on Record," *Donaldsonville (LA) Chief*, September 21, 1872; "The Great Gubernatorial Race," *Louisianian*, September 21, 1872.

23. *Official Journal of the Proceedings of the Senate of the State of Louisiana* (A. L. Lee, 1870), 72, 74, 110, 136, 139–40; William J. Simmons, *Men of Mark: Eminent, Progressive and Rising* (George M. Rewell, 1887), 777–79; "Fastest Race on Record," *Donaldsonville (Louisiana) Chief*, September 21, 1872; "The Great Gubernatorial Race," *Louisianian*, September 21, 1872.

24. Warmoth, *War, Politics, and Reconstruction*, 203; "Fastest Race on Record," *Donaldsonville (Louisiana) Chief*, September 21, 1872; "The Great Gubernatorial Race," *Louisianian*, September 21, 1872.

25. Warmoth, *War, Politics, and Reconstruction*, 203; "Fastest Race on Record," *Donaldsonville (Louisiana) Chief*, September 21, 1872; "The Great Gubernatorial Race," *Louisianian*, September 21, 1872.

26. Warmoth, *War, Politics, and Reconstruction*, 203; Dray, *Capitol Men*, 130–31; Haskins, *The First Black Governor*, 154–55; *New Orleans Republican*, September 20, 1872; *Donaldsonville (Louisiana) Chief*, September 21, 1872; "The Great Gubernatorial Race," *Louisianian*, September 21, 1872.

CHAPTER 8: THIRTY-SIX DAYS THAT CHANGED HISTORY:

1. Report of Committees of the Senate of the United States for the Second Session of the Forty-Third Congress 1874–75: Series of United States Public Documents (Government Printing Office, 1875), 18; Senate Reports, Forty-Second Congress, Third Session, No. 457,541–42; 862–63; "The Muddle: Facts, Rumors, and the Wailings in the Camps of the Contending Factions," undated newspaper clipping, Box 81-2, Series H, Folder 56, Pinchback Papers, Howard University.

2. Report of Committees of the Senate of the United States for the Second Session of the Forty-Third Congress 1874–75: Series of United States Public Documents (Government Printing Office, 1875), 18; Senate Reports, Forty-Second Congress, Third Session, No. 457,541–42; 862–63; Joseph G. Dawson III, *Army Generals and Reconstruction, Louisiana 1862–1877* (Louisiana State University Press, 1982), 136; Henry Dibble to Henry Clay Warmoth, November 20, 1872, Warmoth Papers, University of North Carolina, Chapel Hill; Agnes Smith Grosz, "The Political Career of Pinckney Benton Stewart Pinchback," *Louisiana Historical Quarterly* 27:2 (April, 1944), 558, 559n205; Joe Gray Taylor, *Louisiana Reconstructed, 1863–1877* (Louisiana State University Press, 1974), 244.

3. George H. Williams, Attorney General of the United States, to S. B. Packard, December 3, 1872, in House Executive Documents, Forty-Second Congress, Third Session, VII, No. 91,13, and No. 457,155; Edward Foley, *Ballot Battles: The History of Disputed Elections in the United States* (Oxford University Press, 2016), 113–14; Wikipedia, "Edward Henry Durell," accessed August 26, 2024, https://en.wikipedia.org/wiki/Edward_ Henry_Durell. ().

4. Grosz, "The Political Career," 650–61; Philip Dray, *Capitol Men: The Epic Story of Reconstruction Through the Lives of the First Black Congressmen* (Houghton Mifflin, 2008), 131;

5. Grosz, "The Political Career," 56–561 and 561n72, 73; Haskins, *The First Black Governor: Pinckney Benton Stewart Pinchback* (Africa World Press, 1996), 159–61; Gray, *Louisiana Reconstructed*, 246–47.

6. Ibid.

7. Congressional Globe, House Executive Documents, Forty-Second Congress, Third Session, VII, No. 91 (Office of the Congressional Globe, 1873), 16; Haskins, *The First Black Governor*, 161.

8. New Orleans *Picayune*, December 10, 1872; Grosz, "The Political Career," 561; Haskins, *The First Black Governor*, 162.

9. Congressional Globe, House Executive Documents, Forty-Second Congress, Third Session, VII, No. 91,16; Gray, *Louisiana Reconstructed*, 248.

10. *New Orleans Republican*, December 12, 1872; *Donaldsonville Chief*, December 14, 1872.

11. *New Orleans Daily Picayune*, December 10, 1872; *Louisianian*, December 14, 1872.

12. *Acts Passed by the General Assembly of the State of Louisiana at the Extra Session Convened December 9, 1872* (Government Printing Office), 37.

13. Stephen Packard to George Williams, December 11, 1872 (two telegrams); J. B. Beckworth to George Williams, December 11, 1872; Pinchback to George Williams, December 11, 1872, in House Executive Documents, Forty-Second Congress, Third Session, VII, No. 91,23; LeeAnna Keith, *The Colfax Massacre: The Untold Story of Black Power, White Terror, and the Death of Reconstruction* (Oxford University Press, 2008).

14. *Louisiana Senate Journal*, Extra Session, 1872, 12–13; *Louisianian*, December 14, 1872.

15. *Acts Passed by the General Assembly*, 1873, Extra Session, No. 2, 10, 38–41; *New Orleans Republican*, December 14, 1872; Lerone Bennett Jr., *Black Power U.S.A.: The Human Side of Reconstruction* (Penguin Books, 1976), 262.

16. *New Orleans Republican*, December 13, 14, 1872; *Donaldsonville (LA) Chief*, December 14, 1872; George H. Williams to John McEnery, December 12 and December 13, 1872, in House Executive Documents, Forty-Second Congress, Third Session, VII, No. 91,23; Haskins, *The First Black Governor*, 169.

17. *New Orleans Republican*, December 12 and 14, 1872; P. B. S. Pinchback to President US Grant, and Adjunct-General of the United States Army, to W. H. Emory, December 14, 1872, in House Executive Documents, Forty-Second Congress, Third Session, VII, No. 91,24–25; *Acts Passed by the General Assembly*, 1873, Extra Session), 289: Grosz, "The Political Career," 659–570.

18. "Frederick Douglass on Louisianans," *Louisianian*, May 15, 1872; *New Orleans Republican*, December 19, 1872; Bennett, *Black Power*, 290; Taylor, *Louisiana Reconstructed*, 177–78; Bennett Jr., *Black Power USA.: The Human Side of Reconstruction*, 289.

19. *Louisiana Senate Journal, Executive Session: Extra Session of 1872 and Regular Session of 1873* (Government Printing Office) 216–31; Acts Passed by the General Assembly, 1873, Extra Session, No. 3.,42; "Our New State Government," *Louisianian*, December 14, 1872.

20. *Louisiana Senate Journal, Executive Session: Extra Session of 1872 and Regular Session of 1873*, 216–31; Acts Passed by the General Assembly of the State of Louisiana at the Extra Session Convened December 9, 1872, 40.

21. *Louisiana Senate Journal, Extra Session*, 1872, 22, 215, 217, 219, 221, 230; Mathias Reimann, "The Notary in American Legal History: The Fall and Rise of the Civil Law Tradition?" accessed August 26. 2024, http://www.consiglionotarilevenezia .it/file/news/9/mbCrowg5cA.pdf); Dennis C. Rousey, "Black Policemen in New Orleans During Reconstruction," *The Historian* 49, no.2 (February 1987), 223; Vanessa Flores-Robert, "Black Policemen in Jim Crow New Orleans" (master's thesis, University of New Orleans, 2011), 13; Eric Foner, *Reconstruction: America's Unfinished Revolution, 1863–1877* (Harper & Row, 1988), 356; Wayne Everard and Irene Wainwright, "New Orleans Incorporated: 200 Years of the City Charter," Exhibit, New Orleans Public Library, 19–22, accessed August 26, 2024, https://nutrias.org/~nopl/exhibits/charter/chartercontents.htm; Jo Ann Carrigan, "The Saffron Scourge: A History of Yellow Fever in Louisiana, 1796–1905" (PhD diss., Louisiana State University, 1961), 155, 179, 184, 478; Taylor, *Louisiana Reconstructed*, 154–55.

22. *Louisiana Senate Journal, Executive Session: Extra Session of 1872*, 217, 218, 225; "Notable Character of Old South Dead," *Times-Picayune*, May 8, 1821,9; "Frederick Douglass on Louisianans," reprinted from *New National Era* in *The Louisianian*, May 1872. Pinchback also issued five pardons during his term as governor. See, *Louisiana Senate Journal, Executive Session: Extra Session of 1872*, 219, 220, 224, 229, and *Index of the Executive Documents of the House of Representatives for the Second Session of the Forty-Fourth Congress, 1876–77*, Volume 9 (Government Printing Office, 1877), 392–97.

23. Act No. 4: "An Act to Punish the Crime of Bribery," Acts Passed by the General Assembly of the State of Louisiana, 42–44.

24. Act No. 5: "Relative to Extending the Time of Final Payment of the State Tax Collectors," and Act No. 6: "Providing for the Appointment of a Joint Committee on the Conduct of the Late Election in the State of Louisiana," Acts Passed by the General Assembly of the State of Louisiana, 44–45.

25. Act No. 5: "Relative to Extending the Time of Final Payment of the State Tax Collectors," and Act No. 6: "Providing for the Appointment of a Joint Committee on the Conduct of the Late Election in the State of Louisiana," Acts Passed by the General Assembly of the State of Louisiana, 44–45; *Louisianian*, November 23, 30, 1872; Joe Gray Taylor, *Louisiana Reconstructed, 1863–1877* (Louisiana State University Press, 1974), 239–40; Ella Lonn, *Reconstruction in Louisiana After 1868* (Russell & Russell, 1918), 170–76; 174fn7.

26. Act No. 7: "To Suppress Riots and Unlawful Assemblies," Acts Passed by the General Assembly of the State of Louisiana, 45–47; Haskins, *The First Black Governor*, 175.

27. Act No. 7: "To Suppress Riots and Unlawful Assemblies," 47; Henry Ogden to George H. Williams, January 5, 1873, in Edward McPherson, *Handbook of Politics for 1872: Being a Record of Important Political Action, National and State, From July 15, 1870 to July 15, 1872* (Philp & Solomons, 1873), 108; *New Orleans Republican*, January 5, 1873.

28. Act No. 8: "Prescribing the Duties and Powers of the Governor in Relations to Insubordination in Military Organizations Constituting a Part of the State Militia," 47–48; James W. Illingworth, "Crescent City Radicals: Black Working People and the Civil War in New Orleans" (PhD diss., University of California Santa Cruz, 2015), 380.

29. Act No. 9: "Appropriating Nineteen Thousand and Five Hundred Dollars," 48–49, and Act No. 10: "Making an Appropriation to Pay the Mileage and Per Diem of the Members," 49–50.

30. *New Orleans Republican*, January 14, 1873.

31. Alice Walker, "The Divided Life of Jean Toomer," *New York Times*, July 13, 1980.

32. *Louisianian*, December 14, 1872.

CHAPTER 9: "THE STAR OF MY HOPE"

1. Certificate of Election from P. B. S. Pinchback, December 30, 1872, *House Reports, Forty-Third Congress, First Session*, No. 599,1.

2. Jean Toomer Papers, Box 493, Folder 18, Yale University; Invitation to dinner in honor of P. B. S. Pinchback, US Senator of Louisiana, March 17, 1873, Box 81-2, Series H, Folder 56, Pinchback Papers, Howard University; "Governor Pinchback: Reception by the Leading Colored Citizens of the District," *New National Era*, February 6, 1873; "Ovation From White and Colored People," *Alexandria Gazette*, March 19, 1873.

3. Governor Pinchback (in Baltimore)," *New National Era*, March 27, 1873; Nicholas Patler, "The Startling Career of P. B. S. Pinchback: A Whirlwind Crusade to Bring Equality to Reconstructed Louisiana," in Matthew Lynch, ed., *Before Obama: A Reappraisal of Black Reconstruction Era Politicians* (Praeger Publishing, 2012), 222, 223; Agnes Smith Grosz, "The Political Career of Pinckney Benton Stewart Pinchback," *Louisiana Historical Quarterly* 27:2 (April, 1944)," 598n53; Elizabeth Dowling Taylor, *The Original Black Elite: Daniel Murray and the Story of a Forgotten Era* (Harper Collins, 2017), 26.

4. John Edmond, Gonzales, "William Pitt Kellogg: Reconstruction Governor of Louisiana, 1873–1877," *Louisiana Historical Quarterly* 29:2 (1946), 409–12, 413, 414–16; Roger A. Fischer, *The Segregation Struggle in Louisiana, 1862–1877* (University of Illinois Press, 1974), 51; John E. Fisher, *They Rode with Forrest and Wheeler* (McFarland, 1995), 169–70; Ezra J. Warner, *Generals in Gray: Lives of Confederate Commanders* (Louisiana State University Press, 1959), 284.

5. *Christian Recorder* article reprinted in *New National Era*, April 23, 1873.

6. Ibid.

7. To the Committee of Privileges and Elections of the Senate of the United States of the Forty-Third Congress, Box 81-2, Series H, Folder 56, Pinchback Papers, Howard University;

Grosz, "The Political Career of Pinckney Benton Stewart Pinchback," 592n47; Haskins, *The First Black Governor*, 199.

8. Grosz, "The Political Career," 592–94; Haskins, *The First Black Governor*, 200–201. Patler, "The Startling Career," 224–25.

9. Grosz, "The Political Career," 597; Haskins, *The First Black Governor*, 201; Patler, "The Startling Career," 225–26.

10. "n.d. Draft" of Pinchback defense to the Senate, P. B. S. Pinchback Papers, Box 81-1, Series G, Folder 31, Moorland-Spingarn Research Center, Howard University; Patler, "The Startling Career," 226; Grosz, "The Political Career," 594–94n96.

11. "n.d. Draft," Pinchback Papers; Celeste-Maria Bernier, *If I Survive: Frederick Douglas and Family in the Walter O. Evans Collection* (Edinburgh University Press), 309.

12. "Unvarnished Truth" and "Address of the Committee of Seventy," *Louisianian*, September 26, 1874.

13. Resolution that US Senate recognize validity of Pinchback claim, Pinchback Papers, 81-1, Series C, Howard University; Patler, "The Startling Career," 226–27; Grosz, "The Political Career," 597–98.

14. Pinchback to Bruce, December 3, 1878, Box 81-1, Series B, Folder 2; "n.d. Draft" of Pinchback defense to the Senate, P. B. S. Pinchback Papers, Box 81-1, Series G, Folder 31; and Pinchback narrative regarding the Norton controversy and his right to the Senate seat, Box 81-2, Series H, Folder 56, P. B. S., Pinchback Papers, Howard University; Patler, "The Startling Career," 226–28; *Official Journal of the Proceedings of the Senate of the State of Louisiana* (A. L. Lee, 1870), 230, 257, 284.

15. Untitled Pinchback speech, P. B. S. Pinchback Papers, Box 81-1, Series G, Howard University; Gonzales, 446; Patler, "The Startling Career," 228.

16. Untitled Pinchback speech, P. B. S. Pinchback Papers, Box 81-1, Series G, Howard University; Grosz, 600; Patler, "The Startling Career," 228.

17. "Governor Pinchback at Home: A Grand Ovation," *Louisianian*, March 27, 1875; Daily Picayune, September 16, 17, 19, 25, 30, 1875; Fischer, *The Segregation Struggle in Louisiana, 1862–1877*, 125–27; John W. Blassingame, *Black New Orleans, 1860–1880* (University of Chicago Press, 1973), 116–17.

18. "The City Board of School Directors," *Louisianian*, September 18, 1875; Fischer, *The Segregation Struggle*, 128–29.

19. P. B. S. Pinchback to Frederick Douglas, April 20, 1875, in Bernier, *If I Survive*, 306; *Louisianian*, December 12, 1874 and September 18, 1875; "Column," and "Temporary Abandonment of the Sake of Reform," *New Orleans Bulletin*, September 17, 1875; Fischer, *The Segregation Struggle*, 128–29; Blassingame, *Black New Orleans*, 117–18; Douglas R. Egerton, *The Wars of Reconstruction: The Brief, Violent History of America's Most Progressive Era* (Bloomsbury Press, 2014), 311; Peter J. Breaux, "William J. Brown and the Development of Education: A Retrospective on the Career of a State Superintendent of Public Education of African Descent in Louisiana" (PhD diss., Florida State University, 2006), 165–67.

20. "Column" and "Temporary Abandonment of the Sake of Reform," *New Orleans Bulletin*, September 17, 1875; "People's Column," *Louisianian*, September 18, 1875; Blassingame, *Black New Orleans*, 117–18; A. I. Kennedy, "The History of Public Education in New Orleans Still Matters," *History Faculty Publications* (2006) Paper 5, accessed

August 12, 2024, http://scholarworks.uno.edu/hist_facpubs/5; Breaux, "William J. Brown and the Development of Education," 168.

21. Temporary Abandonment of the Sake of Reform," *New Orleans Bulletin*, September 17, 1875.

22. Grosz, "The Political Career," 600n38, 601; Patler, "The Startling Career," 220, 229.

23. Pinchback's Case Before the County, New York *Herald*, February 12, 1876, Box 81-2, Series H, Folder 56, Pinchback Papers, Howard University.

24. Pinchback speech, Box 81-2, Series H, Folder 56, Pinchback Papers, Howard University.

25. *New York Herald* quoted in *New Orleans Times*, February 17, 1876; Phillip Dray, *Capitol Men: The Epic Story of Reconstruction Through the Lives of the First Black Congressmen* (Houghton Mifflin, 2008), 227–28.

26. *Congressional Record Containing the Proceedings and Debates of the Forty-Fourth Congress, Volume IV*, 1444–45; McFarlin, *Black Congressional Reconstruction Orators and Their Orations*, 10–11.

27. *Congressional Record Containing the Proceedings and Debates of the Forty-Forth Congress, First Session, Volume IV*, 1444–45; McFarlin, *Black Congressional Reconstruction Orators and Their Orations*, 11–12.

28. Grosz, "The Political Career," 601–2n50; Patler, "The Startling Career," 231.

29. *Congressional Record Containing the Proceedings and Debates of the Forty-Fourth Congress, First Session, Volume IV*, 1545, 1550, 1553, 1557; Belknap impeachment debate, 1522–1540; *New Orleans Republican*, March 14, 1876; Patler, "The Starling Career," 230–31, and "The Black 'Consummate Strategist,'" 36–37; Agnes Smith Grosz, "The Political Career of Pinckney Benton Stewart Pinchback," *The Louisiana Historical Quarterly* 27:2 (April 1944), 601–2.

30. Edward E. Bruce Grit, "Draft Statement on PBS Pinchback's 80th Birthday," May 1917, in Bernier, *If I Survive*, 306; Grosz, "The Political Career," 601–2n50; Patler, *The Startling Career*," 211, 212, 231; Lerone Bennett, Jr., *Black Power U.S.A.: The Human Side of Reconstruction, 1867–1877* (Baltimore Penguin Books, 1967), 296.

31. "Pinchback," *New Orleans Democrat*, March 9, 1876; "Political Talk," *New Orleans Bulletin*, March 10, 1876; Frederick Douglass, "The Country Has not Heard the Last of P. B. S. Pinchback: An Address Delivered in Washington, DC on 13 March 1876," in Bernier, *If I Survive*, 308; Patler, "The Startling Career," 232; Pinchback Speech, Box 81-2, Series H, Folder 56, Pinchback Papers, Howard University.

CHAPTER 10: AFTER RECONSTRUCTION

1. Pinchback to Bruce, October 14, 1878, and Pinchback to Bruce, September 29, 1879, Bruce Papers, Box 9-2, Folder 69, Moorland-Spingarn, Howard University.

2. Pinchback to Francis Nicholls, undated correspondence, Box 81-1, Series B, Folder 4; "The President's Southern Policy: Letter to Hon. O.P. Morton," Box 81-1, Series E, Folder 27, Pinchback Papers, Moorland-Spingarn, Howard University; Matthew Lynch, "John Roy Lynch's Account of the Republican Abandonment of the Negro," in Matthew Lynch,

ed., *Before Obama: A Reappraisal of Black Reconstruction Era Politicians* (Praeger, 2012), 144–45; Luis-Alejandro Dinnella-Borrego, *The Risen Phoenix: Black Politics in the Post-Civil War South* (University of Virginia Press, 2016), 119; William Ivy Hair, *Bourbonism and Agrarian Protest: Louisiana Politics, 1877–1900* (Louisiana State University Press, 1969), 20–23; Robert A. Fischer, *The Segregation Struggle in Louisiana, 1862–1877* (University of Illinois Press, 1974), 136–37; Taylor, *Louisiana Reconstructed*, 499–500.

3. Steven Hahn, *A Nation Under Our Feet: Black Political Struggles in the Rural South from Slavery to the Great Migration* (Harvard University Press, 2003), 319–20, 330–31, 360–61.

4. Fischer, *The Segregation Struggle in Louisiana*, 144–45; Pinchback to T. I. Galbraith, June 17, 1879, Pinchback Papers, Box 81-1, Series B, Folder 2, Moorland-Spingarn Research Center, Howard University.

5. Constitution of the State of Louisiana, 1879, adopted in convention at New Orleans, July 23, 1879 (J. S. Cosgrove, 1879), 46; Germain A. Reed, "Race Legislation in Louisiana, 1864–1920," *Louisiana History: The Journal of the Louisiana Historical Association* 6:4 (Autumn 1965), 391; P. B. S. Pinchback to Doctor, November 24, 1884, Box 81-1, Series B, Folder 2, and Pinchback, untitled speech, n.d., Box 81-2, Folder 45, Pinchback Papers, Howard University.

6. Constitution of the State of Louisiana, 1879, 7. Today, the P. B. S. Pinchback Engineering Building is located on the Baton Rouge campus, and a plaque on it summarizes his life and work.

7. Robert Peterson, *Only the Ball Was White: A History of Legendary Black Player and All-Black Professional Teams* (Oxford University Press, 1970), 38; Dale A. Somers, *The Rise of Sports in New Orleans* (Louisiana State University Press, 1972), 120–21, 181–83, 186–90, "The Pinchbacks Baseball Brigade," *Times-Democrat* (New Orleans), August 28, 1888.

8. P. B. S. Pinchback Speech on Constitutionality of State Constitutions, Testimonial Banquet, Box 81-1, Series G, Folder 37, Pinchback Papers, Howard University; J. Morgan Kousser, "Before Plessy, Before Brown: The Development of the Law of Racial Integration in Louisiana and Kansas," Social Science Working Paper 681, October 1988,26, note 68, Division of Humanities and Social Sciences, The California Institute of Technology; Henry Dumas, "Speech of Hon. Henry Dumas on the Separate Car Bill, Delivered to the Senate at Baton Rouge, July 8, 1890," *The (New Orleans) Crusader*, July 19, 1890; Germaine A. Reed, "Race Legislation in Louisiana, 1864–1920," *Louisiana History: The Journal of the Louisiana Historical Association* 6:4 (Autumn 1965), 383, 387, 388.

9. Jean Toomer Papers, Series II, Box 18, Folder 493, Yale University.

10. Jean Toomer Papers, Series II, Box 18, Folder 493, Yale University; Gatewood, *Black Aristocrats of Color*, 4, 191; Elizabeth Dowling Taylor, *The Original Black Elite: Daniel Murray and the Story of a Forgotten Era* (Amistad/HarperCollins, 2017), 85. Today the house still stands, but Bacon Street has been changed to Harvard Street.

11. P. B. S. Pinchback's eulogy/speech of Frederick Douglass, Series G, Box 81-2, Howard University.

12. Kerman and Eldridge, *The Lives of Jean Toomer*, 23–24, 25–26, 27, 28, 29; Gatewood, *Black Aristocrats of Color*, 4, 191; McKay, *Jean Toomer, Artist: A Study of His Literary Life and Work, 1894–1936* (University of North Carolina Press, 1984), 20; Kent Anderson Leslie and Willard B. Gatewood, Jr., "'The Father of Mine . . . A Sort of Mystery': Jean Toomer's Georgia Heritage," *The Georgia Historical Quarterly* 77:4 (Winter 1993), 789, 790, 793, 798.

13. "*Washington Bee*, March 12, 1898; "An Appeal to the Governors Legislators and Judicial Officers of the Southern States," Box 81-2, Series H, Box 56. Pinchback Papers, Howard University; Taylor, *The Original Black Elite*, 175–76–177, 181–83, 204–5, 248.

14. Nina, who had remarried and was happily living in Rochelle, New York, "died suddenly after an operation for appendicitis at her home," likely from an infection, *Washington Bee*, July 3. 1809. Standard Certificate of Death for P. N. Pinchback, Maricopa, Arizona (Pinckney Napoleon Pinchback [1863–1900] , accessed October 1, 2024, https://www.findagrave.com/memorial). Pinckney Jr. had been a pharmacist in Philadelphia and is believed to have been the first African American graduate of the Philadelphia College of Pharmacy, see Daniel Flanagan, "Earliest Known Black Graduates of the Philadelphia College of Pharmacy," *History of Pharmacy and Pharmaceuticals* 60: 1&2 (2018), 29.

15. P. B. S. Pinchback Speech on State Constitution Amendments, Box 81-2, Series G. Folder 43 and 44; P. B. S. Speech Delivered at A. M. E. Zion Church, Box 81-2, Series G, Folder 49; and "Our Advice to the Negroes," Box 81-2, Series H, Folder 56, Pinchback Papers, Howard University; Taylor, *The Original Black Elite*, 147–78.

16. Gatewood, *Aristocrats of Color*, 304; Booker T. Washington, *My Larger Education: Being Chapters From My Experience* (Doubleday, Page., 1911), 104; Charles Scruggs and Lee Vademarr, *Jean Toomer and the Terrors of American History* (University of Pennsylvania Press, 1998), 44–45; Louis R. Harlan, *Booker T. Washington: The Wizard of Tuskegee, Volume II, 1910-1915* (Oxford University Press, 1983), 77; Louis Harlan and Raymond W. Smock, eds., *The Booker T. Washington Papers, Volume 6: 1901-02* (University of Illinois Press, 1977), 86n1; P. B. S. Pinchback Speech Delivered at A. M. E. Zion Church, Box 81-2, Series G, Folder 49, Pinchback Papers, Howard University; P. B. S. Pinchback to Whitefield McKinlay, August 18, 1912, Whitefield McKinlay Papers, Carter G. Woodson Collection, Library of Congress.

17. Jean Toomer Papers, Series II, Box 18, Folder 493, Yale University; Kerman and Eldridge, *The Lives of Jean Toomer*, 24–25, 32; Barbara Foley, *Jean Toomer: Race, Repression, and Revolution* (University Of Illinois Press, 2014), 278–79n41; Jean Toomer to *The Liberator*, August 19, 1922, in Frederik L. Rusch , ed., *A Jean Toomer Reader: Selected Unpublished Writings* (Oxford University Press, 1993), 16: Taylor, *The Original Black Elite*, 380.

18. Darwin Turner, ed., *The Wayward and the Seeking: A Collection of Writings by Jean Toomer* (Howard University Press, 1983) 24,70–71; Kerman and Eldridge, *The Lives of Jean Toomer*, 32–33, 34; Byrd and Gates, "Afterword," *Cane*, 170.

19. Rudolph P. Byrd and Henry Louis Gates Jr., "Afterword," in Jean Toomer, *Cane* (Liveright, 2011), 169–70, 188–90, 191–92, 193: in all census records between 1850 and 1910, "Jean Toomer's mother, father, grandfather and grandmother all self-identified as Negroes," 232; Turner, ed., *The Wayward and the Seeking*, 70–71.

20. Turned, ed., *The Wayward and the Seeking*, 89, 117, 118, 122; Byrd and Gates, "Afterword," 199–200; Taylor, *The Original Black Elite*, 380–81.

21. Byrd and Gates, "Afterword," 207, 208–9; Turner, ed., *The Wayward and the Seeking*, 124.

22. Jean Toomer, *Cane* (Liveright Publishing Corporation, 2011), 117.

23. Byrd and Gates explain that this was "one of his last admissions of his awareness of the primacy of his own Negro ancestry in the shaping of his cultural and ethnic identity." Foley, *Jean Toomer: Race, Repression, and Revolution*, 75, 179; Byrd and Gates, "Afterword,"

172; Jean Toomer to *The Liberator*, August 19, 1922, in Rusch, ed., *A Jean Toomer Reader*, 16; Darwin Turner, ed., *Cane: An Authoritative Text, Backgrounds, and Criticisms* (Norton, 1988), 156.

24. Turner, ed., *The Wayward and the Seeking*, 124.

25. P. B. S. Pinchback death certificate, Orleans Parish Death Certificates, Volume 0, Page, 4683, Louisiana State Archives, Baton Rouge. Walter died in 1938. He was a graduate of Howard Law School, had served as a lieutenant in the Spanish-American War, practiced law in Washington, and became a local activist there, working for Black and female suffrage, (2LT Walter Alexis Pinchback [1871–1938] accessed October 1, 2024, https://www.findagrave.com/memorial). Bismarck died in 1924 and had been employed as an auditor for the Navy Department for twenty years, "B. R. Pinchback Dead," *Washington Times*, February 28, 1924. His cause of death is unknown.

26. Haskins, *The First Black Governor*, 258; Kaelin Maloid, "Prominent New Orleans' Activist Dies," March 27, 2019, *New Orleans Data News Weekly*, accessed August 14. 2024, https://ladatanews.com/prominent-new-orleans-civil-rights-activist-dies-at-89/); Louisiana Justice Institute Profile: Reverend Sampson "Skip" Alexander, posted by Justin Flaherty, March 3, 2010, accessed August 14, 2024, https://louisianajusticeinstitute.blogspot.com/search?q=skip+alexander

27. S. Pinchback to Francis Grimke, July 12, 1916, in Carter G. Woodson, ed., *The Works of Francis J. Grimke, Volume IV: Letters* (The Associated Publishers, Inc., 1942), 179.

BIBLIOGRAPHY

ARCHIVES AND COLLECTIONS

Beinecke Rare Book and Manuscript Library, Yale University
    Jean Toomer Papers
Caswell County, NC Historical Association
Holmes County Chancery Office, Lexington, Mississippi
    Deeds Records
    Mississippi Census
    Will Abstracts
Lexington, Mississippi, Public Library
    William Pinchback File
Library of Congress, Manuscript Division
    Whitefield McKinlay Papers
    Carter G. Woodson Collection
Louisiana State Archives, Baton Rouge
    P. B. S. Pinchback Death Certificate
Moorland-Spingarn Research Center, Howard University
    P. B. S. Pinchback Papers
    Blanche Kelso Bruce Papers
New Orleans Public Library, Louisiana Division
    Pinchback/Hawthorn Marriage License
University of Illinois, Urbana-Champaign
    Booker T. Washington Papers
Wilson Library, University of North Carolina
    Henry Clay Warmoth Papers
North Carolina Collection

GOVERNMENT RECORDS AND DOCUMENTS

Acts Passed by the General Assembly of Louisiana
    Third Session of the First Legislature
    Extra Session, 1872
    Extra Session, 1873
Acts of the State of Louisiana
Congressional Globe, Forty-Second Congress
Third Session, House Executive Documents
Congressional Record, Forty-Second Congress
    First Session, Appendix
Congressional Record, Forty-Fourth Congress
    First Session, Special Session
Congressional Record, Forty-Sixth Congress
    Second Session
Francis Newton Thorpe, ed., *The Federal and State Constitutions, Colonial Charters, and Other Organic Laws of the States, Territories, and Colonies Now or Heretofore Forming the United States of America*
House Executive Documents, Forty-Second Congress
    Third Session
House Miscellaneous Documents, Forty-Second Congress
    Second Session
House Reports, Forty-Third Congress
    First Session
Index of the Executive Documents of the House of Representatives for the Second Session of the Forty-Fourth Congress
Louisiana Senate Journal 1868, 1869, 1870, Extra Session of 1872
Louisiana House Journal
Official Records of the Union and Confederate Navies in the War of the Rebellion
Official Journal of the Convention for Framing a Constitution for the State of Louisiana, 1867–1868
Official Journal of the Proceedings of the House of Representatives of the State of Louisiana
Official Journal of the Proceedings of the Senate of the State of Louisiana
Official Report of the Proceedings, Addresses and Resolutions of the Republican State Convention of Louisiana
Proceedings of the National Republican Convention Held at Philadelphia, June 5 & 6, 1872
Reports of Cases Argued and Determined in the Supreme Court of Louisiana
Series of United States Public Documents, 1875
Southern Reporter, Volume Containing All the Decisions of the Supreme Courts of Alabama, Louisiana, Florida, Mississippi, Volume 42
The Congressional Globe and the Debates and the Proceedings of the Third Session Forty-Second Congress
1840 US Federal Census, Ancestry.com

NEWSPAPERS

Alexandria (LA) Democrat
Alexandria (LA) Gazette
New Orleans Crusader
Atchison (KS) Daily Champion
New Orleans Daily Picayune
New Orleans Republican
New Orleans Crescent
New Orleans Commercial Bulletin
New York Commercial Advertiser
Natchitoches (LA) Times
Opelousas (LA) Journal
New Amsterdam News
New York Herald
New National Era
New Orleans Times
New Orleans Bulletin
New York Times
New Mexico Sentinel
Rochester (NY) Democrat and Chronicle
Washington Bee
Bossier (LA) Banner
Louisianian
South-Western (Shreveport, LA)
Terre Haute (IN) Tribune Star
Weekly Echo (Lake Charles, LA)
Louisiana Democrat
Morning Star and Catholic Messenger (New Orleans)
Philadelphia Evening Bulletin
Donaldsonville (LA) Chief

BOOKS

Barry, John M. *Rising Tide: The Great Mississippi Flood of 1927 and How It Changed America.* Touchstone Books, 1997.

Bash, Dana and David Fisher. *America's Deadliest Election: The Cautionary Tale of America's Most Violent Election in American History.* Hanover Square Press, 2024.

Behrend, Justin. *Reconstructing Democracy: Grassroots Black Politics in the Deep South After the Civil War.* University of Georgia Press, 2015.

Bennett Jr., Lerone. *Before the Mayflower: A History of the Negro in America, 1619–1964.* Penguin Books, 1970.

Bennett Jr., Lerone. *Black Power USA: The Human Side of Reconstruction, 1866–1877*. Penguin Books, 1967.

Berlin, Ira, et al., eds., *Freedom: A Documentary History of Emancipation, 1861–1867*, Series II. New York 1982.

Bernier, Celeste-Maria. *If I Survive: Frederick Douglas Family in the Walter O. Evans Collection*. Edinburgh University Press, 2018.

Blassingame, John W. *Black New Orleans*. University of Chicago Press, 1973.

Bontemps, Arna. *One Hundred Years of Negro Freedom*. Dodd, Mead, 1961.

Buchanan, Thomas E. *Black Life on the Mississippi: Slaves, Free Blacks and the Western Steamboat World*. Chapel Hill: The University of North Carolina Press, 2004.

Burgess, John. *Reconstruction and the Constitution, 1866–1876*. Charles Scribner's and Sons, 1907.

Byrd, Rudolph P. and Henry Louis Gates Jr., "Afterword," in Jean Toomer, *Cane*. Liveright Press, 2011.

Campbell, Will D. *Providence*. Baylor University Press, 2002.

Coulter, E. Merton. *The South During Reconstruction, 1865–1877*. Louisiana State University Press, 1947.

Current, Richard Nelson. *Those Terrible Carpetbaggers*. Oxford University Press, 1988.

Dawson III, Joseph G., ed. *The Louisiana Governors: From Iberville to Edwards*. Louisiana State University Press, 1990.

Dawson, Joseph G. *Army Generals and Reconstruction, Louisiana 1862–1877* (New Orleans: Louisiana State University Press, 1982.

Devol, George. *Forty Years a Gambler on the Mississippi*. Home Book Company, 1887.

Dineen-Wimberly, Ingrid. *The Allure of Blackness among Mixed-Race Americans, 1862–1913*. University of Nebraska Press, 2019.

Dinnella-Borrego, Luis-Alejandro. *The Risen Phoenix: Black Politics in the Post-Civil War South*. University of Virginia Press, 2016.

Dowling Taylor, Elizabeth. *The Original Black Elite: Daniel Murray and the Story of a Forgotten Era*. Amistad/HarperCollins, 2017.

Dray, Phillip. *Capitol Men: The Epic Story of Reconstruction Through the Lives of the First Black Congressmen*. Houghton Mifflin Co., 2008.

Du Bois, W.E.B. *Black Reconstruction in America, 1860–1880*. Free Press, 1998.

Dunning, William Archibald. *Reconstruction Political and Economic, 1865–1877*. Harper Brothers Publishers, 1907.

Egerton, Douglas R. *The Wars of Reconstruction: The Brief, Violent History of America's Most Progressive Era*. Bloomsbury 2014.

Faulkner, Carol. *Women's Radical Reconstruction: The Freedmen's Aid Movement*. University of Pennsylvania Press, 2004.

Finkelman, Paul and Stephen E. Gottlieb, eds. *Toward A Usable Past: Liberty Under State Constitutions*. University of Georgia Press, 2009.

Fisher, John E. *They Rode with Forrest and Wheeler*. McFarland, 1995.

Fischer, Robert A. *The Segregation Struggle in Louisiana, 1862–77*. University of Illinois Press, 1974.

Fogel, Robert William. *Without Consent or Contract: The Rise and Fall of American Slavery*. W. W. Norton, 1994.

Foley, Edward. *Ballot Battles: The History of Disputed Elections in the United States.* Oxford University Press, 2016.
Foner, Eric. *Reconstruction: America's Unfinished Revolution, 1866–1877.* Harper & Row, 1988.
Foner, Eric. *Freedom's Lawmakers: A Directory of Black Officeholders During Reconstruction.* Louisiana State University Press, 1996.
Franklin, John Hope. *From Slavery to Freedom: A History of Negro Americans.* Alfred A. Knopf, 1969.
Gatewood, Willard. B. *Black Aristocrats of Color: The Black Elite, 1880–1920.* Indiana University Press, 1990.
Grant, Richard. *Dispatches From Pluto: Lost and Found in the Mississippi Delta.* Simon & Schuster, 2015.
Gordon-Reed, Annette. *The Hemingses of Monticello.* W. W. Norton, 2008.
Hahn, Stephen. *A Nation Under Our Feet: Black Political Struggles in the Rural South from Slavery to the Great Migration.* Harvard University Press, 2005.
Hair, William Ivy. *Bourbonism and Agrarian Protest: Louisiana Politics, 1877–1900.* Louisiana State University Press, 1969.
Hairston, L. Beatrice W. *A Brief History of Danville, Virginia, 1728–1954.* The Deitz Press Incorporated, 1955.
Haskins, James. *P. B. S. Pinchback: The First Black Governor.* Africa World Press, 1996.
Harlan, Louis R. *Booker T. Washington: The Wizard of Tuskegee, Volume II, 1910–1915.* Oxford University Press, 1983.
Harris, William H. *The Day of the Carpetbagger: Republican Reconstruction in Mississippi.* Louisiana State University Press, 1979.
Hollandsworth Jr., James G. *The Louisiana Native Guards: The Black Military Experience During the Civil War.* Louisiana State University Press, 1995.
Houzeau, Jean-Charles. *My Passage at the New Orleans Tribune: A Memoir of the Civil War Era.* Louisiana State University Press, 1984.
Hume, Richard L. and Jerry B. Gough. *Blacks, Carpetbaggers, and Scalawags: The Constitutional Conventions of Radical Reconstruction.* Louisiana State University Press, 2000.
Ingham. John and Lynne B. Feldman. *African American Business Leaders: A Biographical Dictionary.* Greenwood Press, 1994.
Kein, Sybil. *Creole: The History and Legacy of Louisiana's Free People of Color.* Louisiana State University Press, 2000.
Kerman, Cynthia Earl and Richard Eldridge, *The Lives of Jean Toomer: A Hunger for Wholeness.* Louisiana State University Press, 1987.
LaRoche, Cheryl Janifer. *The Geography of Resistance: Free Black Communities and the Underground Railroad.* University of Illinois Press, 2014.
Lankford, George E., ed., *Bearing Witness: Memories of Arkansas Slavery: Narratives From the 1930s WPA Collection.* University of Arkansas Press, 2003.
Lau, Peter F. ed., *From the Grassroots to the Supreme Court: Brown v. Board of Education and American Democracy.* Duke University Press, 2004.
Litwack, Leon F. and August Meier, eds., *Black Leaders of the Nineteenth Century.* University of Illinois Press, 1991.

Loewen, James. *Lies My Teacher Told Me: Everything Your American History Textbook Got Wrong*. The New Press, 1994.

Lynch, ed., Matthew. *Before Obama: A Reappraisal of Black Reconstruction Era Politicians*. Praeger Publishing, 2012.

Keith, LeeAnna, *The Colfax Massacre: The Untold Story of Black Power, White Terror, and the Death of Reconstruction*. Oxford University Press, 2008.

McCaul, Robert L. *The Black Struggle for Public Schooling in Nineteenth-Century Illinois*. Southern Illinois University Press, 1987.

McKay. *Jean Toomer, Artist: A Study of His Literary Life and Work, 1894–1936*. University of North Carolina Press, 1984.

McPherson, Edward. *Handbook of Politics for 1872: Being a Record of Important Political Action, National and State, From July 15, 1870 to July 15, 1872*. Philp & Solomons, 1873.

Mitchell, Brian K., Barrington S. Edwards, and Nick Weldon, *Monumental: Oscar Dunn and His Radical Fight in Reconstruction Louisiana*. The Historic New Orleans Collection 2021.

Nordhoff, Charles. *The Cotton States in the Spring and Summer of 1875*. D. Appleton, 1876.

Painter, Nell Irvin. *Creating Black Americans: African American History and Its Meanings, 1619 to Present*. Oxford University Press, 2007.

Patler, Nicholas. *Jim Crow and the Wilson Administration: Protesting Federal Segregation in the Early Twentieth Century*. University Press of Colorado, 2007.

Payne, Charles M. and Adam Green, ed., *Time Longer Than Rope: A Century of African American Activism, 1850–1950*. New York University Press, 2003.

Peterson, Robert. *Only the Ball Was White: A History of Legendary Black Player and All-Black Professional Teams*. Oxford University Press, 1970.

Redding, J. Saunders. *They Came in Chains: Americans from Africa*. Lippincott, 1950.

Redkey, Edwin S., ed. *A Grand Army of Black Men: Letters from African American Soldiers in the Union Army, 1861–1865*. Cambridge University Press, 1992.

Reid, Whitelaw. *After the War: A Tour of the Southern States, 1865–1866*. Reprint from 1866: Harper Torch Books, 1965.

Rhodes, James Ford. *History of the United States from the Compromise of 1850 to the McKinley-Bryan Campaign of 1896, Volume VII*. MacMillian 1920.

Roberts, Alasdair. *America's First Great Depression: Economic Crisis and Political Disorder After the Panic of 1837*. Cornell University Press, 2012.

Rousseve, Charles. *The Negro in Louisiana*. Xavier University Press, 1937.

Rusch, Frederick L., ed. *A Jean Toomer Reader: Selected Unpublished Writings*. Oxford University Press, 1993.

Sapp, Andrew L. *The Doom of Reconstruction: The Liberal Republicans in the Civil War Era*. Fordham University Press, 2006.

Satcher, Buford. *Blacks in Mississippi Politics, 1865–1900*. University Press of America, 1978.

Scruggs, Charles and Lee Vademarr, *Jean Toomer and the Terrors of American History*. University of Pennsylvania Press, 1998.

Shugg, Roger. *Origins of Class Struggle in Louisiana: A Social History of White Farmers and Laborers During Slavery and After, 1840–1875*. Louisiana State University Press, 1939.

Simmons, William J. *Men of Mark: Eminent, Progressive and Rising*. George M. Rewell, 1887.

Stern, Walter C. *Race and Education in New Orleans: Creating the Segregated City, 1764–1960.* Louisiana State University Press, 2018.
Somers, Dale A. *The Rise of Sports in New Orleans.* Louisiana State University Press, 1972.
Taylor, Elizabeth Dowling. *The Original Black Elite: Daniel Murray and the Story of a Forgotten Era.* Harper Collins, 2017.
Taylor, John Gray. *Louisiana Reconstructed, 1863–1877.* Louisiana State University Press, 1974.
Taylor, Nikki. *Frontiers of Freedom: Cincinnati's Free Black Community, 1802–1868.* Ohio University Press, 2005.
Toomer, Jean. "Jean Toomer to Waldo Frank, September 1923." In *Cane: An Authoritative Text, Backgrounds, and Criticisms,* edited by Darwin Turner. Norton, 1988.
Trotter, James M. *Music and Some Highly Musical People.* Lee and Shepard, 1881.
Turkel, Stanley. *Heroes of the American Reconstruction: Profiles of Sixteen Educators, Politicians and Activists.* McFarland, 2005.
Turner, Darwin, ed. *The Wayward and the Seeking: A Collection of Writings by Jean Toomer.* Howard University Press, 1980.
Twain, Mark. *Life on the Mississippi.* Reader's Digest Association, 1987.
Vincent, Charles. *Black Legislators in Louisiana During Reconstruction.* Louisiana State University Press, 1976.
Warner, Ezra J. *Generals in Gray: Lives of Confederate Commanders.* Louisiana State University Press, 1959.
Warmoth, Henry Clay. *War, Politics, and Reconstruction: Stormy Days in Louisiana.* University of South Carolina Press, 2006.
Washington, Booker T. *My Larger Education: Being Chapters From My Experience* (Doubleday, Page, 1911.
White, Allyson. *A Chosen Exile: A History of Racial Passing in American Life.* Harvard University, 2014.
Williams, T. Harry. *Huey Long: A Biography.* Penguin, 1969.
Willis, John C. *Forgotten Time: The Yazoo-Mississippi Delta After the Civil War.* University Press of Mississippi, 2000.
Wilson, Joseph Thomas. *The Black Phalanx: A History of the Negro Soldiers in the Wars of 1775, 1812, 1861–1865.* Reprint Wentworth Press, 2016.
Wiltshire, Betty Couch. *Holmes County, Mississippi Pioneers.* Heritage Books, 1995.
Woodson, Carter G. and Charles H. Wesley, *The Negro in Our History.* Associated Publishers, 1962.
Woodson, Carter G. and Charles H. Wesley. *The Works of Francis J. Grimke, Volume IV: Letters.* Associated Publishers, 1942.
Yafa, Stephen. *Big Cotton: How a Humble Fiber Created Fortunes, Wrecked Civilizations, and Put America on the Map.* Penguin, 2005.

JOURNAL ARTICLES AND OTHER COMPILATIONS

Belz, Herman. "Origins of Negro Suffrage During the Civil War," *Southern Studies* 17, no. 2 (Summer 1978).

Binning, Wayne. "Carpetbagger's Triumph: The Louisiana Election of 1868." *Louisiana History* 14 (Winter, 1973).

Crenshaw, Gwendolyn. *Bury Me in a Free Land: The Abolitionist Movement in Indiana, 1816–1865*. Indiana Historical Bureau, 1993.

Davis, Donald W. "Ratification of the Constitution of 1868—Record of Votes." *Louisiana History: The Journal of the Louisiana Historical Association* 6, no. 3 (Summer 1965).

Fisher, Roger A. "A Pioneer Protest: The New Orleans Streetcar Controversy of 1867." *Journal of Negro History* 53, no. 3 (July 1968).

Flanagan, Daniel. "Earliest Known Black Graduates of the Philadelphia College of Pharmacy." *History of Pharmacy and Pharmaceuticals* 60, nos. 1/2 (2018).

Franke, Catherine M. "Becoming a Citizen: Reconstruction Era Regulation of African American Marriages." *Yale Journal of Law and the Humanities* 11, no. 2 (Summer 1999).

Gonzales, John Edmond. "William Pitt Kellogg: Reconstruction Governor of Louisiana, 1873–1877." *Louisiana Historical Quarterly* 29, no. 2 (1946).

Grosz, Agnes. "The Political Career of P. B. S. Pinchback." *The Louisiana Historical Quarterly* 27, no. 2 (April 1944).

Grenier, Judson A. "'Officialdom': California State Government, 1849–1879." *California History* 8, nos. 3/4 (2003).

Jones, Howard. "Biographical Sketches of Members of the 1868 Louisiana State Senate." *Louisiana History*, 19, no. 1 (Winter 1978).

Leslie, Kent Anderson and Willard B. Gatewood Jr. "'The Father of Mine . . . A Sort of Mystery:' Jean Toomer's Georgia Heritage." *The Georgia Historical Quarterly* 77, no. 4 (Winter 1993).

Lynch, Matthew. "John Roy Lynch's Account of the Republican Abandonment of the Negro." In Matthew Lynch, ed., *Before Obama: A Reappraisal of Black Reconstruction Era Politicians* (Praeger, 2012).

McDaniel, Hilda Mulvey. "Francis Tillou Nicholls and the End of Reconstruction," *Louisiana Historical Quarterly* 32 (April 1949).

Patler, Nicholas. "The Startling Career of P. B. S. Pinchback: A Whirlwind Crusade to Bring Equality to Reconstructed Louisiana." *Before Obama: A Reappraisal of Black Reconstruction Era Politicians* (Praeger, 2012).

Perkins, A. E. "James Henri Bruch and Oscar James Dunn in Louisiana." *Journal of Negro History* 22 (July 1937).

Perkins, A. E. "Some Negro Officers and Legislators in Louisiana." *Journal of Negro History* 14 (October 1929).

Porter, Betty. "The History of Negro Education in Louisiana." *Louisiana Historical Quarterly* 25 (July 1942).

"Reconstructing Pinchback: The Story of Gov. P. B. S. Pinchback." February 10, 2011, *Ezine Articles*.

Reed, Germain A. "Race Legislation in Louisiana, 1864–1920." *Louisiana History: The Journal of the Louisiana Historical Association* 6, no. 4 (Autumn 1965).

Reynolds, Donald E. "The New Orleans Race Riot of 1866." *Louisiana History: The Journal of the Louisiana Historical Association* 5, no. 1 (Winter 1964).
Rousey, Dennis C. "Black Policemen in New Orleans During Reconstruction." *The Historian* 49, no. 2 (February 1987).
Staples, Brent. "Escape into Whiteness." *New York Times Book Review*, November 24, 2011.
Taylor, Alrutheus. "Negro Congressmen a Generation Later." *The Journal of Negro History* 7, no. 2 (April 1922).
Vincent, Charles. "Negro Leadership and Programs in the Louisiana Constitutional Convention of 1868," *Louisiana History: The Journal of the Louisiana Historical Association* 10, no. 4 (Autumn, 1969).
Weisberger, Bernard A. "The Carpetbagger." *American Heritage* 25, no. 1 (1973).

DISSERTATIONS/THESES/PAPERS

Binning, Francis Wayne. "Henry Clay Warmoth and the Louisiana Reconstruction." PhD diss., University of North Carolina, 1969.
Breaux, Peter J. "William J. Brown and the Development of Education: A Retrospective on the Career of a State Superintendent of Public Education of African Descent in Louisiana." PhD diss., Florida State University, 2006.
Carrigan, Jo Ann. "The Saffron Scourge: A History of Yellow Fever in Louisiana, 1796–1905." PhD diss., Louisiana State University, 1961.
Christensen, Matthew. "The 1868 St. Landry Massacre: Reconstruction's Deadliest Episode of Violence." Master's thesis, University of Wisconsin-Milwaukee, 2012.
Davis, Henry Ian. "For Civilization and Citizenship: Emancipation, Empire, and the Creation of the Black-Citizen Soldier Tradition." PhD diss., Mississippi State University, 2021.
Devore, Donald E. "Race Relations and Community Development: The Education of Blacks in New Orleans, 1962–1960." PhD diss., Louisiana State University, 1989.
Flores-Robert, Vanessa. "Black Policemen in Jim Crow New Orleans." Master's thesis, University of New Orleans, 2011.
Gates Jr., Paul H. "Toward a Common Goal: Jean-Charles Houzeau, P. B. S. Pinchback and New Orleans' Black Press, 1862–1882." Unpublished paper, College of Journalism and Communications, University of Florida, 1993.
Griffin Jr., John Chander. "Jean Toomer: American Writer (A Biography)." PhD diss., University of South Caroline, 1976.
Hall, Douglas M. "Public Education in Louisiana During the War Between the States with Special Reference to New Orleans." Master's thesis, Louisiana State University, 1940.
Illingworth, James W. "Crescent City Radicals: Black Working People and the Civil War in New Orleans." PhD diss., University of California Santa Cruz, 2015.
Kousser, J. Morgan. "Before Plessy, Before Brown: The Development of the Law of Racial Integration in Louisiana and Kansas." Social Science Working Paper 681, October 1988, p. 26, note 68, Division of Humanities and Social Sciences, California Institute of Technology.

Lynn, Louis August. "A History of Teachers' Institutes of Louisiana, 1870–1921." PhD diss., Louisiana State University, 1961.

Mitchell, Brian. "Oscar J. Dunn: A Case Study in Race & Politics in Reconstruction Louisiana." PhD diss., University of New Orleans, 2011.

Patler, Nicholas. "An Early 'Human Rights' Movement on the Frontier: Building an Underground Railroad Community in Wayne County, Indiana, 1820–1850." Master's thesis, Bethany Theological Seminary, Richmond, Indiana, 2012.

Peller-Semmens, Carin. "Unreconstructed: Slavery and Emancipation in Louisiana's Red River, 1820–1880." PhD diss., University of Sussex, 2016.

Tunnell Jr., Ted B. "Henry Clay Warmoth and the Politics of Coalition." Master's thesis, North Texas State University, 1966.

Yamanaka, Mishio. "Erasing the Colorline: The Racial Formation of Creoles and the Public School Integration Movement in New Orleans, 1867–1880." Master's thesis, University of North Carolina at Chapel Hill, 2013.

SYMPOSIA/INTERVIEWS

Masur, Kate. "Black Civil Rights Activism During Reconstruction: A National View." *The Historic New Orleans Collection's 2021 Symposium*, New Orleans, Louisiana, March 5–7, 2021.

Mitchell, Brian K, Barrington E. Edwards, and Nick Weldon. "Oscar Dunn and His Radical Vision for Louisiana." *The Historic New Orleans Collection's 2021 Symposium*, New Orleans, Louisiana, March 5–7, 2021.

Shaik, Fatima, Caryn Cossé Bell, and Libby Neidenbach. "Much More Than Music: Economy Hall and the Struggle for Civil Rights." *The Historic New Orleans Collection's 2021 Symposium*, New Orleans, Louisiana, March 5–7, 2021.

Stern, Walter C. "How New Orleans Schools Created a Segregated City." Interview with Jess Clark, WWNO, May 17, 2018.

ONLINE SOURCES

Blake, Tom, transcriber. "St. Landry Parish: Largest Slaveholders from 1860 Slave Census Schedules and Surname Matches for African Americans on 1870 Census," accessed August 7, 2024, https://freepages.rootsweb.com/~ajac/genealogy/lastlandry.htm.

"C. S. Sauvinet vs. J. A. Walker: A Brief on Behalf of Plaintiff & Appellee," Supreme Court of Louisiana, no.3513 (L'Avenir, 1871), accessed August 7, 2024, https://babel.hathitrust.org/cgi/pt?id=hvd.32044018647792&seq=5&q1=filleul. "C. S. Sauvinet vs. J. A. Walker," Supreme Court of Louisiana, No. 3513 (St. Louis: L'Avenir Job Office (C. S. Sauvinet Vs J. A. Walker: A Brief on Behalf of Plaintiff & Appellee: E. Filleul: Free Download, Borrow, and Streaming: Internet Archive)

"City Government: The Three Municipalities," *Historic New Orleans*, http://www.storyvilledistrictnola.com/neworleans_three_municiplaities.html.

"Constitution Adopted by the State Constitutional Convention of the State of Louisiana," March 7, 1868, *Internet Archive*, https://archive.org/details/constitutionadop1868loui/page/n3/mode/2up.

Douglass, Frederick. "The Country Has not Heard the Last of P. B. S. Pinchback: An Address Delivered in Washington, D.C., on March 13, 1876," https://frederickdouglasspapersproject.com /s/digitaledition/item/18198.

Evans, Farrel. "America's First Black War Correspondent Reported from the Civil War's Front Lines," updated January 3, 2024, https://www.history.com/news/first-black-war-correspondent-civil-war-thomas-morris-chester.

Everard, Wayne and Irene Wainwright, "New Orleans Incorporated: 200 Years of the City Charter," Exhibit, New Orleans Public Library, accessed August 26, 2024. https://nutrias.org/~nopl/exhibits/charter/chartercontents.htm.

"The Exceptionally Cold Spring of 1837," Netweather Community, https://www.netweather.tv/forum/topic/76238-the-exceptionally-cold-spring-of-1837.

Kennedy, A. I. "The History of Public Education in New Orleans Still Matters", *History Faculty Publications* (2006) Paper 5, http://scholarworks.uno.edu/hist_facpubs/5.

Louisiana Constitution of 1974, https://senate.la.gov/Documents/LAConstitution.pdf. Louisiana Justice Institute Profile: Reverend Sampson "Skip" Alexander, posted by Justin Flaherty, March 3, 2010, https://louisianajusticeinstitute.blogspot.com/search?q=skip+alexander.

Maloid, Kaelin, ed. "Prominent New Orleans Civil Rights Activist Dies at 89." *New Orleans Data News Weekly*, March 27, 2019. https://ladatanews.com/prominent-new-orleans-civil-rights-activist-dies-at-89/.

Mobley, Suzanne-Juliette." "Streetcar Protest 1867." *New Orleans Historical*, accessed June 10, 2023, https://neworleanshistorical.org/items/show/1433.

Pinchback Family Genealogy, US African American Griots, http://sites.rootsweb.com/~aagriots /NC/WmPinchback.htm.

"Tobacco in Caswell County, North Carolina," Caswell County Historical Association, March 20, 2012; "History of Caswell County," Caswell County Historical Association (www.rootsweb.ancestry.com)

INDEX

Page numbers in **bold** indicate photo and illustrations.

abolitionists/abolitionism, 18, 38, 69, 172
Africa/Africans, 16, 34, 35, 37, 40, 41, 43
Alabama speaking tour, 38, 44, 45, 46, 52, 60
Alonzo Child (steamboat), 26
Antoine, C. C. (Caesar), 77, 78, 79, 87, 88, 96, 103, 112, 133, 146, 179n5; lieutenant governor, 103, 133, 146
Article 13 (Civil Rights Article), 61, 64, 72, 75, 154
Article 135 (Public School Integration Clause), 61

Banks, Nathaniel, 36, 45, 81
Bash, Dana, 8
Battle of Liberty Place, 140
Beckwith, J. R., 124
Belot, Octave, 75
Bennett, Lerone, Jr., ix, 6, 7, 125, 127, 148
Big Black River (MS), 16
Black Codes, 39, 44, 46, 62, 70
Black enslaved women, 14, 75
Black exodus, 151, 153
Black women during Reconstruction, 113, 114
Blaine, James G., 114
Blassingame, John, 69
Bontemps, Anna, 40
Brady, Matthew, 28, **29**
Bovee, George C., 120
Brown, William, 78, 112
Brown vs. Board of Education, 84

Bruce, Blanche Kelso, 111, **138**, 146, 159, 160
Bruch, J. Henri, 113, 181n30
Butler, Benjamin, 26, 27, 31, **32**, 33, 34, 36
Byrd, Rudolph P., 161, 165, 176n3, 194n23

Caddo Parish, 60
Cane, 5, 157, **163**, 164, 171n15
Canonge, Jeffrey (P. Z.), 98
Campbell, Hugh J., 126
Caroll Parish, 136
Carter, George, 91
Caswell County, NC, ix, 11, **13**
Central Executive Committee of the Louisiana Republican Party, 52
Central High School, 142, 143, 144
Chandler, William, 114, 115, 116
Choctaw people, 171n16
Cincinnati, OH, 18, **19**, 21, 22, 29, 36, 37, 39, 59, 69, 126
Cincinnati Enquirer, 126
Civil Rights Bill, 64, 71, 73, 74, 75, 143
Claiborne, William, 165
Colfax, Schuler, 114
Colfax Massacre, 124
Columbia Heights (DC), **156**
Committee of Public Education, 60, 61
Congressional Investigations, 1871–72, 80, 86, 117
Congressional Reconstruction, 47, 48
Congo, Wimba and August, 34, 35

Constitutional Convention (Louisiana): 1864 Convention, 45–46; 1867–68 Convention, 9, 48, 49, 50, 51–63, **53**, 65, 66, 68, 74, 77, 82, 92, 93, 107, 112, 126, 169n16; 1879 Convention, 151; 1974 Convention, 9
Conway, William, 81, 83
Corbin, Henry, 114, 120
Corps d'Afrique, 37
Coupland, Theodore, 96
Creoles, 3, 32, 33, 35, 41, 46, 48, 62, 129, 156
Custom House faction, 91, 92, 110, 112

Daily Picayune, 3, 84
Davis, Alexander, 103
de le Guerra, Pablo, 104
DeFeriet, Gabriel, 118
Democrats, 52, 53, 55, 66, 67, 68, 80, 83, 85, 89, 91, 93, 109, 110, 111, 113, 122, 127, 129, 131, 145, 147, 148, 151
Deslonde, Pierre, 112, 127
Devol, George, 23, 24, 34
Dibble, Henry C., 83
Dinella-Borrego, Louis-Alejandro, ix, 8
Dinneen-Wimberly, Ingrid, ix, 8, 176n4
Donaldson (LA) Chief, 116
Douglas, Frederick, 4, 6, 28, 43, 101, 107, 110, 127, 129, 137, 140, 143, 148, 156; admiration for Pinchback, 110, 127, 140, 148; eulogy by Pinchback, 156–57
Dray, Philip, ix, 8, 105, 116, 172n34
Du Bois, W. E. B., 5, 28
Dunn, Oscar J., 35, **65**, 66, 72, 74, 75, 76, 81, 84, 90, 91, 92, 93, 94, 95, 96, 98, 101, 103, 123; lieutenant governor, 103; untimely death/rumors of murder, 90, 94–95, 123
Dunning, William Archibald, 167–68n8
Durrell, Edward Henry, 119

Economy Hall, 38
Edmonds, E. J., 144
Education Act (Act 121), 38
Elmore, William, 118, 122, 123, 125
Eustis, J. B., 145
excessive spending accusations, 85–88

Federal Civil Rights Act of 1875, 72, 75, 152
Field, A. P., 123, 124, 132
Finney, William, 58
First Cavalry Regiment, 37
First Regiment Infantry, 27
Fourth Ward, 48, 49, 50, 52, 93
Fourteenth Amendment, 54, 152
Franklin, John Hope, 8
Freedmen's Bureau, 44, 56, 58, 59, 68, 81
Fusionists, 117, 118

Gates, Henry Louis, Jr., 161, 165
Gayarre, Charles, 122
General Order No. 63, 31
Gilmore School, 18, 19, 172n36
Gleaves, Richard, 21, 103; South Carolina lieutenant governor, 103
Grant, Ulysses, 66, 71, 75, 76, 77, 80, 81, 99, 109, 111, 112, 114, 117, 118, 121, 122, 123, 124, 125, 126, 130, 131, 132, 138, 139, 140, 142, 146, 151
Great Rail Race, 114–16
Greely, Horace, 118
Grimke, Francis, 166
Grosz, Agnes Smith, ix, 7, 85, 86, 88

Harlem Renaissance, 5, 13, 28, 41, 157, 162, 163
Harris, A. B., 114, 115
Harris, J. S., 111
Harvey, David Archibald, 147
Haskins, James, 16, 17
Hawthorn, Nina (Pinchback), 25, 40, **45**
Hayes, Rutherford B., 18, 128, 148; Hayes-Tilden Compromise of 1877, 148
Hemings, Sally, 12
Highgate, Edmonia, **59**
Hill, James, 137
Holeman, David, 20, 21
Holeman, Lydia, 20
Holmes County, MS, ix, 11, 15, 16, **17**, 18, 19, 20–21, 26, 37, 171n16; author's description, 16, 18, 171n17; census, 15; William Pinchback deed, 20–21
Hopkins, George, 15, **155**
Houzeau, Jean-Charles, 43, 57

Ingraham, James, 60, 78, 85, 96, 120; school integration, 60
Isabelle, Robert, 71, 74, 83; assault by white people, 71; Civil Rights Bill, 71; school integration, 83

Jacobs, William, 20–21
Jefferson, Thomas, 12
Jewell, E. L., 64, 66, 67, 68

Kabnis (*Cane*), 163–64
Keeling, William F., 35
Kellogg, William, 112, 117, 118, 119, 120, 121, 122, 124, 125, 127, 130, 131, 133, 134, 137, 138, 139, 141, 142, 145, 146

Langston, John Mercer, 14, 18, 163
Langston, Lucy, 14
Legal Interracial and Common Law Marriage (Act 210), 68–70
Lewis, John, 23, 96–97, 112, 136
Liberal Republican(s), 109, 110, 186n10
Logan, John, 147
Lonn, Ella, 131
Louisiana Constitution of 1868, 9, 51–63; Article 13, 61–62; Article 99, 54–55; Article 135, 56–61; Black delegates, 52, **53**; Black male suffrage, 54; convention officers from both races, 52–53; "magnificent for its liberal principles," 51; ratification of, 62
Louisiana Native Guards, 31, 33, **34**, 36, 37, 43, 60, 71, 103
Louisiana Question, 139
Louisiana State Militia, 126
Louisiana State Senate, 64–89; controversy over Pinchback seat, 66–67; Pinchback campaigning for, 64; Pinchback gunfight with S. C. Morgan, 67; Pinchback's final legislative session, 85–88; Pinchback's first session, 68–70; Pinchback's second session, 70–77; Pinchback's third session, 80–81
Louisianian, 78, **79**, 86, 128, 143
Long, Huey, 10
Longstreet, James, 126

Lowen, James, 6
L'Union, 43
Lusher, James, 81
Lynch Board, 118, 119

Macon, GA, 11, 14, 165
Manard, John Willis, 72
manumission/manumitted, 13, 21, 33
Mardi Gras, 109–10
Marshall, Thurgood, 60
McCreery, Thomas, 141, 147
McEnery, John, 117, 118, 119, 121, 122, 123, 124, 125, 126, 127, 130, 131, 132, 134, 137, 139, 140
McMillen, William M., 137
Mechanics Institute, 46, **99**, 100, 101, 119
Memphis, TN, 23, 25, 26, 40, 46, 115
Metairie Cemetery, 165, **166**
Metropolitan Police Force, 126, 127, 128, 133
Mississippi River Packet Company, 76, 87
Mobile, AL, 44
Montgomery, AL, 44
Morgan, S. C., 67, 68, 129
Morris, T. Chester, 95, 98
Morton, Charles, 139, 141, 148
Moore, Thomas, 32

National Republican Convention of 1872, 111
New National Era, 28, 110, 140
New Orleans, 3, 4, 5, 7, 8, 10, 11, 15, 18, 23, 25, 26, 28, 31, 33, 34, 35, 47, 48, 52, 55, 56, 57, 60, 64, 67, 68, 69, 72, 88, 93, 98, 99, 100, 101, 102, 105, 109, 110, 114, 136, 139, 140, 148, 150, 153, 165; Black activism, 43, 45; Black/Creole Confederates, 33; Black Union officers/Creoles, 33–36; and efforts to integrate public schools, 81–86, 142–44; fall of in the Civil War, 26; great railway race to, 115–16; Louisiana Constitutional Convention, 1867–68, 51–63; Louisiana State Senate 1869–71, 64–89; Mardi Gras during Pinchback's term as lieutenant governor, 109–10; New Orleans Pinchbacks, 3, 154, **155**; New Orleans Riot, 1866, 46, 56; Nina Hawthorn's possible birth city, 40;

Port of New Orleans, **47**; Pinchback & Antione, Commission Merchants, 77, **79**; Pinchback organizing Fourth Ward Republican Club, 48; Pinchback starts *Louisianian*, 77–**79**; Pinchback's regiment, 34–35; Pinchback's term as governor, 117–35; Pinchback's term as lieutenant governor, 90–102; Southern University, 7, **153**; Union occupation of during Civil War, 26–33; William/Eliza and family migration to, 11, 15

New Orleans Commercial Bulletin, 75, 142

New Orleans Crescent, 67, 68

New Orleans Evening Times, 119

New Orleans Pinchbacks, 3, 154, **155**

New Orleans school board, 57, 83

New Orleans Tribune, 43, 55, 57, 58, 60, 74

New York Amsterdam News, 160

New York Herald, 35, 145, 146

Nichols, William, 39

Nicholls, Francis, 151

Norton, Emery Ebenezer, 139, 140

Norton bribery controversy, 4, 129, 139, 140, 141, 144

Oberlin College, 18

Ogden, Henri, 132

Ohio River, 19

P. B. S. Pinchback Engineering Building, 154

Pacheco, Romualdo, 104

Packard, Stephen B., 98, 111, 118, 119, 122, 124

Passing, 27–31, 105–8

Pinchback (Hawthorn), Nina (wife), 25, 40–43, **45**, 46, 70, 76, 104, 113, 136, 140, 147, 155, 162; ambition and outspokenness, 113–14; barred from first-class Pullman berth, 76; controversy over marriage date, 42, 70; Jean Toomer's description of, 40–41, 42–43

Pinchback (Toomer), Nina (daughter), 42, 155, 157, **158**

Pinchbacks (New Orleans baseball team), 3, 154, **155**

Pinchback, Adeline (sister), 20, 21, 22, 29, 30, 31, 41, 171n27, 172n28; letter to brother, 29–31

Pinchback, Bismarck (son), 42, 44, 137, 155, 161, 162, 165, 195n25

Pinchback, Mary Louisa (daughter), 20–21

Pinchback, Napoleon (brother), 14, 18, 20, 21, 22

Pinchback, Nathaniel (brother), 20, 30

Pinchback, Pinckney Benton Stewart: advocacy for Act 188, 151–**52**; and appropriation to start Southern University, 153–54; birth, 11; death, 165–66; and deaths of loved ones, 159; and efforts to integrate New Orleans public schools, 81–86, 138, 142–44; elected Congressman-at-large, 136; erasing from history, 5–6; eulogy for Frederick Douglass, 157; exile in Cincinnati, 21–22; fight for US Senate seat, 136–**49**; First Regiment Infantry, 27; friendship with Blanche Kelso Bruce, **138**, 146–47; friendship with George Devol, 23, 24, 34; Gilmore School, 18; gunfight with S. C. Morgan, 67–68; Holmes County, MS plantation, ix, 11, 15, 16, **17**, 18, 19, 20–21, 26, 37; knife fight and arrest, 27; Louisiana Constitutional Convention, 1867–68, 51–63; Louisiana Constitutional Convention, 1879, 151–54; Louisiana State Senate 1869–71, 64–89; Mardi Gras during term as lieutenant governor, 109–10; marriage to Nina Hawthorn, 42; moves into Columbia Heights house, 155; moves into U Street apartment, 160; New Orleans Pinchbacks, 3, 154, **155**; Pinchback & Antione, Commission Merchants, 77, **79**; post-Reconstruction life and career, 150–65; organizing Fourth Ward Republican Club, 48; racial indeterminacy/passing, 27–31, 105–8; racism from white Union officers, 35–36; railway race to New

Orleans, 115–16; regiment, 34–35; relationship with Henry Clay Warmoth, 93–94, 97; relationship with Jean Toomer, 105–8, 157, 160–66, **163**; relationship with Oscar Dunn, 95–96, 98; relocation to Washington, DC, 155–**56**; rise in the Republican Party, 48–50; rumors of corruption, 4–5, 85–88; shooting incident, 98; Southern University, 7, **153**; speaking tours, 38, 43–45; starts *Louisianian*, 77–**79**; stint in New York, 155; streetcar sit-in, 38–39; support for Booker T. Washington, 159–60; support of Democrat governor, 151–52; term as governor, 117–35; term as lieutenant governor, 90–102; work on steamboat, 22–23
Pinchback, Pinckney Napoleon, Jr. (son), 42, 44, 84, 104, 136, 155; forced enrollment in white school, 104
Pinchback, Walter (son), **158**
Pinchback, William (father), 165; birth of P. B. S. Pinchback, 11; cotton planter, 17–18; death, 18–19; deed of family sale, 20–21; description of Holmes County, MS plantation, **17**, 18; enslaved persons, 15; migration to New Orleans/Holmes County, MS, 14–16; relationship with Eliza Stewart, 12–14; tobacco planter, 11–12; William's white family, 11, 15
Pinchback, William Henry (brother), 20, 30
Pinchback & Antione, Commission Merchants, 77, **79**
Pinchback Lake, **17**
Pinchback Plantation, 17
Pinchback vs. Jackson Railroad, 76, 87
Plessy vs. Ferguson, 154
Port Hudson, LA, battle of, 37
Presidential Reconstruction, 46, 47

Quakers/Quakerism, 162
Quarles, Ralph, 14

Ransier, Alonzo, 103
Rapides Parrish, 49

Ray, John, 96
Reconstruction, 105, 117, 119, 121, 124, 126, 128, 129, 131, 133, 134, 135, 145, 150, 153, 154
Reconstruction Act of 1867, 54
Republicans: liberal, 109, 110, 186n10; radical, 39, 47, 55, 58, 93, 110, 111; regular, 110, 118
Revels, Hiram, 8, **108**, 137, 172n36
Roxborough, 143
Rudd, Lavinia (William Pinchback's white wife), 11, 15

Sauvinet, Charles: damages for refused service in white saloon, 75; enrolled daughter in all-white New Orleans school, 82
scalawag, 91
school integration, 81–86, 104, 138, 142–44
Selma, AL, 44
Sheridan, George, 136
Sheridan, Philip, 49
Simmons, William J., 6
slavery, 26, 31, 33, 39, 44, 68, 71, 95, 107, 113, 157, 165; Eliza enslaved in Caswell County, NC, 13, 14; enslaved persons on Holmes County, MS plantation, 16
Soule' Chapel School, 58
Southern University, 7, **153**
Sparta, GA, 163
St. Albin, Charles, 75
St. Landry Parrish, 80, 81
steamboats, 22, 23, 24, 25, 73, 76, 77, 87, 96
Stewart, Eliza (mother), 136, 165; birth of P. B. S. Pinchback, 14–15; children, 171n27; description by Jean Toomer, 13; enslaved in Caswell County, NC, 13, 14; freed from bondage, 11, 12; forced migration to Cincinnati, 20; Metairie Cemetery burial, **166**; relationship with son, 17, 18, 20, 30–31, 70, 108, 148, 157; relationship with William Pinchback, 12–14; relationship with William's white family, 12, 15; sales/protection in deed, 20–21
streetcar sit-in, 38–39
Sumner, Charles, 109

Taliaferro, J. G., 120
Taylor, Joe Gray, 7, 97, 101
Terre Haute, IN, 24
tobacco plantation, 11–12, **13**, 15
Toomer, Jean (Nathan Pinchback Toomer Jr.), 15, 21, 28, 34, 44, 50, 172n28; accompanied Pinchback's coffin to Metairie Cemetery, 165–**66**; authored novel *Cane*, **163**; caregiving for elderly Pinchback, 162–63; description of great-grandmother, 13; description of Pinchback's diverse social gatherings, 137, 156; memories of grandmother, 40–**41**, 42–43; moved into Pinchback's DC home, 157; passing in the Pinchback family, 30; on Pinchback's anger and political motivation, 10, 17, 20, 30–31; on Pinchback's experience of racism, 37–38; on Pinchback's racial indeterminacy, 105–6; relationship with Pinchback, 5, 105–8, 157, 160–66; struggle with racial identity, 161–62; trip to Sparta, GA as inspiration for novel, 163; writing *Cane/Kabnis* by bedside, 164–65
Toomer, Nathan (Jean Toomer's father), 157
Traditionalists, 5–6, 9, 88, 159, 167n8
Treaty of Dancing Rabbit Creek, 171n16
Trotter, James, 187n21
Trotter, William Monroe, 187n21
Turner Hall, 91, 93

U Street Apartment (Washington, DC), 160
US Senate, 93, 113; Pinchback's fight for seat, 136–42, 144–49

Vincent, Charles, ix, 7

Warmoth, Henry Clay, 4, 71, 86, 96, 109, 111, 117, 118, 136; alleged bribe to John Lewis, 96–97; approved Civil Rights Act, 75; break with Oscar Dunn, 76; campaign for governor, 66; controversy over commitment to Black rights, 107; efforts to get Pinchback lieutenant governor's seat, 94–102; expanding powers as governor, 80, 81; opposition to Article 13, 71, 72, 73, 74; physical description, 65–66; Pinchback's state senator campaign, 67; rail race with Pinchback, 114–16; relationship with Pinchback, 92–94, 95, 104, 106; struggle against Pinchback for governor, 117–35; struggles to hold onto power, 90, **92**, 92
Washington, DC, 28, 33, 34, 75, 77, 78, 109, 112, 113, 119, 122, 124, 125, 126, 137, 138, 140, 142, 144, 148, 155, 156, 159, 160, 162, 166
Weed, C. E., 119
White League, 140, 142, 143, 151
Williams, George H., 125, 132
Williams, Harry T., 106
Wilderness (federal ship), 98, 99, 107
Wilson, Henry, 114, 115
Wilson, Woodrow, 160
women during Reconstruction, 75, 78, 113, 114n19
Woodson, Carter G., ix, 7, 168n11
Works Progress Administration, 8
Wycliffe, George, 59, 60, 61

Yazoo City, MS, 26
Yazoo River, 16

ABOUT THE AUTHOR

Photo courtesy of Katie C. Savage

NICHOLAS PATLER is a published historian focused on African American history, particularly in the reconstruction, progressive, and civil rights eras. He has a master's in liberal arts from the Harvard Extension School, with a focus on government and history, and a master's in arts from Bethany Theological Seminary in Richmond, Indiana, with a focus on historical studies and the African American experience in Islam.

www.ingramcontent.com/pod-product-compliance
Lightning Source LLC
Chambersburg PA
CBHW030107170426
43198CB00009B/531